1502

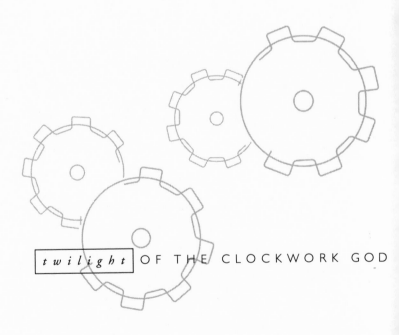

twilight OF THE CLOCKWORK GOD

twilight

of *the*
CLOCKWORK
GOD

*Conversations
on Science and
Spirituality at the
End of an Age*

BY JOHN DAVID EBERT

COUNCIL OAK BOOKS

TULSA / SAN FRANCISCO

Twilight of the Clockwork God
Council Oak Books
Tulsa, OK 74120
Printed in the United States of America
03 02 01 00 99   5 4 3 2
Library of Congress Cataloging-in-Publication Data
Ebert, John David, 1968-
    Twilight of the clockwork God : conversations on science and spirituality at the end of an
age / John David Ebert.
            p. cm.
    Includes bibliographical references.
    ISBN 1-57178-079-3
    1. Science—History. 2. Religion and science—History. 3. Philosophy, European—History.
4. Scientists—Interviews.
I. Title.
Q125.E362   1999
501--dc21   98-32417
                              CIP

Book and cover design by Carol Stanton

Grateful acknowledgment is made to the following periodicals in which versions of some of
these chapters first appeared:

"Terence McKenna and the Evolution of Consciousness Part I." *Magical Blend*. May, 1997.
"Life, Lindisfarne and Everything: William Irwin Thompson Speaks Out." *Alexandria* 4, 1997.
"Terence McKenna and the Evolution of Consciousness Part II." *Magical Blend*. August, 1997.
"From Cellular Ageing to the Physics of Angels: A Conversation with Rupert Sheldrake." *The
Quest*. Spring, 1998.
"God and the Quantum Vacuum: A Conversation with Brian Swimme." *Lapis* 7, 1998.

THIS BOOK IS DEDICATED TO

MELYNDA CHRISTOFF,

WITHOUT WHOM IT SIMPLY WOULD NOT HAVE BEEN POSSIBLE.

"IN THIS VERY CENTURY, I PROPHESY, THE CENTURY OF SCIENTIFIC-CRITICAL ALEXANDRIANISM, OF THE GREAT HARVESTS, OF THE FINAL FORMULATIONS, A NEW ELEMENT OF INWARDNESS WILL ARISE TO OVERTHROW THE WILL-TO-VICTORY OF SCIENCE. . . . THE SEPARATE SCIENCES — EPISTEMOLOGY, PHYSICS, CHEMISTRY, MATHE-MATICS, ASTRONOMY — ARE APPROACHING ONE ANOTHER WITH ACCELERATION, CONVERGING TOWARDS A COMPLETE IDENTITY OF RESULTS. THE ISSUE WILL BE A FUSION OF THE FORM-WORLDS, WHICH WILL PRESENT . . . A SMALL GROUP OF THEORIES . . . WHICH IN THE END WILL BE SEEN TO BE MYTHS . . . UNDER MODERN VEILS. . . ."

— OSWALD SPENGLER

THE DECLINE OF THE WEST (1918)

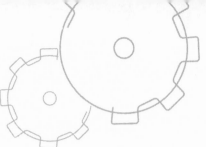

C O N T E N T S

FOREWORD

John David Ebert's *Twilight of the Clockwork God* is a valediction, a funeral oration to a dream that died. In its inception, it was a dream of a perfectly ordered universe, with each part smoothly fitting into its neighbor like the cogs of a Swiss clock. It was a dream that unified the earth and heavens within the three laws of Newtonian mechanics and allowed scientists to predict everything from the return of a comet a century into the future, to the exact time of high tide one month hence. But it was also a dream whose domain rapidly expanded beyond the boundaries of the physical sciences to embrace everything from the study of history to human psychology. And so the dream turned into a nightmare, for there was no room for human consciousness and values within such a clockwork cosmos. Indeed, life itself was reduced to nothing more than a chemical accident on a planet orbiting a nondescript star in an indifferent universe.

It was a nightmare replete with hubris. The ability to predict eclipses and the flight of cannon balls soon gave rise to the illusion that everything could be predicted. And what can be predicted, through a detailed analysis of cause and effect, can therefore be controlled. A century after Newton's *Principia*, the philosopher Jeremy Bentham was proposing to engineer human society along strict scientific principles in order to produce a Utilitarian world having "the greatest happiness of the greatest number." So even pleasure and pain were to be brought within the scope of scientific measurement in a clockwork world of endless progress.

This part-dream part-nightmare should have been laid to rest by the great scientific revolutions of the early twentieth century, culminating in the current explosion of interest in Chaos Theory. Today we are no longer passive observers of a cosmos created by a Clockwork God but full members of a participatory universe. Our abilities to predict and control the world are strictly limited. And we now know that only those systems which are open and responsive to their environments will, in the long run, survive.

Implications of this revolution for our perception of the world, and for ourselves, have already diffused into the arts. The mechanical universe was nowhere to be found in Virginia Woolf or James Joyce. Indeed, its intimations were already present in the paintings of Cézanne, in which the artist was clearly an active participator in the scene before him. Likewise, we have come to realize that a world based upon a single, monolithic culture is an unhealthy place to live and so we are more willing to enjoy a plurality of views and readings.

Yet in other areas of life, the mechanical universe keeps ticking on. Its ticks can still be heard in our schools, hospitals, legislatures and seats of government. Some cognitive psychologists believe that consciousness and human behavior can be reduced, like a computer program, to a series of algorithms. The motives for the human genome project and the desire to manipulate plants and animals are all gathered under the unfortunate umbrella of genetic engineering. Politicians are still too quick to resort to military force as a way to resolve international disputes or dominate a population. Only slowly are businesses and corporations learning from nature's living systems, that self-organization is more successful than rigid hierarchy. Likewise, despite its enormous successes, modern medicine, by virtue of its mechanization, tends to dehumanize the patient into a defective machine that requires expert repair.

Each one of us desires a better life for the next generation. Yet do we always take into account the impact of our actions on the environment and the simple fact that unlimited progress is not possible on a finite planet? The

Clockwork God should have been put to rest and yet we continue to maintain faith in the absolute power of our scientific knowledge and believe that, in the end, more technology will resolve the problems that surround us. At the same time, the inner cities and the lakes decay. Violence abounds. Populations starve. Disease can reach epidemic proportions. And the possibility of unemployment and an unrewarding life dehumanizes youth, while governments seem more interested in diverting funds to wage war on drugs.

That is why Ebert's *Twilight of the Clockwork God* is so important. It argues powerfully for the new vision of nature, and ourselves, that emerged in this century. For the book's conversations, Ebert has selected the leading figures of the new paradigm. And if there are those occasional moments in which the experts don't always agree on the direction in which we are heading, this makes the book all the more exciting. It shows that the new thinking is not monolithically hierarchical. Rather it is a human, and a humane, attempt to celebrate our living universe and understand our position within it. Reading *Twilight of the Clockwork God* gives us a sense of the new spirit of the age and our responsibility towards it. Ebert has done his job well, his co-conversationists have expressed their positions. Yet in this new world we are all responsible, all participators. And so the rest is up to us.

F. David Peat

Introduction:

THE GENESIS AND DISINTEGRATION OF THE MECHANICAL WORLD PICTURE

I. The Dialogue of Myth and Science

From Carl Jung's descriptions of his various dinner conversations with Einstein, it is apparent that the two understood very little of what the other was up to. "He was often in my house," Jung has remarked, "and I pumped him about his relativity theory. I am not gifted in mathematics and you should have seen all the trouble the poor man had to explain relativity to me. . . . But one day he asked me something about psychology. Then I had my revenge."[1] The thought of the two greatest geniuses of the twentieth century sciences of Nature and of the Spirit talking past each other is ironic, since both were engaged in a similar dismantling of the mechanical universe. The year was 1911, and Carl Jung was at work on his masterpiece, *Psychology of the Unconscious,* the volume that would mark his departure from the rationalistic psychology of Sigmund Freud.[2] This was Jung's first exploration into the realm of myth, and it was here that the groundwork was laid for his theory of the collective unconscious. In 1905 physics had been turned upside down with the publication of Einstein's little paper "On the Electrodynamics of Moving Bodies," in which he announced that the concepts of time, space and mass — for centuries unquestioned absolutes — were now to become variable properties of matter in motion approaching light speed.

As the philosopher Michel Serres has theorized, the facility with which two parties communicate is a function of how well they are able to exclude the "third man," which Serres terms "the parasite," a mythic personification of the various forms of entropy which threaten to garble communication in the form of noise, static, misunderstandings, language barriers and so forth.[3] The ability of science and spirituality to exclude this third party has increased significantly since the days of Jung and Einstein, for now they seem to have more to say to each other. Quantum physicist Erwin Schrödinger, for example, continuing in the tradition of Arthur Schopenhauer a century before him, supposed Hindu philosophy to be essentially equivalent to the phenomenological insights of modern physics, while Catholic priest Teilhard de Chardin spent his life endeavoring to join the evolutionary world picture of the sciences with Christianity. The physicist David Bohm spent much of his later years engaged in dialogues with Jiddu Krishnamurti, while the conversations between Fritjof Capra and Brother David Steindl-Rast were published as *Belonging to the Universe* in 1991. And two of the protagonists of this book, Brian Swimme and Rupert Sheldrake, have continued the tradition through collaborations with theologian Matthew Fox.

Not long ago, I sat through a five-part video documentary of a conference that took place in Europe called "Art Meets Science and Spirituality in a Changing Economy."[4] What struck me was that neither the artists nor the economists had much to contribute to the four-way dialogue, whereas the various representatives of the sciences and religion had intelligent, interesting things to say both for themselves and to each other. Theologians such as Huston Smith, Sogyal Rinpoche, or the Dalai Lama did not seem at all threatened by the eloquence of the scientists who — for me, anyway — stole the show. Rupert Sheldrake, Ilya Prigogine, David Bohm, Francisco Varela and Fritjof Capra were by far the most articulate, exciting speakers at the conference, and it was clear that the really *new* ideas were coming from that quarter.

But the sciences these days are not as autistic as they once were, for a new generation has arrived which takes myth seriously. Frazer's attitude in *The Golden Bough*, is no longer appropriate to the *Zeitgeist*, for he insisted that civilization had followed a sequence of three phases that moved, irreversibly, from magic to religion to science, and that once the latter stage had been achieved, the former would vanish for good, since they had only been rough draft sketches of a "scientific" approach to the world, which is really what earlier cultures had been aiming at all along. With the publication, however, in 1918 of Oswald Spengler's *Decline of the West* and then in 1934, Ludwik Fleck's *Genesis and Development of a Scientific Fact*, the "progress" stencil through which Frazer — and everybody else in the nineteenth century — had traced his theory of cultural development had become outdated.

It was Jean Gebser who, in 1949, with his *Ever-Present Origin*, surpassed Frazer's theory of cultural development with one of his own, in which the stages of history became a series of structures of consciousness which, once crystallized, were not so much rendered obsolete by subsequent phases as miniaturized to perform specific functions in the overall map of human consciousness. In Gebser's sequence, the Archaic, Magical, Mythic and Rational stages of culture history were followed in the nineteenth century by the Aperspectival (also known as Integral), in which all other structures and points of view were taken up into a new relativistic phase space in which conflicting philosophies coexist like the geometrical icons of corporate data in the cyberspace of William Gibson's novels.

And so, consistent with Gebser's portrait of our contemporary world, it is my contention that a new generation of scientists is emerging, one for which magic, myth and science are part of the same spectrum of human cultural activity. Ideas like the Gaia hypothesis, Chaos theory, Ilya Prigogine's self-organizing structures, or David Bohm's holographic cosmos all exhibit the presence of images from earlier, more mythic cosmologies. The magical structure of consciousness which characterized the outlook of man's primordial childhood is resurfacing, for example, in the Princeton Engineering Anomalies Research Program headed by Robert Jahn and Brenda Dunne, who have meticulously documented the reality of such paranormal phenomena as telepathy, psychokinesis and remote viewing. Rupert Sheldrake's morphogenetic fields are a kind of scientific transform of the ancient *anima mundi*, the soul of the world which, even as late as the time of Leibniz, still infused the minutest particle with teeming, sentient consciousness. Medical doctors such as Richard Gerber, Larry Dossey or

Deepak Chopra, likewise, are taking seriously the ancient microcosmologies that most academic scientists discarded long ago, seeing in thought systems like Kundalini yoga or acupuncture the rudiments for a whole new science of "vibrational medicine," in which the *pranic* channels and pathways of the subtle body can become superconductors for states of consciousness leading to higher health.

This phenomenon, furthermore, is not just another manifestation of pop culture or the latest New Age narcissism, for it has been gaining ground steadily throughout the course of the twentieth century, expanding into larger and larger spheres of influence amongst the population. Its audience, consequently, is both popular and elite, including bestsellers like Michael Talbot's *Holographic Universe*, Fritjof Capra's *The Tao of Physics*, or Paul Davies's *God and the New Physics*, as well as more refined works like William Irwin Thompson's *Gaia* anthologies or Francisco Varela's *Gentle Bridges: Conversations with the Dalai Lama on the Sciences of Mind*, or even the recent academic work by Kitty Ferguson, *The Fire in the Equations: Science, Religion and the Search for God*.

So, the topic is on a lot of minds these days, and this book is intended as a modest contribution to the subject. Its focus is on the relationship between the imagery shared by archaic myth and contemporary science, with a glance backward at the historical matrix from out of which this dialogue has emerged.

II. THE DIVINE CLOCKWORK

Rewinding the film strip of European history back to the thirteenth and fourteenth centuries we find, perhaps to our surprise, that the creation of the mechanical universe originated in the imagination of a series of Gothic monks. For men such as Robert Grossetteste, Petrus Peregrinus, Roger Bacon and Witelo, the medieval cosmos apotheosized by Dante was a sort of giant perpetual motion machine: the nested hierarchy of translucent spheres bearing within their orbs the five planets did not turn by themselves, as they had for Aristotle and Pythagoras, but were governed by hordes of bioluminescent angels who turned the spheres with eternal, undissipated motion. The great Gothic cathedrals, in turn, were imagined as earthly miniaturizations of this cosmic machine, for their flying buttresses, stained glass windows, and ribbed-barrel vaulting embodied the closest man could come to imitating the organization of the divine architecture.

It was Lewis Mumford's opinion that the first mechanical clocks were built by Benedictine monks in the thirteenth century for the purpose of regulating the seven canonical hours of the day. But it seems more likely, as Jean Gimpel has pointed out,[5] that the first clocks were primarily astronomical calendars, and as such, derive their origins from an attempt to imitate the perpetual motion machine of the heavens. One of the oldest mechanical clocks we know of was found off the island of Antikythera and dates from the Hellenistic epoch. It is a rectangular box within which an elaborate series of gears and wheels are used to turn a number of dials on its exterior, apparently for the purpose of charting the sun's journey through the zodiac.[6]

Around the year 1090, the Chinese invented a mechanical clock tower which was powered by a waterwheel that turned an armillary sphere and a celestial globe. In Europe about the year 1150, an Arabic text of an astronomical treatise by the Hindu mathematician Bhaskara was translated into Latin, and seems to have contained the first reference to the idea of a perpetual motion machine encountered by Westerners. Bhaskara's machine is a kind of self-turning wheel that operates by leaking mercury from a series of hollow rods, and one of the earliest references to a mechanical clock seems to refer to it, for the clock that is illustrated in a book from the court of Alfonso X of Castile around 1276 is shown bearing an astrolabe for a dial, powered by a weight and verge escapement which rotates by means of a revolving drum leaking mercury. Both machines, in turn, seem to have been conceived as earthly reflections of the ever-cycling wheels of the cosmos. "The time-telling clock which dominates our lives," Gimpel remarks, "was only a by-product of the astronomical clock."[7]

Thus, the invention of the mechanical clock by monks — one way or another — during this age was inspired by an image of the cosmos as a perpetual motion machine, since clocks approximated for the medieval mind the ideal of a self-moving miniature cosmos better than any other machine. As Oswald Spengler puts the matter:

Here, if anywhere, the religious origins of all technical thought are manifested. These meditative discoverers in their cells, who with prayers and fastings *wrung* God's secret out of Him, felt that they were *serving* God thereby. . . . And so they created the *idea of the machine* as a small cosmos obeying the will of man alone.[8]

Many a monk busied himself in his cell with the idea of *Perpetual Motion.* This . . . idea never thereafter let go its hold on us, for success would mean the final victory over "God or Nature" . . . a small world of one's own creation moving like the great world, in virtue of its own forces and obeying the hand of man alone. To build a world *oneself,* to be *oneself* God — that is the Faustian inventor's dream, and from it has sprung all our designing and redesigning of machines to approximate as nearly as possible to the unattainable limit of perpetual motion.[9]

These monks were already analyzing the properties of matter for new and more intricate ways of harnessing the mysterious forces contained therein, which only God or the Devil knew about. They examined mirrors and lenses, the properties of light and magnetism, and Roger Bacon, who was thrown into prison for public suspicion of having made Faustian bargains with the Devil, was already dreaming of steam engines and flying machines. As Spengler, again, comments, ". . . he who was not himself possessed by the will to power over all nature would necessarily feel all this as *devilish*, and in fact, men have always regarded machines as the invention of the Devil." For in the popular mind, power over the earth was uncomfortably identified with Satan's temptation of Christ, in which the Devil leads him up to a hill and promises him all the kingdoms of the world, if he will only submit to worship him.

Thus, the Faust myth that crystallized in the Western imagination between the years 1000 and 1500 catalyzed a series of technological innovations that constitutes one of the greatest explosions of mechanical genius that has ever occurred. Mirrors, water mills, sawmills, the spinning wheel, the treadle loom, eyeglasses, the compass, guns, windmills, cannons, paper and the printing press all emerged out of this Cambrian burst of technical mutations.

Jung's disciple Erich Neumann has characterized the significance of this epoch as "the reappearance of the earth archetype, in opposition to the heaven archetype that had dominated the Middle Ages."[10] This shift in the orientation of Western sensibilities was evident, for example, in such developments as the invention of depth perspective in painting simultaneously with the almost daily revising of maps resulting from the discoveries of Prince Henry the Navigator, Diaz, Columbus, Vasco da Gama and Magellan. The series of classical sculptures that began rising up from the depths of the earth, where they had been buried since Roman times, was strangely fortuitous also, for these Venuses and Laocöons stamped works of art by Botticelli and Michelangelo with an unmistakably pagan character not possessed by works of Christian art in the preceding centuries. These works were decidedly unmedieval in their interest in the details of human anatomy, and likewise in the paintings of Leonardo da Vinci there is a new interest in rendering with accuracy the folds of a robe or the feathers of an angel's wing. Look again at the sparrow's wings he has given to Gabriel in his *Annunciation* or the atmospheric effects of the blue horizons of his backgrounds.

In the sciences, meanwhile, the atomist hypothesis had been revived by a fifteenth-century translation of Lucretius's *De Rerum Natura* and eventually this new ontology of matter was taken up by the great minds of the seventeenth century, including Descartes, Gassendi, Bacon and Hobbes. In the words of Newton:

> It seems probable to me that God in the beginning formed matter in solid, massy, hard, impenetrable, movable particles, of such sizes and figures, and with such properties, and in such proportion to space, as most conduced to the end for which He formed them; and that these primitive particles being solids, are incomparably harder than any porous bodies compounded of them; even so very hard, as never to wear or break in pieces; no ordinary power being able to divide what God Himself made one in the first creation.[11]

Aristotle's theory of the four elements, consequently, was displaced and along with it such spiritual disciplines as alchemy, in which the central endeavor to render an epiphany of the spirit embedded within matter depended upon the notion of the elements composing the structures of all things in varying ratios. And for alchemy's celestial counterpart, astrology, an equally dire fate lay in store, for the burgeoning new science of astronomy was in the process of collapsing the heaven-earth dichotomy that made up the framework of the medieval cosmos. In the Babylonian creation epic, *Enuma Elish*, the male warrior gods destroy the goddess Tiamat and cut up her body to make a cosmos out of it. Likewise, the philosopher scientists of the sixteenth and seventeenth centuries attacked Plato's cosmic Living Being, and began to strip the flesh from its skeleton until only a dead thing remained.

"My vision," Kepler wrote, "is to show that the celestial machine is to be likened not to a divine organism but rather to a clockwork." So Kepler, in ironic imitation of Plato's Demiurge, hammered the celestial circles of the planets into ellipses, while Galileo turned Aristotle's vision of motion upside down with his articulation of the Law of Falling Bodies, for which the primary visual schema was the parabolic arc made by the trajectory of a cannonball. Newton then fused together the two worlds of the heavens and the earth, split asunder by the Medieval mind, into a single continuum by joining a pair of Galileo's paraboloid arcs end to end in order to derive Kepler's elliptical orbits of the planets, which could now be regarded as falling objects that somehow never managed to hit their targets. For Newton, the mechanical clock was a perfect analogue for his vision of the cosmos, or nearly so, for his calculations indicated to him that the orbits of the planets were inherently unstable and would eventually crash into the sun without recourse to a *deus ex machina*, the god that had to rewind his clockwork periodically in order to avoid chaos.

III. THE DEMON IN THE MACHINE

By the end of the nineteenth century, the steam engine had come to replace the clock as the primary image of the cosmos. Whereas the mechanical clock derived its origins from the heavens, the steam engine was invented in the late seventeenth century as a pump for drawing water from mine shafts, and so, as it were, came up from the depths of the earth itself.

There is an archetypal opposition working itself out here, for even though it was known that the laws of the heavens and those of the earth were absolutely identical — since Newton's work had shown them to be so — there nevertheless persisted in the collective imagination an association of the heavens with the realm of eternity and timelessness, for the image of a cosmic clock is one in which *becoming* is abrogated by the repetition of cycles within cycles ad infinitum. In Newtonian mechanics, time is simply nonexistent, since all processes and their equations are theoretically reversible. But we *know* that the events in real, lived time are *not* reversible — that has been, for example, one of the secrets known to great tragedians — and the earthly archetype has been classically associated with the rhythms of time: generation and corruption, growth and decay.

Thermodynamics, accordingly, evolved directly out of a meditation on the steam engine, which is an earthly machine if there ever was one. All four of the classical elements are involved in its operation: earth in the form of coal, fire that heats the coal which, in turn, sets the water boiling into steam — a form of moist air — that is used to do the work of pushing the piston; and when the steam is cooled back into water, the cycle begins anew. And so, the steam engine gave rise to its own science, thermodynamics, in which, contrary to Newtonian mechanics, time is *not* a negligible quantity but is of the essence, for it flows in only one direction: forward.

It was the publication in 1824 of Sadi Carnot's *Reflections on the Motive Power of Fire* that established the basic metaphysical postulates of thermodynamics. Carnot asked himself why it was that steam engines operated with such low efficiency, for even the technical innovations of Watt conferred on them an efficiency rate below 10 percent. This led him to a profound meditation on the metaphysics of the steam engine, in which he visualized an ideal Platonic heat engine that would run without friction and at a constant temperature. He realized that its efficiency was a direct function of the tension between how hot the water was heated before it was used to do work and how cold it became afterwards. The greater the temperature difference, the more efficiently the engine's energy reserves could be converted into work. But Carnot saw that even the most reliable engine would never have an efficiency rate of 100 percent, since usable energy was always lost when the cycle reset itself.

With Carnot's ideal heat engine, the Faustian dream of perpetual motion became an impossibility, since such a machine, in order to keep itself going, would have to continually create energy out of nothing. When Kelvin and Clausius discovered Carnot's work in mid-century, they realized that within it lay an implicit formulation of what Clausius termed Entropy, which he formulated thus: heat always flows from the hotter body to the colder. Once the temperature difference is equalized, furthermore, there is no longer an energy gradient, and the system has reached thermal equilibrium. Thus, the two great laws of thermodynamics may be expressed as follows: "The total energy content of the universe is constant and the total entropy is continually increasing."[12]

And so from a meditation on the steam engine, the idea of the end of the world arose, for entropy in a closed system must always increase, and to all appearances, the universe is a closed system. With the gradual dissipation of available energy throughout the universe, there would be none left for any further transformations. Stars could no longer pour their heat into the cold space surrounding them, for a homogeneity of temperature would reign and the universe would gradually fill with armies of disbanded atoms floating like weary troops incapable of rousing themselves into fresh phalanxes for battle. Thus, the universe was imagined as a sort of gigantic heat engine gradually running itself down.

The savior of this thermodynamic apocalypse, however, arose in the form of Maxwell's demon, a tiny little being reminiscent of those medieval angels who turned the planetary spheres. James Clerk Maxwell imagined how it might be possible to reverse the second law of thermodynamics: he envisioned this demon sitting at the threshold of a box partitioned into two halves and throughout which a gas had reached thermal equilibrium in the form of a constant temperature. This being would catch the faster moving molecules and herd them off into one compartment, while leaving the other filled with the slower moving ones, thereby reestablishing a temperature difference and setting up a new gradient for energy to flow. Carnot's engine would turn out to be a perpetual motion machine, after all, since it would not have to be supplied with fresh energy to restart its cycle.

But of course, the idea was only one of those scientific myths like that of the Leibnizian homunculus, for Maxwell was stepping outside the laws of the phenomenal world in order to bring in a being from the numinous realm to restart Carnot's engine, just as Newton's clockwork vision of the planets required him to resort to the idea of a God who had to keep resetting the planets to make his calculations come out safely. The apocalyptic substructure of Maxwell's demon rises to the surface like a palimpsest when we compare it with the vision of Christ at the Last Judgment sorting out the saved with his right hand and the damned with his left, casting the latter into the pits of a fiery hell, while the former take up their abode in the (presumably balmy) climates of heaven. The history of science abounds with such mythic structures, for science is never as "objective" as its priesthood would have us believe, since it too is a production of the human imagination and subject to the same archetypal contours as that of myth. The apocalyptic vision of a universal heat death, after all, has much in common with the Scandinavian Ragnarok, the Day of Doom in which the world will be destroyed in a final conflagration. Wagner and Hebbel, not coincidentally, were working out their Nibelung dramas while the thermodynamicists were putting an end to the clockwork cosmos.[13]

IV. OF DYNAMOS AND MONADS

When Henry Adams stood in awe before the hall of dynamos at the Great Exposition of 1900, he realized that he was in the presence of a whole new type of machine, one with the power to radically alter the Western imagination:

> . . . to Adams [as he writes] the dynamo became a symbol of infinity. As he grew accustomed to the great gallery of machines, he began to feel the forty foot dynamo as a moral force, much as the early Christian felt the Cross. . . . Between the dynamo in the gallery of machines and the engine-house outside, the break of continuity amounted to an abysmal fracture for a historian's objects. No more relation could he discover between the steam [engine] and the electric current than between the Cross and the cathedral. The forces were

interchangeable if not reversible, but he could see only an absolute *fiat* in electricity as in faith.[14]

And so, for the dawning twentieth century, the dynamo was to become the symbol of the transformation of the mechanical universe of Newton into Einstein's vision of time and space as a humming latticework of curved geodesics. Einstein's cosmology in many ways actually resembles that of his Jewish-German predecessor Spinoza — one of his favorite philosophers — for Spinoza had imagined time and space as attributes of a single underlying substance which he identified with God. For Einstein, likewise, time and space are attributes of mass-energy, for time slows down and space contracts as objects approach light speed; and in the presence of intense gravitational fields near massive objects, clocks move slower and space is deformed. Mass is really bound energy, and all objects are capable of resolution back into it. Einsteinian relativity announced the beginning of a cultural meltdown of the earth archetype.

For instance, the conception of atoms in quantum mechanics, emerging at about the same time, was also undergoing a gestalt shift. The atoms of Newtonian mechanics had been tiny solid objects of varying shapes and sizes, whose combinations made up the order of things. The modern conception of atoms, however, is more ethereal, for these tiny units of aggressive force binding enormous reserves of energy have more in common with Leibnizian monads than anything else. Furthermore, their ghostly wave-particle and non-locality properties defy the binary categories of classical logic, while the spontaneous radioactive decay of uranium, thorium and plutonium atoms does not seem to be susceptible of a causal interpretation.

In the arts, meanwhile, something similar had been going on since Cézanne's invention of aperspectival space. The history of twentieth century painting reveals a gradual dissolution of solid objects into the energetic wellsprings from out of which they initially concretized. First, in the generation of Picasso, Klee and Miro, the objects blooming over their canvases like Japanese water flowers are manifestations from the realm of the dreaming mind, the forms of which glow with their own internal radiance, like the bioluminescent fish which inhabit the darkest abysses of the ocean. What the great film director David Cronenberg said of his own work applies equally here: "People say, 'What are you trying to do with your movies?' I say, 'Imagine you've drilled a hole in your forehead and that what you dream is projected directly onto a screen.'"

In the second phase, that of Jackson Pollock, Willem de Kooning and Mark Rothko, these protean forms are resolved into the energetic sources which have given them birth, for the visions of their canvasses are manifestations of pure energy, what the Hindus call *shakti* or in the case of Rothko, the Void of the Buddhists. These are the causal zones of manifestation from out of which the forms of dream and myth spring, and from which, in turn, the physical world itself has arisen.

So it is evident to me, anyway, that the five centuries in which the earth archetype has dominated the collective imagination of the West are at an end, and so too, the various philosophies of materialism that it spawned. And though a significant portion of our modern scientists remain fixated in the nineteenth century, their world belongs to the past and not the one that is presently unfolding before us.

V. THE SECOND RELIGIOUSNESS

There is a novella by Doris Lessing called "The Temptations of Jack Orkney," which perfectly captures the sort of bifurcation in our collective unconscious that is the focus of this book. The story recounts a middle-aged socialist who has spent his life engaged in various causes, organizing protest marches, and writing trashy adventure novels of his travels around the world. With regard to his religious views, as Lessing puts it, "he . . . wore atheism like a robe of honour. Not to believe in an after-life was like a certificate of bravery and above all, clarity of thinking."[15]

As the story opens up, he is called to his father's death bed, where he encounters his brother and sister, whom he discovers to his surprise are no longer religious, either. His father dies and Jack returns home to his wife and his political activities. Only now, he finds that he can no longer sleep at night because of a series of terrifying dreams. He has never been afraid of death, at least not in the diffuse existential sense to which Heidegger refers in *Being and Time*, but every night tormenting dreams come to him of being buried alive with his father or confronting a mysterious white-robed woman pointing the way to a promised land. He loses interest in his political activities, and to the astonishment of all his friends, finds himself attending church one Sunday morning. But this doesn't feel right to him, either, and as the dreams become worse, he decides to study comparative religion and anthropology, while reading Chardin and Simone Weil. The story ends on an ominous note as he decides to repudiate religiosity altogether, even while his dreams continue to grow progressively worse.

I see Lessing's story as a perfect analogy for what is presently going on within Western civilization, which has spent the past two hundred years or so living in a spiritual vacuum covered up by one materialism or another, and as a result, its neglected soul has been trying to get our attention in the form of the nightmarish catastrophes of the twentieth century. As the great German Indologist Heinrich Zimmer writes:

> All the gods and powers are within us, the body expands to a cosmos, and woe to him who disregards it. This divine being in us can never . . . be asleep or away on a voyage; if it seems to sleep or to be far off, that is a sign that it is angry, because we have lost our relation to it and have not been able to preserve it. In that event, we no longer enjoy its grace: it is already in process of metamorphosing into a dangerous devil, which, like all stupidity and despair must behave malignantly toward us.[16]

From Copernicus to Newton, to the Kant-Laplacian theory of the origin of the solar system, Hutton's geological uniformitarianism, Darwin's *Origin of Species*, relativity and quantum mechanics, science has gradually eroded the once magnificent edifice of the Biblical vision of the cosmos to little more than a ruined Gothic church like those which haunt the forests in a Caspar David Friedrich painting. Nature, it would seem, has triumphed over spirit, for the vision of the cosmos painted by science is one of hard, immutable laws that give rise, of necessity, to stars and planets and great spiraling galaxies that go pinwheeling through space until they crash into each other. Rogue stars wander like pirate ships into stable solar systems where they disrupt the careful balance of gravitational attractions, sending whole systems into chaos, while black holes quietly drain the life out of burgeoning young stars, like spiders feasting on captive prey. There seems little room in all of this for the tiny, feeble productions of man, whose once mighty thought systems are dwarfed to nothing by these incomprehensible magnitudes. Man has apparently been scaled down in this new cosmos to little more than an industrious insect.

He has certainly behaved like one throughout the twentieth century, for what else shall we make of the mustard gas attacks of the first World War, or Stalin's massacre of nine million peasants, or Hitler's gas chambers with their dark commodities of soap and lampshades made from human remains? Or the bombing of Hiroshima? Or the recent nerve gas attacks in Tokyo subways by the Aum Shinrikyo doomsday cult? Indeed, one is tempted to suspect that there is a connection between the disintegration of our religious cosmologies during the past two or three hundred years and the corresponding increase in human savagery that has taken place since. It would seem that the absence of a spiritual vision of the cosmos which makes a place for man somewhere within it, leads directly to the sort of existentialist despair expressed in phrases like, "nothing is true, everything is permitted," for twentieth century man has certainly given himself permission to do as he pleases.

It is, however, the thesis of this book that the world view of materialism is currently undergoing transubstantiation into a more spiritually-informed way of regarding the cosmos. I believe that this is what the disintegration of the earth archetype in the twentieth-century imagination of culture amounts to, although I do not mean by this to imply "progress" of the technological or economic kind. Oswald Spengler, for example, predicted in *The Decline of the West* that by century's end we would be entering a "second religiousness," by which he had nothing in mind like "progress," either. The "second religiousness" is the inevitable sequel to a materialistic way of life pushed to its limits, and for Spengler it carried the same kind of evolutionary necessity that communism had for Marx when he insisted that it was the inescapable outcome of capitalism. By *second* religiousness, Spengler meant something like the image of the serpent biting its tail, for he saw culture as a species of organism with a life cycle of growth and decay that was directly analogous to the seasons of a year or the stages of a human lifetime. The *first* religiousness is the childhood of a culture, which, for us Northern Europeans, began with the Christian Middle Ages. The intellectual cycle that a culture grows through follows the sequence: Religious, Philosophical, Prosaic (or materialistic), and then back to Religious. Once this latter stage has been achieved, the culture in question has reached thermodynamic equilibrium and may remain for centuries in a kind of suspended decrepitude — like India or the Muslim world today.

While it is my belief that we are thoroughly immersed in this "second religiousness," I do not intend the profiles that make up the contents of the following chapters as a catalogue of cultural senescence. Rather, it is that the shift in our culture which Spengler foresaw — from materialism to religiousness — is directly analogous to the kind of transition from the practice of mechanistic science to the spiritual one that is embodied by the thinkers in this book. The appearance of a new species of scientist who takes myth seriously does not signify the end of Western civilization, but rather the end of an *epoch* in which the cultural canon that has shaped the imagination of the West for five centuries is disintegrating. As Erich Neumann writes of such transitional periods:

> This chaos and the attendant atmosphere of doom are by no means diminished by the approach of other archetypes, which may actually have ushered in the collapse of the old cultural canon. Just as in antiquity and the Middle Ages, people today are afraid when stars fall, when comets move across the heavens and when terrifying changes in the firmament and other signs announce the end of an epoch, which for the generation in question seems to be the end of the whole world.
>
> For just as, archetypally, every New Year . . . is a perilous time of judgment and doom, so is the beginning of every new cultural epoch bound up with all that characterizes the end of an era. Only at rare intervals, when the clouds part in the dark sky of the crumbling canon, do a few individuals discern a new constellation, which already belongs to the new canon of transpersonal values and foreshadows its configuration.[17]

The appearance of such new constellations is precisely what this book is about, for in contradistinction to the mechanistic universe, its chapters are filled with visions of a cosmos that is alive and sentient, capable of remembering the past and interacting with our lives on the most intimate level. Ghosts, telepathy, angels, reincarnation and the existence of the soul are discussed here by scientists who take them seriously, rather than dismissing them out of hand, and so there is a radical difference between the way in which these scientists go about the practice of science and the way it has been done in the past.

Such a metanoiac shift from materialism to spirituality, furthermore, has been taking place on a microcosmic scale throughout the individual lives of a number of significant minds of the twentieth century, and indeed, one may gauge the climate of a cultural noosphere at any particular point in its history by examining the intellectual development of its more imaginative minds. Doris Lessing herself underwent such a transformation, from her involvement in the Communist Party and the writing of her early novels of social realism, to the more mystically inspired masterpieces of her later career, such as the *Canopus in Argos* series. Arthur Koestler, a generation before, had also become disillusioned with communism and moved on to author famous books of countercultural science like *The Ghost in the Machine* and *The Act of Creation*. The engineer Arthur Young, inventor of the Bell helicopter, also underwent this transformation, as he chronicles in his diaries *The Bell Notes: A Journey from Physics to Metaphysics*. Young's masterpiece, *The Reflexive Universe*, is a grand synthesis of science and spirituality and I regard it — along with Carl Jung's autobiography *Memories, Dreams, Reflections* and William Irwin Thompson's *Imaginary Landscape: Making Worlds of Myth and Science* — as one of the key sacred gospels for the epoch that I set forth in this book.[18]

VI.

CONCERNING AN IMAGINARY *DOPPELGÄNGER* OF THIS BOOK WITH THE ALTERNATIVE CAST OF MARY CATHERINE BATESON, JOANNA MACY, CAMILLE PAGLIA, JAMES LOVELOCK, ILYA PRIGOGINE, FRANCISCO VARELA, JAMES HILLMAN AND KEN WILBER

My initial vision of this book differed in certain respects from the present result. I had intended to interview a much larger group, for one thing. But as I went along, I realized that more would not necessarily have been better, since a smaller cast enabled me to devote more time to each particular person. The resulting interviews are therefore longer and more detailed than what appears in most such "collections."

I began this project with the intention to create a number of bridges between culture worlds. Not only did I want to span the chasm between the sciences and the humanities, but also to create a pair of scales, of sorts, evenly weighted between the West coast approach of science to myth and spirituality, and that of the East coast. Contingencies of time and place have tipped the scales in favor of the Pacific, which, in the present cast, is comprised of Deepak Chopra, Stanislav Grof, Brian Swimme, Terence McKenna, Ralph Abraham and Rupert Sheldrake (who, though he is British and still resides in England, also spends a great part of his time in the West-coast circles). My Atlantic representatives have turned out to be Lynn Margulis and William Irwin Thompson (and here again, although Thompson was born and raised in Los Angeles, the cultural world with which he most identifies is that of the East coast. In our interview, his contrast between the symposia which he conducted at the Cathedral of Saint John the Divine in New York City and the classes which he taught briefly at California Institute of Integral Studies makes the point clear). In this respect, I deeply regret having been late in getting to Mary Catherine Bateson, who was not available for an interview due to prior commitments, or not having had the pleasure to interview the physicist Arthur Zajonc.[19]

On the other hand, it is just as well, since the twilight of the clockwork god is not something taking place exclusively in American science, but in science globally. Europeans like Ilya Prigogine and Michel Serres are just as much a part of the cultural noosphere in this book as are any of the American scientists. Thus, to have framed the book in terms of the tension between the coasts would have been perhaps a moot point from the outset. But let me just note here in passing, that the East coast approach to science differs quite dramatically from that of the West coast, since the former is more conservative, uptight, critical, formal, academic and generally less tolerant of experimentation with psychedelics or drugs of any kind, whereas the California approach is more informal, populist and experiential. The differences can be summed up in the contrast of the California workshop approach to that of New England journal science.

In choosing to interview the eight personalities whose work comprises the chapters of this book, I have deliberately cast a wide net so that my purview would include domains such as psychology and culture history as well as more traditionally scientific areas such as biology and physics. However, these protagonists are only a small sampling of the general transubstantiation of science. They should in no way be taken to represent its core nucleus, for I chose to interview them simply because they are favorites of mine. Someone else writing a book with exactly the same thesis might have chosen a different cast, because the core group is actually quite large, as the list at the end of this chapter will indicate.

As a means of somewhat redressing my initial vision, then, I will briefly sketch out the existence of an imaginary *doppelgänger* of this book concerning an alternative cast which, in a perfect world, I would like to have included in the present book. The following is a group of eight other scientists and philosophers that I personally find intriguing and whose work is of equal importance to those I have profiled in *Twilight of the Clockwork God*.

— ANTHROPOLOGY: *Mary Catherine Bateson*: As I have already mentioned, I regret not having reached Ms. Bateson for an interview sooner, since her inclusion would have enriched the book immeasurably. Not only would it have balanced my East coast / West coast scales somewhat more properly, but since Bateson is a personal friend of both Lynn Margulis and William Irwin Thompson, she would have helped to enrich the description of the particular cultural milieu surrounding Lindisfarne, the organization built by William Irwin Thompson for the purpose of creating an ecology of consciousness bridging the worlds of science and spirit. Bateson is the daughter of the biologist/anthropologist Gregory Bateson and the famous anthropologist Margaret Mead. Gregory Bateson spent most of his final years at Esalen, the cultural matrix which helped produce Stan Grof, the astrologer Richard Tarnas,[20] Fritjof Capra and Terence McKenna. Bateson wrote his final work, *Mind and Nature* while residing at Lindisfarne. Mary Catherine Bateson's memoirs of her parents are contained in her book *With A Daughter's Eye*.

Bateson herself has written a series of unique and fascinating books which attempt to eradicate what Lynn Margulis terms "academic apartheid."

She is both a professor of English as well as Anthropology at George Mason University, and has written about everything from Arabic love poetry to the changing roles of women in society. Her book *Composing A Life* examines the "complex expectations that are part of the baggage of most women."[21] Other books such as *Our Own Metaphor*, *Peripheral Visions*, and *Angel's Fear*, have been extremely influential.

— ECOLOGY: *Joanna Macy*: Part of the culture world of California Institute of Integral Studies, she has written a series of important books such as *World as Lover, World as Self* which discuss the interface between Buddhism, General Systems Theory and Deep Ecology. Once again, this multidisciplinary approach (she has also translated the poetry of Rilke) is what this book is all about. Only in the larger patterns which connect the various disciplines to each other, and ourselves with the web of the earth, will we gain the necessary perspective to see our current problems as functions of wrong living.

— CULTURE HISTORY: *Camille Paglia*: Like William Irwin Thompson, Ms. Paglia is a culture historian with, however, an emphasis in art history. Her book *Sexual Personae* is a narrative of Western culture from the Paleolithic to the present day. (The second volume still hasn't appeared.) Her approach is contentious, multidisciplinary and wide-ranging. Her thesis that Western culture is built out of a series of unique and bizarre personalities and that it is their very uniqueness which gives our culture the dynamism and energy which it has resonates with the tradition of Oswald Spengler and Joseph Campbell, and yet, unlike them, she champions decadence and perversion as a vital source of creativity. In her view, Maplethorpe and Madonna have as much to offer as feminism, the cinema, astrology and the great classics.

— GEOSCIENCES: *James Lovelock*: The counterpart of Lynn Margulis and originator of the Gaia hypothesis. Lovelock is fascinating not only for Gaia — which is discussed with Margulis below — but for his insistence that Big Science is absolutely unnecessary for re-visioning the world. As such, he works not at a university but out of a laboratory which he has built in his own home near Wales. There, he invents machines like the electron capture detector which helped give Rachel Carson the data for her book *Silent Spring*, the first of the ecological apocalypses (1962).

— THERMODYNAMICS: *Ilya Prigogine*: The thermodynamicist who made himself famous with the concept of dissipative structures is one of the foremost architects of the new world view coming out of science, which Eric Jantsch describes in his book *The Self-Organizing Universe*. The idea of self-organization is inherently mythic. Cosmogonic creation accounts like that from the *Brihadharanyaka Upanishad*, or some of the pre-Socratic cosmologies, are inherently descriptive of a self-organizing immanent universe in contradistinction to one that is made by an architect like Yaweh who is external to it. The concept of dissipative structures — self-organizing structures that are fragile, temporary, membrane-bounded and eject their entropy into their environment — is one of the most important images in the new cosmologies which are emerging to put Humpty Dumpty back together again.

— COGNITIVE SCIENCE: *Francisco Varela*: Like Prigogine, Varela's work is essential for understanding the new pictures of the cosmos that are emerging. With Humberto Maturana, he originated the concept of autopoiesis, "self-making" structures, in order to describe the cognitive basis of the worlds which organisms bring forth for themselves. Varela's bridges between cognitive science, epistemology, immunology and Buddhism are impressive and important alternatives to the hard-core reductionism of much mainstream science.

— PSYCHOLOGY: *James Hillman*: Here the contrast of West coast and East coast could not be more striking. Both he and Stan Grof are heirs to the Jungian throne, yet the way in which each has built from the work of Jung has led to the creation of two totally different psychologies. For Hillman, LSD is eschewed — or any kind of drug for that matter — as a means of accessing the visionary dimensions of the psyche, and is tantamount to a mechanical hi-jacking of the soul by the spirit. This is typical of the more conservative approach of the East coast. Hillman's distinctions between soul and spirit are rooted in the Neoplatonic tradition. Unlike Plotinus, however, he has chosen to side with soul and all its pathologies, against the spirit with its disdain for the earthly world, and so has inverted the value system of Neoplatonism, which always looks up. Hillman looks down into the individual soul and studies its sicknesses, depressions and suicidal tendencies in a quest of the mythic archetypes that are operating within.

— PHILOSOPHY: *Ken Wilber.* If Hillman stands for the claims of the soul, then it can be said that Wilber represents those of what Hillman defines as the spirit. In reading Hillman, one often has the feeling of a lack of structure, but in Wilber, there is almost nothing but. Wilber, consequently, has been accused of being "soulless," but there is something to be said for his hyper-analytical approach to this field. Often, in New Age literature, there is not enough criticism and differentiation, but Wilber is like a surgeon performing an anatomy lesson on the spirit and there is much to be gained from a study of his work. It would have been fun to include him in the present book, since he is discussed at several points. (My letter requesting an interview went unanswered.)

And so, as a final note here, I would like to append a list of names of scientists and philosophers — people who have come to my attention — whose work is contributing to the death of the mechanical world view, and who are taking myth, religion and spirituality seriously. This list encompasses both popular science and the more esoteric reaches of journal science and so it is not intended to draw distinctions about what constitutes "real science" and what does not. Its purpose is to delineate in the broadest possible contours, the size of the arena in which this transformation is taking place, highbrow culture as well as low. All of these people are inhabiting with varying degrees of emphasis the same phase space of myth, science and culture: Henri Atlan, Fritjof Capra, David Darling, Paul Davies, Larry Dossey, Brenda Dunne, Michel Gauquelin,* Richard Gerber, Marija Gimbutas,* Steve Hagen, Willis Harman,* Michael Harner, James Hillman, Wes Jackson, Robert Jahn, Eric Jantsch,* Stuart Kauffman, Stanley Krippner, Ervin Laszlo, Lawrence LeShan, James Lovelock, Joanna Macy, Humberto Maturana, Raymond Moody, Michael Murphy, Brian O'Leary, Susan Oyama, F. David Peat, Wilder Penfield, Karl Pribram, Ilya Prigogine, Howard Puthoff, Kenneth Ring, Peter Russell, Michel Serres, Percy Seymour, Saul-Paul Sirag, Charlene Spretnak, Ian Stevenson, Michael Talbot,* Russell Targ, Charles Tart, Evan Thompson, John and Nancy Todd, Francisco Varela, Frances Vaughan, Andrew Weil, Brian L. Weiss, John Anthony West, Ken Wilber, Fred Alan Wolf, and Arthur Zajonc.

Several ghosts also hover over these proceedings, men who represent the prophets, as it were, of this era. I would love to have had conversations with any one of them: Gregory Bateson, Henri Bergson, David Bohm, Joseph Campbell, Teilhard de Chardin, Karlfried Graf Durckheim, Jean Gebser, Carl Jung, Marshall McLuhan, Oswald Spengler, Arnold Toynbee, Immanuel Velikovsky, Alfred North Whitehead, Arthur Young, and others.

Therefore, this book is an apocalypse, of sorts, announcing the twilight of the mechanical world view. That world is most emphatically coming to an end, and the new one that is rising from out of its ruins is the one that will shape the imagination of the twenty-first century. I have been privileged to be living at a moment in the history of our culture when the mutation of a new species of scientist is beginning to proliferate. Yet, mechanists remain in abundance. As this book reveals, their magnificent ship has not only hit its iceberg, but is sinking. Slowly.

* Deceased.

*"This brings me to . . .
an idea that is expressed
in the old myths, in
Plato, in almost every
religion: that of a fall,
a descent into matter,
often though not always
followed by an ascent
back to celestial spheres
and a higher state of
being."*

— ARTHUR YOUNG

Part One:

THE

DESCENT

TO

EARTH

We begin with origins. In a discussion with mathematical cosmologist Brian Swimme, we explore the creation and evolution of the universe, which, in the words of Abbé Georges Lemaître, "can be compared to a fireworks display that has just ended. A few red wisps, ashes and smoke. Standing on a well chilled cinder we study the slow fading of suns, and try to recapture the vanished brilliance that gave rise to the origin of worlds."

Then, in a movement that evokes the shift in the imagination of Plotinus from the unknowable One to the unfolding of Nous, the Mind of the cosmos, biologist Rupert Sheldrake sketches for us the Cosmic Memory which guides and shapes this process. With Sheldrake, we linger for a time amongst the disembodied souls and ghosts that inhabit the astral plane, and explore the paranormal abilities of human beings.

Then, from our contemplation of God and the swarming magnitudes of his angels, we hover above Chaos with Ralph Abraham, for whom the swirling vortices that give rise to the creation of forms possess an inherent orderliness. Abraham's fractal landscapes are evocative of Leonardo da Vinci's imagination of the earth as a living being, whose rocks were like bones and whose ever-circulating rivers, lakes and turbulent streams like the arteries and veins of a huge, dreaming giant.

Finally, our descent to earth is completed with Lynn Margulis's descriptions of the genesis and evolution of Gaia. Margulis emerges from the center of the drama like the goddess Erda in Wagner's *Ring* cycle who periodically rises from the earth to remind Wotan in his battles with destiny that all the universe is encompassed within her Fate and not even the gods can escape their doom. Margulis reminds us that whatever we humans do, we are firmly encompassed by Gaia, and she will destroy us if she sees fit, regardless of what we do to her.

GOD AND THE

QUANTUM VACUUM:

A CONVERSATION WITH

BRIAN SWIMME

It was a Catholic priest, Georges Lemaître, who in 1927 drew the initial sketch for the big bang hypothesis when he said that the universe must have originated from a sort of "cosmic egg" of matter and energy. Consciously or not, Lemaître was invoking ancient myth, for the image of the cosmic egg as the origin of the universe goes back to the Orphic cults of Greece, and even beyond, to Egypt. For when the human mind is confronted with realms which transcend the bounds of experience, the mythic imagination goes to work, populating the dark hinterlands of our maps with dragons and chimeras. The narratives of science, accordingly, almost always conceal mythic patterns, if you look closely enough.[1]

Another Catholic priest, Teilhard de Chardin, attempted a more deliberate synthesis of science and religion, but the veneer of scientific imagery which he painted over his theology was more like a vast, crumbling Diego Rivera mural of evolution beneath which the older canvas of Christianity and its mythic structures is still visible. Chardin's two main cosmic principles are really God and the Devil in disguise: the benevolent force of Evolution is driving the cosmic drama to its Omega Point, in spite of the resistance put up by the dark force of Entropy. It is the same drama, precisely, in Zoroastrianism, in which the god of light, Ahura Mazda, is in cosmic contention with the lord of darkness, Angra Mainyu, and as in Chardin's narrative, the victory of the former at the end of time is already assured.

Science and religion may have a lot more in common than most of us realize, and on the basis of these shared archetypal patterns, a reconciliation of sorts might be built. That they may share identical archetypes, however, does not mean that they perform the same functions. The function of religiosity is to awaken a sense of awe with respect to the mystery of the cosmos, and to do so through a transformation of consciousness. The function of science, on the other hand, has never been the alteration of human consciousness, but to render an accurate knowledge of the cosmos through an explanation of its processes. Science is addressed to the intellect, whereas religion normally bypasses the intellect to galvanize emotional energies. The Scholastic debates of the middle ages between Aristotelian rationality and Augustinian faith have reawakened for us, today, in the conflict between science and religion.

For mathematical cosmologist Brian Swimme, resolving this antinomy has been something of a life task. He was educated at Santa Clara, a Catholic university, where he discovered the works of Teilhard de Chardin, who first introduced him to the interface between science and theology. When attending graduate school at the University of Oregon, he realized that this interface was of no interest to most of the scientists there, and in fact, was largely an embarrassment because "as scientists we were trained not to ask these deeper questions." Although he took his Ph.D. in gravitational dynamics, the nature of the cosmos as a numinous revelation remained for him the primary interest. He taught at the Institute of Culture and Creation Spirituality at Holy Names College in Oakland, California from 1983 to 1990. His first book *Manifesto for a Global Civilization* (written in collaboration with Mathew Fox) is a brief exploration into the shortcomings of Augustinian theology and the mechanistic paradigm, emphasizing the need for a synthesis of science, religion and ecology.

In 1984, he published *The Universe is a Green Dragon*, a delightful Socratic dialogue sketching out the lineaments of this synthesis. The book was dedicated to Thomas Berry, his most important mentor.[2] Berry's lifetime of investigation into the religions of the Far East and current ecological concerns immediately caught Swimme's attention when in 1980 he came across a paper written by him, called "The New Story." For Swimme, the paper echoed his own thinking about the possibility for a new cosmology that transcended the antagonism of science and religion. For the next decade or so, he and Berry worked out the contours of this synthesis, which was published in 1992 as *The Universe Story.*

He has also produced a series of video courses: *Canticle to the Cosmos* (1990), *Soul of the Universe* (1991), *The Hidden Heart of the Cosmos* and *The Earth's Imagination.* His most recent book is *A Walk Through Time: From Stardust to Us.* Currently, he teaches at California Institute of Integral Studies in the Philosophy, Cosmology and Consciousness Program.

JE: In your first book, Manifesto for a Global Civilization, *you write, "whereas the machine was the primary symbol for the world in the previous age, in the emerging age, the primary symbol for the world is music." Can you elaborate on that?*

BS: Well, the main idea there is the sense of presence. Where is something? Where does it exist? And at least from the point of view of modern science, the simple way of talking about it was that something exists where its atoms are. But our discoveries have deepened our understanding of that and so we don't think of an atom as being in one particular place anymore. We think of it as having a presence that is co-extensive with the universe. So we've begun to conceive of a reality that's interpenetrating, that somehow or another, even at the level of atoms, we can't think of them as simply located in one spot. And so if we have a reality where the parts are woven into the whole and they are in some way present throughout the universe, then I was trying to imagine what would be a way of capturing that image of an interpenetrating whole and I thought of music. The simple analogy is that instead of atoms, we have notes and the notes themselves are all interwoven to make this new thing, a chord.

But even beyond that, if you're in the middle of a song and you really are present to the music, the beginning is there, as well. As the music goes on, the whole is always present, so that to hear the last notes of a song really well is to be feeling the first notes. So if you're watching a lizard scampering around in the dust, to really be present to it, you have to feel the ancestry of the lizard. You know, the backbone came from the fish and so the lizard is making this whole story present. And that, to me, is like listening to a work of music.

JE: You also state that in order for science to thrive in the coming global civilization, its mystical core should be celebrated. Does this mean that science should be transformed into something that more closely resembles the function of religion?

BS: I'm not suggesting you're saying this, but let me just make it clear that I don't think science should become religion. I think science is a distinct activity. Religion and philosophy are distinct intellectual achievements, but they're really not separate and to pretend that they are is no longer viable. During the nineteenth century, scientists were happy striving after knowledge; the questions beyond that somehow were seen as non-scientific, whereas today there's a realization that every activity of the human has multiple implications. When I talk about the mystical core, I think the urge of the scientist to understand is ultimately mystical. It has to do with a deep desire to taste and touch reality. So it's not that science should become religion, but that science and religion should work together toward something else.

Niles Eldredge is a paleontologist and he is now giving talks on the sixth great extinction that we're in. He is talking about how we have to start thinking about reducing the human population.[3] It would have been inconceivable even a couple of decades ago that a paleontologist would be talking about human population. But he's gone beyond that type of rigid separation in a very admirable way. So that would be closer to what I was talking about. His love of life is now, as a scientist, leading him to speak on these huge issues that sometimes we would say should just be dealt with by religion.

JE: You also suggest in your first book that Augustine's various dualisms, spirituality versus sensuality, God versus the cosmos and so forth, should be done away with in favor of a cosmology that transcends the separation of the divine and the physical world. Can you describe what this sort of a cosmology would be like?

BS: Well, for example, the Deism of the seventeenth century, where you have a god that's separate from the universe and the universe, then, is wholly separate from the divine origin; that doesn't appeal to me, particularly, because then it's easier to think of the universe as a sort of neutral stuff. So the religious writers that have impressed me more are pantheists. They're the ones that speak of a divine reality that is interpenetrating all physical reality. And that seems to be a much more attractive theology.[4]

JE: How certain are we of our model of the Big Bang? What's the evidence for it?

BS: The evidence would be threefold: the first is the expansion. If you look at other galaxies in the universe, they're moving away from the Milky Way. And if you look at galaxies that are twice as far away, they're moving twice as fast. So if you think about that for a minute, it means that the universe is moving apart like some rapid expansion from an initial point. And so that would be one major piece of evidence.

The second would be — and Lemaître was the first to speculate about this — that if this began at the great explosion, there should be evidence of that explosion around. George Gamow and his collaborators actually calculated that the remnants from that explosion would be a form of radiation at ten degrees above absolute zero. Then in 1965, Penzias and Wilson actually located this background radiation at 2.75 degrees. So it was lower than even Gamow calculated it, but again, a remarkable discovery.

The third major piece of evidence is the presence of hydrogen and lithium and helium in the Big Bang scenario. Early on in the universe there was a moment when light elements could be created, but only in a certain amount. There are exact predictions made in the model about how much hydrogen, helium and lithium there would be in the universe and these have been remarkably consistent with the empirical findings. So the background radiation pretty well eliminated the other models,[5] but since that time more of this has come in. The most recent one would be from the COBE satellite, discovering the ripples from around 300,000 years after the birth that we now think gave rise to the galaxies.

JE: Stephen Hawking is excited about these quantum fluctuations. Can you explain why they're significant?

BS: If we go back 15 billion years, we have this expanding universe. If the universe is perfectly symmetric and homogeneous — and we imagine that's how it began — then the universe would simply expand forever and never form any structures. But for structures to actually come about there had to be some break in symmetry, some sort of fluctuation. One way to imagine this is that at the quantum level we have this foaming of material, space and time and energy. Our current theory is that this initial foaming was inflated very rapidly so that those fluctuations at the quantum level suddenly became macro fluctuations — and those are what Mather and Smoot captured on the COBE satellite. They're what gave rise to the structure of the universe.

You see, if the universe were perfectly symmetric, then early on, for every particle of matter there would be another particle of anti-matter. Everything would just annihilate and there would be nothing left but light. But there's a slight, tiny, tiny asymmetry. So for every billion anti-protons, there turns out to be a billion plus one protons, and so this strange little piece of asymmetry is what gave rise to everything. The same thing could be said now about the structure of the universe in terms of the galaxies: these fluctuations at a micro scale are what enable the Milky Way and Andromeda and other things to come into being. It's just overwhelming.[6]

JE: Where does the idea of God fit into our current cosmological narratives?

BS: I would say most scientists would just ignore the question. But many really good scientists have thought about it, too, and there would be a variety of opinions there. My own way of relating a sort of classical theological thought with this modern scientific story is to think in terms of the origin of the universe coming out of emptiness. That would be the way in which some scientists would talk about it. We would say that the quantum vacuum, really, is the origin of the universe. And the quantum vacuum is a mysterious realm. It has nothing in it; there's no thing there, but it's a realm of generativity. This is remarkably similar to the kinds of speculations coming from such theologians as Meister Eckhart, who talked about the super essential Darkness of God. Now obviously, when they're investigating the quantum vacuum, scientists are not saying to themselves, "I'm investigating the Godhead!" I'm simply pointing out that there is a remarkable correspondence between these two ways of investigating ultimate reality. If you simply identify them and say that the quantum vacuum really *is* a scientific way of exploring the Godhead then you begin to see the contours of a new kind of theology, one that would draw upon both traditional sources and contemporary science.

JE: You contrast the current view of time given by our scientific narratives as essentially linear and irreversible, to that of the old mythic view of cyclical time. Can you describe what implications our current cosmology has for cyclical views of time and history?

BS: There are cyclical patterns that we're involved with and we're quite aware of them. There's winter, and new people are born, new people are dying, and they go through this cycle over and over again. And that I think is a deep understanding from cosmologies all around the world. But the scientific one adds to that the discovery of irreversible time. For instance, we have no way of validating the statement that if life extinguished on earth, it would recreate itself. But rather, the mainstream theory would be that the emergence of life on planet Earth is a one-time event because the actual emergence of life alters the conditions which enable life to come about. So that irreversible aspect to creativity, I think, adds a degree of drama to the other cosmologies that they would not otherwise have. There's something dramatic and even tragic about the loss of a form of life. For instance, we're on the verge of losing the higher primates, like the gorillas. Well, in a cyclical cosmology one could fail to really feel the depth of that event because there would be a sense of earth replenishing itself and the gorillas would come back. But in our understanding the gorillas would never come back, ever.

JE: James Lovelock and Lynn Margulis have put forth their model of the Gaia hypothesis, in which the earth seems to behave like a living organism. Likewise, you have suggested that the universe can be thought of as analogous to an organism. Can you describe how the universe can be seen as a self-organizing being?

BS: Well, for instance, Lovelock and Margulis point out that the percentage of oxygen in the atmosphere is not a random number. It's the highest concentration that the atmosphere can really bear and support life. If it were much higher, you would have spontaneous combustion. So there would be a big destruction of life. If it were much lower, the more complex organisms would not have come into being. So, one of the things they point out is, it's not an accident that the earth organizes itself so that oxygen will be around 21 percent.

In an analogous way, if you look at the universe as a whole and go back to the expansion of the galaxies, you see they're moving away from each other at a certain rate, and you can measure the rate, but it turns out that it isn't random. Again, like the percentage of oxygen, if the rate of expansion had been just slightly higher, then looking back over fifteen billion years, we would have a situation where the universe would have expanded rapidly and never would have formed a structure. The formation of a structure is such a delicate event. So even a slight change in the expansion would have made the galaxies impossible. On the other hand, if you slow the expansion down just slightly, even a trillionth of a trillionth of a trillionth of one percent, the universe would have expanded out and then collapsed back into a massive black hole after maybe a million years.

So you can think about the expansion of the universe as a way in which the universe is proceeding so that life might come forth. Now, that statement I just gave you would be a cosmological assumption. Some people call it the strong Anthropic Principle. I'd just like to point out that in a certain sense, it's a conception of the universe that's new. The idea that the universe could be involved with its own unfolding simply wouldn't have been conceivable scientifically a hundred years ago. Now, in no way has it been advanced as a theory, it's simply in the minds of some scientists as a new way of thinking about the universe as a whole.

JE: In your lecture series Canticle to the Cosmos, *you draw an analogy between chlorophyll and human beings when you say that the reason the universe created chlorophyll was to capture sunlight and that the reason the universe created the human being was to capture the depth of things. What did you mean by that?*

BS: I meant that there seems to be the possibility of developing human sensibilities so that we can become deeply moved by the magnificence of existence. Now, it's quite possible to avoid that kind of development and to throw yourself into a more simplistic pursuit of money or whatever else, and that too is a human life. But I just mean there is the possibility for evoking sensitivities and sensibilities that respond very deeply to the majesty of the universe. So it seems to me that the whole tradition of poetry and music and art and religious expression comes out of humans who have developed this capacity to be moved to awe.

But to give one example: a person can go outside and look up and see Andromeda galaxy. You can see it with your naked eye, no telescope or anything, it's just there. It's slightly different than the other stars and if you have really good eyesight or a set of binoculars you can actually see that it's a galaxy. You can see the spiral structure. And it's just so remarkable because as you're looking at that, the light that's entering your eyes took two and half million years to get here. It left Andromeda right when the first humans were discovering how to use stone tools. The eye that I'm using to see Andromeda has been shaped by two and a half million years of human development, starting with those first stone tools. You know, it involved mathematics and language and all this; and eventually we've arrived at a place where we can now see Andromeda and know what we're seeing. And the light that we're seeing has been traveling toward us all that time, for two and a half million years. So that to experience Andromeda is to experience not only the depth of the galaxies, it's also to experience the depth of the human. I just mean that kind of experience is something like what a chlorophyll molecule does in capturing sunlight. We capture instead wonder or amazement that so easily could have been missed otherwise.

JE: In your book The Hidden Heart of the Cosmos, *you suggest that drug abuse is actually built into the structure of a materialistic society. What is the connection between our current views of the cosmos as a collection of dead objects and the high volume of drug usage?*

BS: The consumer culture seems to be something like the opposite of what I'm talking about in that the focus is on an ephemeral and I would say, shallow experience of things. The whole idea is not to cherish, because if you're going to cherish things it's going to be harder to throw them away and buy some new things. So the drive in consumerism seems to be to get us to be attracted to things. And so we want them and we get them. Simultaneously, once we get them, we're bored by them and we want to throw them away and get some new ones. So it's based on the conviction that the things themselves are really important to get and then really important to get rid of. This isn't the whole story on drug abuse by any means, but if we are putting so much energy into a culture that is convincing us that things are ephemeral and to be cast aside easily, then that makes it even more likely that people will resort to drugs to break out of that superficiality and at least taste something deep and real at whatever cost.

So I think there is a relationship. More important would be to point to a cosmological tradition — and this is something that every indigenous people I've looked at knew very well — that would spend enormous amounts of energy teaching gratitude and appreciation so that instead of a throwaway attitude, there would be a profound reverence for everything. I think it's really this reverence that would be a way of tasting the depths of things.

JE: In your book The Universe is a Green Dragon, *you articulate a philosophy of cosmic allurement. Can you explain that?*

BS: It's just the idea that in physics we're always looking for what causes things to happen and we've arrived at four fundamental interactions: the gravitational, the electrical and then the strong and weak nuclear forces. Basically everything we've looked at in the universe involves a combination of these forces. There's nothing we've found that doesn't involve these. So I was reflecting on that and I realized that if you look at fifteen billion years of cosmic evolution, it means that everything that's happened is a weaving of these fundamental interactions. It doesn't matter what level you look at: asteroids, stars, galaxies, planets, the first cells or multicellularity — at any level these four will be at work.

So then I thought, well, what if you looked at the human world from that perspective? If you look at the galaxy, the reason stars are moving about the center is this common gravitational attraction. I realized when I thought about my own life that so much of what I do comes down to fundamental attractions of various sorts to things that I was interested in or drawn to. And we say, "well, I'm interested in studying cosmology because I find it fascinating and whatnot," but *why* do you find it fascinating? See, ultimately, it comes down to this power we call fascination, so it's similar to trying to understand why a star goes around a galaxy. It's attracted by gravity. Well, but why? What's gravity? So it's a way of simply pointing to the fact that things happen in the universe because of these fundamental powers and one of them is the power of attraction. On the plane of stars, we use the word "gravity" but we're really using the word "gravity" to point to a fundamental power of attraction. And on the level of the human, we say "fascination" or "interest." But once again, that's pointing to the same power of attraction, just in a different form.

Much of my work is always an attempt to understand the human in terms of the cosmos because during the last 300 years we've isolated the human from the cosmos. We think of ourselves as an appendage or an addendum, but it's so wrong now that we understand it's all one story. So I was trying to reflect on the ways in which our understanding could be deepened if we embedded it in the larger story of the galaxy or of the earth. It's simply a way of recognizing that what fascinates us, what draws us as individuals is utterly mysterious. There's no reason for it, it's something we discover and experience that's at the core of our lives. And it's to be explored with a real sense of awe.

JE: You co-authored with Thomas Berry a book called The Universe Story. *In that book, both of you say that we are moving into an Ecozoic Era. Can you explain what that means?*

BS: The Ecozoic Era would be a vision, and our hope is that the human species will move in this direction. It's a fundamental shift. If we look at our situation today on the planet, there's a great deal of destruction taking place. In our own thinking, a lot of this comes from the gap between the human and the natural world. So if we're talking about human rights, the natural world has no rights. Or if we talk about the GNP we're talking about *human* economics. We're not thinking about the economics of the birds. In terms of our religions, we're talking about the relationships between the human and God and we don't imagine that the natural world is the locus of God. So there's a separation between the human and the natural world that permeates society and the Ecozoic Era would simply be an era when we would see ourselves as embedded within the earth community. We would begin with the fundamental respect for all of life, in fact, all of the components of the earth. That would be the basic orientation of the

Ecozoic. And the one challenge of entering the Ecozoic would be to invent a way of human life that is mutually enhancing throughout the natural world. So rather than just focusing on human benefits, we would look for a way of increasing human benefits while at the same time increasing the benefits to the natural world.

FROM CELLULAR AGING

TO THE PHYSICS OF ANGELS:

A CONVERSATION WITH

RUPERT SHELDRAKE

Can there be a science of metaphysics? The question was posed by Immanuel Kant in 1781 with his monumental cathedral of a book, *The Critique of Pure Reason*. Deeply embedded within the towering spires and vaulted arches of its frame — with its ornate tracery of axioms and foliated scrollwork of concepts within concepts repeating like Cantor sets to infinity — was to be found, for the patient reader, Kant's answer: there can *never* be a science of metaphysics because science, by its very nature, is concerned with a recondite analysis of tangible things *within* the world of space and time. Metaphysics, on the contrary, is concerned with such *transcendent* intangibles as God, the soul, freedom and immortality. Theology has never been the province of science, the primary aim of which is a *coniunctio* of the categories of the mind *with* the impressions of the senses. Classical metaphysics, confined by the rigid nexus of logic, has always looked askance at the earthly plane for confirmation of the validity of its "truths."

The question is still relevant today, for some of our most creative scientists have begun trespassing into the territory of metaphysics, which Kant had insisted should remain separate from science in order to preserve the domain of human freedom and religiosity from being absorbed by the machine of the Newtonian cosmos. Kant knew very well what would happen to society if its citizens came to believe that free will was an anachronism and that the events of one's own life were to be regarded strictly as functions of the impersonal laws of a secularized environment. And indeed, with the publications of the works of Darwin, Marx, Freud and Skinner throughout the nineteenth and early twentieth centuries, precisely what Kant had feared came into manifestation with the unfolding of these various materialisms. T.S. Eliot's poems "The Waste Land" and "The Hollow Men" have become emblematic of the spiritual climate of the twentieth century, particularly since every one of the classical domains of the humanities has been colonized by the expanding empire of mechanistic science. But now, as the twentieth century spirals to its finale, it would seem that science is very much in need of a blast of wind from the pneumatic spirit to set its stagnant waters in motion once again.

Rupert Sheldrake is one of the few scientists who has no reservations whatsoever about discoursing on those metaphysical topics which engaged the famous banqueters of Plato's tables, such as the existence of the soul, reincarnation, or the *anima mundi*. He is the biologist who made himself famous with the concept of morphogenetic fields, which he articulated in his first book, *A New Science of Life* (1981), as a creative response to the challenge set by nineteenth century debates between mechanists and vitalists over the development of organisms. In the 1920s, the "organicists" first proposed the idea of morphogenetic fields as a mean between the extremes of mechanism and vitalism. The models proposed by these thinkers, however, tended towards Platonism with their vision of morphogenetic fields as transcendent "laws" of organization. But Sheldrake's innovation was to see these fields as themselves evolving along with the forms which they produce.

Indeed for Sheldrake the "laws" of the universe may not be laws at all, but rather deeply ingrained habits of action which have been built up over the many eons in which the universe has spun itself out. Like the ancient riverbeds on the surface of Mars left behind by the pressures of flowing water over billions of years, so too, the "laws" of the universe may be thought of as runnels engraved in the texture of space-time by the endless flow of repetitive activity. And the longer particular patterns persist, the greater their tendency to resist change. Sheldrake terms this habitual tendency of nature "morphic resonance," wherein present forms are shaped by the forms of the past. Morphic resonance is transmitted by means of "morphogenetic fields," which are analogous to electromagnetic fields in that they transmit information, but differ in that they do so without using energy, and are therefore not diminished by transmission through time or space.[1]

Sheldrake illustrates his idea with the analogy of a television set. Though we can alter the images on our screens by adjusting components or distorting them — just as we can alter or distort the phenotypical characteristics of organisms through genetic engineering — it by no means follows that the images are coming from *inside* the television set. They are in fact encoded as information coming from *outside* in the form of electromagnetic frequencies which the skillful arrangement of the transistors and circuits within the television set enables us to pick up and render *visible*. Likewise, it is not at all necessary for us to assume that the physical characteristics of organisms are contained *inside* the genes, which may rather be analogous to transistors tuned in to the proper frequencies for translating invisible information into visible form. Thus, morphogenetic fields are located invisibly in and around organisms, and may account for such hitherto unexplainable phenomena as the regeneration of severed limbs by worms and salamanders, phantom limbs, the holographic properties of memory, telepathy, and the increasing ease with which new skills are learned as greater quantities of a population acquire them.

When Sheldrake's first book was published, needless to say, there was great controversy in the academic journals regarding the value of his hypothesis. The editor of *Nature* magazine described the book "as the best candidate for book burning there has been for many years." One recalls here the anxieties of Saturn which impelled him to devour his children when he learned that Zeus was coming to put an end to his Golden Age.

Sheldrake's first book was followed by his magnum opus, *The Presence of the Past* (1988), a philosophical and cultural amplification of ideas presented academically in the first volume. This was followed by *The Rebirth of Nature* (1991) in which he traced the birth, rise, and inevitable senescence of the materialistic world view that is presently crumbling beneath the onslaught of such fresh thought worlds as chaos theory, the Gaia hypothesis, cellular symbiosis, and morphic resonance. Sheldrake's next book, *Trialogues at the Edge of the West* (1992), was a series of discussions with friends Terence McKenna and Ralph Abraham regarding the current state of cosmology.

In 1995, Sheldrake's little gem, *Seven Experiments That Could Change the World* was proposed as a do-it-yourself guide to science in the spirit that some of its great ideas have come from amateurs and dilettantes outside the formal academic world (Leeuwenhoek, for instance, was a janitor; Faraday a self-educated printer's apprentice; and of course, Mendel was a monk). Sheldrake presents a series of experiments in which he invites the reader to participate in the investigation of such unexplained phenomena as pets who know when their owners are coming home, the strange homing powers of pigeons, or the phenomenon of phantom limbs.

Most recently he has collaborated with theologian Matthew Fox on two sets of dialogues, *Natural Grace* and the *Physics of Angels* (1996) in which the ongoing conversation between science and spirituality finds fresh incarnation. Another set of conversations with Abraham and McKenna, entitled *The Evolutionary Mind: Trialogues at the Edge of the Unthinkable*, was published in 1998.

In the following interview, Sheldrake and I discuss his ideas about aging, the existence of the soul, reincarnation, ghosts, telepathy and angels. For despite Kant's insistence on keeping the two spheres separate, it is important to know what the changing perspectives of science have to say about traditional spiritual beliefs. The elementary ideas of the human imagination — gods, spirits, the category of the holy — have been ubiquitous throughout the development of human cultural evolution. There is no reason to think that the death of orthodox Christianity at the hands of an increasingly arrogant mechanistic science means that these ideas are merely vestigial relics from man's "superstitious" past. On the contrary, as Carl Jung often pointed out, modern man's lack of contact with these ideas has left him vulnerable to all sorts of political, social and economic hysterias which have plagued the course of the twentieth century with one mass catastrophe after another.[2] It is therefore important to bring the two perspectives together in order to heal the schism between the sciences and the humanities which has rendered that famous inability to communicate with each other remarked upon by C. P. Snow.

> *JE: One of the first papers that you wrote was on the aging, growth and death of cells. Can you say a few words about the theory of aging that you proposed in that paper?*

RS: I think aging is inherent in all forms of life because accidents occur, things go wrong, just like they do in a house; there's always something that goes wrong and needs repairing. But living cells have limited repair capacities. And so, when there are mistakes that can't be repaired, they tend to accumulate. That I think is the basis of aging. My proposal was that what happens in regeneration is that cells can be regenerated only by growing so fast that they dilute these breakdown products, these seeds of death that build up as a result of aging.

Or, that cells divide asymmetrically — that is, they divide in an unequal way, so that one of the daughter cells gets the seeds of death in an unfair measure, while the other one is regenerated. Asymmetrical cell division is very common in both animals and plants, in tissues which go on growing indefinitely, like the skin, the blood cells, or the growing tips of plant shoots. It's also found in the way egg cells are formed in both animals and plants, where, for every egg cell that's made, there are three highly mortal cells which are cast aside as the new regenerated egg cell is formed. So this was the basis of the cellular theory of aging as I proposed it in my *Nature* paper.[3]

JE: Joseph Campbell once suggested that the idea of morphogenetic fields reminded him of the Hindu concept of maya *— the field of space-time that gives birth to the forms of the world.[4] You wrote your first book,* A New Science of Life, *while living in an* ashram *in India. Do you think that the content of your book was influenced at all by a resonance with the traditions of Indian thought?[5]*

RS: I think it probably was, but the basic idea of morphic resonance and morphic fields came to me while I was in Cambridge, before I went to live in India. My thinking about morphogenetic fields was influenced by the holistic tradition in developmental biology, where these fields are fairly widely accepted. The idea of an influence through time — the morphic resonance idea — in fact, was inspired by Henri Bergson in his book *Matter and Memory*, where he argues that memory is not stored in a material form in the brain. I realized that Bergson's ideas on memory, which were to me completely new and incredibly exciting, could be generalized, and it was really through reflecting on Bergson's thought that I came to this idea.

However, when I went to work in India in an agricultural institute, I went on thinking about these ideas, and indeed they had much in common with Indian thought. I discovered, when I was first thinking about these things in Cambridge, that many people there simply couldn't understand what I was going on about — particularly scientists — and thought the idea was too ridiculous to be worth taking seriously. When I arrived in India and discussed it with Hindu friends and colleagues, they took the opposite approach; they said, "There's nothing new in this, it was all known millennia ago to the ancient *rishis*." So, they found the ideas perfectly acceptable; the only thing was, they weren't particularly interested in extending them into a scientific hypothesis.

I worked for five years in an agricultural institute before I went to live in the *ashram* to write my book. The climate of Indian thought was a very fertile one for me, and it enabled me to go on thinking about these ideas in a much more favorable environment than if I'd been doing it in Cambridge. But the germs of these ideas, the roots of my own thought, are in Western philosophy and science rather than Oriental philosophy. So, it's a kind of convergence.

> *JE: You see evolutionary history as a tension between the two forces of habit — or morphic resonance — and creativity, which involves the appearance of new morphic fields. But in the case of mass extinctions, you suggested once that "the ghosts of dead species would still be haunting the world, that the fields of the dinosaurs would still be potentially present if you could tune into them."* [6] *Would you mind commenting on how it might be possible for extinct species to reappear?*

RS: Well, I don't have in mind some kind of *Jurassic Park* scenario. What I was thinking of was that the fields would remain present, but the conditions for tuning into them are no longer there if the species is extinct; so they're not expressed. However, it's a well known fact in evolutionary studies that some of the features of extinct species can reappear again and again. Sometimes this happens in occasional mutations, sometimes it turns up in the fossil record. And when these features of extinct species reappear, they're usually given the name, "atavism," which implies a kind of throwback to an ancestral form. Atavisms were well known to Darwin, and he was very interested in them for the same reasons I am, that they seem to imply a kind of memory of what went before.

JE: Do you think that morphic fields could account for the existence of ghosts in any way?

RS: Well, the fields represent a kind of memory. If places have memories, then I suppose it's possible for ghostly-type phenomena to be built into their fields. This is a very hazy area of speculation and not one I've thought through rigorously. I've had no incentive to think it through rigorously because it's so hard to think of repeatable experiments with ghosts. But ghosts do seem to be a kind of memory thing, and morphic fields have to do with memory, so there may well be a connection.

JE: Karl Pribram suggests that memories are spread throughout the brain like waves, or holograms, and you go further in suggesting that memories may not be stored in the brain at all, but rather that the brain acts as a tuning device and picks up memories analogous to the way a television tunes in to certain frequencies. Furthermore, you've suggested that if memories aren't stored in the brain at all, this leaves the door open for the possibility of the existence of the soul. Can you explain how your ideas on the existence of the soul fit into this paradigm?

RS: Well, we should clarify the terms here. The traditional view in Europe was that all animals and plants have souls — not just people — and that these souls were what organized their bodies and their instincts. In some ways, therefore, the traditional idea of soul is very similar to what I mean by morphic fields. The traditional view of the soul in Aristotle and in Saint Thomas Aquinas was not the idea of some immortal spiritual principle. It was that the soul is a part of nature, a part of physics, in the general sense. It's that which organizes living bodies. In that sense, all morphic fields of plants and animals are like souls.

However, in the case of human beings the additional question arises as to whether it's possible for the soul to persist after bodily death. Now, normally, souls are associated with bodies. And the theory I'm putting forward is one that would see the soul associated with the body and memories coming about by morphic resonance. If it's possible for the soul to survive the death of the body, then you could have a persistence of memory and of consciousness. From the point of view of the theory I'm putting forward, there's nothing in the theory that says the soul has to survive the death of the body, and there's nothing that says that it can't. So, this is simply an open question. But it's not one that can be decided on *a priori* principles.

> *JE: In your book,* The Presence of the Past, *you have an interesting theory of reincarnation.[7] You suggest that people who have memories of past lives may actually be tuning in to the memories of other people in the morphogenetic field, and that they may not actually represent reincarnated people at all. Would you care to comment on that?*

RS: Yes. I'm suggesting that through morphic resonance we can all tune in to a kind of collective memory, memories from many people in the past. It's theoretically possible that we could tune into the memories of specific people. That might be explained subjectively as a memory of a past life. But this way of thinking about it doesn't necessarily mean this has to be reincarnation. The fact that you can tune in to somebody else's memories doesn't prove that you *are* that person. Again, I would leave the question open.

But, you see, this provides a middle way of thinking about the evidence for memories of past lives; for example, that collected by Ian Stevenson[8] and others. Usually the debate is polarized between people who say this is all nonsense because reincarnation is impossible — the standard scientific, skeptical view (I should say, the standard skeptical view; it's not particularly scientific.) — and the other people who say this evidence proves what we've always believed, namely, the reality of reincarnation. I'm suggesting that it's possible to accept the evidence and accept the phenomenon, but without jumping to the conclusion that it has to be reincarnation.

> *JE: So your theory that information can be transmitted by these non-material morphic fields makes plausible a paradigm in which phenomena such as telepathy or ESP can be understood. Can you explain how your paradigm makes sense out of this type of phenomena?*

RS: Well, if people can tune in to what other people have done in the past, then telepathy is a kind of logical extension of that. If you think of somebody tuning in to somebody else's thought a fraction of a second ago, then it becomes almost instantaneous and approaches the case of telepathy. So telepathy doesn't seem to be particularly difficult in principle to explain, if there's a world in which morphic resonance takes place.

Morphic fields also extend beyond the body. I think that when a person looks at something else or somebody else, the image that they're seeing is not located in their brain, but in the place where it seems to be. For example, if I looked at you, then my image of you would not be inside my head, but where you actually are. So I think that in perception we project our fields of perception, which are one kind of morphic field, which link the person who's doing the looking to what is being looked at. This, I think, means that people can affect other people or things just by looking at them through these fields. This is what underlies my current interest in the sense of being stared at, the feeling many people have of being looked at from behind.[9] I discuss this in my book *Seven Experiments That Could Change the World*, and since that book was published we've done many further experiments that convince me this is indeed a real phenomenon. So, that's not one of the things that parapsychologists usually talk about, but it's something which follows quite naturally from the idea of morphic fields.

I think that some of the other phenomena of parapsychology are hard to explain from the point of view of morphic fields and morphic resonance. For example, anything to do with precognition or premonition doesn't fit into an idea of influences just coming in from the past. So, I don't think this is going to give a blanket explanation of all parapsychological phenomena, but I think it's going to make some of it, at least, seem normal rather than paranormal.

JE: In your book Seven Experiments That Could Change the World, *you point out that the expectations of experimenters have a great deal to do with the outcome of their experiments. And you even suggest that they might influence their experiments through psychokinesis or telepathy. Would you mind discussing how that might work?*

RS: Yes, it's well known that in psychology and in medicine, the experimenter's expectations can and do influence the outcome of experiments, which is why people use blind experimental techniques to try and minimize this. The second point is a new one that I've just discovered by doing a survey of the literature and scientific practice of laboratories from different branches of science. And this reveals that in the physical sciences and in most of biology, people never do blind experiments. There's no protection whatever against possible experimenter effects. It seems to me quite possible that experimenters could be biasing the way they record their data. I would be very surprised if that doesn't happen in conventional science.[10]

But I think something more surprising and alarming might be happening, as you suggest: namely, a possible psychokinetic influence over the actual experimental system. Scientists would be completely unprepared for this if it were happening; they'd take no precautions against it. The culture of institutional science dismisses it as impossible. So, there would be a great vulnerability to this effect, if it's going on, and it might be happening quite commonly in science.

We know from the psychokinetic studies of Robert Jahn of Princeton that people can influence random number generators in a rather surprising way, even at a distance.[11] And since quantum events and random number generators are not unlike the quantum events occurring in physical, chemical and biological systems, there's already a precedent in experimental data for this kind of mind-over-matter effect. In Jahn's experiments, people are simply doing a kind of harmless game. In scientific experiments, where the experimenter has a lot invested in the outcome of the experiment, a lot of hopes and tensions and funding proposals hinging on what happens, the intensity of expectation may be much greater, and the consequences far larger than anything detected by Jahn. But this is an unexplained area. In that book I suggest several experiments that could be done in order to test for this effect in conventional science.

JE: Your books Natural Grace *and* The Physics of Angels, *co-written with Matthew Fox, are explorations into the interface between science and spirituality. There have been other important scientists — such as David Bohm and Fritjof Capra — who have also taken an interest in cross-breeding science and spirituality. In what ways do you see these two areas of discourse intersecting and what kinds of cultural hybrids do you see resulting from this fusion?*

RS: There are many areas of potential intersection. One is the cosmological, because when science is talking about creation, it's getting into a realm that has been very much the preserve of religion for a long time. I'm not now thinking simply of, "where did the big bang come from?" If we focus too much on the initial moments of creation, about which we know practically nothing, we get into a situation rather like that of the eighteenth century Deists, who thought of God making the world machine and starting it up and then standing back and letting it go on by itself.

I'm more interested in the ongoing creativity, which is expressed in the evolutionary process — and the evolutionary process must have an inherent creativity — and we know that our universe is creative at all levels, physical, biological, or mental, cultural and so on. So, what is the source of this creativity? Well, it's really a metaphysical question and materialist science has no other suggestion than chance; which really means that it's unintelligible, we can't think about it. However, this does overlap with traditional areas of theological and spiritual enquiry. Therefore this is one area of discussion.

Another is the nature of the soul, the psyche, consciousness, which science, until very recently, has had almost nothing to say about but which is obviously of crucial importance to our understanding of ourselves and of nature. And as I show in my book with Matthew Fox, there are yet further areas, such as the question of prayer and how it works. If people praying for things to happen on the other side of the world have a statistically measurable effect on what does happen, you've got a kind of action at a distance, which is in the purview of science to investigate. This is precisely what people who pray claim *can happen*. So I think there are quite a number of areas of fruitful discourse and enquiry. I think that as science breaks out of this narrow mechanism that has been its straitjacket for so long, approaching a more holistic view of nature, then much more possibility of fruitful interaction occurs between science and the spiritual.

JE: You mention that your new book, The Physics of Angels, *was inspired by the similarity of Saint Thomas Aquinas's descriptions of angels as without mass or body, and the modern view of science that particles of light — photons — also have neither mass nor body. Can you elaborate on the significance of this?*

RS: When Matthew Fox and I were first talking about angels together, this was one of the points we raised. We both found it quite fascinating. I think that Aquinas was trying to think as logically and as rationally as he could about what it would mean to be a being with no mass which could yet move and act. If you think in those terms, I suppose you come to rather similar conclusions with people like Einstein and other pioneers in the present century, when thinking about relativity and quantum theory. You're driven to very similar conclusions. Einstein's photons of light have remarkable parallels to Aquinas's discussions of the movements of angels. I think it's because they were starting from similar premises, and thinking in a similarly logical way about the consequences.

RALPH ABRAHAM

AND THE

FOUNDATIONS

OF CHAOS

The strata of Western cosmogonic myths have been built up out of layer upon sedimentary layer of peoples, races and tongues which the ebb and flow of time has fossilized into the broken torsos and fallen colossi which crowd our historical landscapes. A random sample taken from this deposit — like a cross-section from a slab of Cambrian shale — reveals to us at least two quite distinct species of genesis narrative. The Babylonian epic, *Enuma Elish*, is a specimen of the first kind. The core of its narrative describes how the solar god Marduk confronts Tiamat — the goddess of the watery abyss — and like a Paleolithic hunter closing in on his prey, captures her with a net and shoots an arrow into her belly. Then he slices her in half to create a sort of cosmic dwelling out of her body; for just as the mammoth hunters built houses out of the interlocking bones of their prey in order to signify that the animal *was* the cosmos within which they lived, so the ancient Leviathanic skeleton of Tiamat becomes the cosmic frame of the habitation within which the gods dwell. We find a similar account in *Genesis 1*, where Tiamat reappears transformed as *tehom*, the watery abyss out of which Yahweh separates the firmament above from the firmament below. And in Plato's *Timaeus*, the Demiurge confers order on the disordered realm of the four elements by hammering the world into being from out of their substance.

The best example of the other species of myth has been preserved for us in Hesiod's *Theogony*. For it is there that Chaos, the yawning void, spontaneously generates an ordered cosmos of deities, the firstborn of which is the goddess Gaia, the seedbed from which her husband, the sky god Ouranos, grows like a plant. Examples of this self-generation of the cosmos survive even in pre-Socratic philosophies of the origins of the world. In Anaximander, for instance, the Infinite spins the world into being by an eternal motion which has the effect of separating out the pairs of opposites hot and cold, wet and dry. And in Anaxagoras, this undifferentiated substance containing the seeds of all things is whirled into being by an immanent Mind that sets it in motion. Even in the atomist philosophy of Democritus there is an echo of this myth as the primordial motion of the atoms knock against each other until a vortex forms and begins the process of creation.

Myths of self-generation are, of course, older than those of the first kind, based upon the organic paradigm of a plant growing with spiral motion from out of its mother soil: these myths stem ultimately from the Neolithic Age, with its worship of the goddess earth as a self-generating matrix of creativity. Those of the first kind, however, are based upon the idea of a cosmic architect who creates the universe through an act of renovation by destroying the old foundations and building anew. They are consequently of a masculine nature, rooted in the Indo-Aryan paradigm of the warrior and his blacksmith-magician. These myths have been the foundation of most Western cosmogonies for the past four thousand years.

However, it has been the particular emphasis of the work of chaos theoretician Ralph Abraham to demonstrate that the earlier mythologies in which chaos was the self-generating vortex which gave rise to the universe is returning under the guise of a branch of mathematics known as dynamical systems theory, which is based upon the creation of mathematical models of dynamical processes in nature. In dynamical systems theory, chaos is no longer regarded as "noise" to be purged from mathematics in order to maximize Platonic purity. The fractal contours and rough edges of nature are the earth goddess herself who, in the guise of storms, flowing rivers, beating hearts and jagged shorelines, has begun to enter the traditionally masculine domain of mathematics.

Chaos theory deals with the processes of the world of nature not in any ideal sense but in a very concrete way. Through the aid of computer graphics, it has been discovered that when systems enter states of turbulence — boiling water, epileptic seizures, mob riots — they are in fact entering into states of organization so infinitely complex that they only appear to the unaided eye to be disordered. In fact, they are states of semi-random activity governed by a mathematical geometry known as a chaotic attractor, which configures the apparent chaos into states of complex order. In the words of William Blake, "I was walking among the fires of hell, delighted with the enjoyments of Genius; which to Angels look like torment and insanity."

Ralph Abraham's fascination with these self-organizing properties of chaos has provided him with the central vector guiding his career as a mathematician and philosopher. In the late sixties while Abraham was teaching mathematics in Princeton, the eclectic scholar of history Immanuel Velikovsky happened to be giving informal lectures to a group of students on the stability of the solar system. Velikovsky had published a most sensational book in 1950, entitled *Worlds in Collision*, in which he articulated the unpopular view that a comet had nearly collided with the earth in 1500 B.C.E., and that its passage not only caused hurricanes, floods, and earthquakes, but tilted the earth off its axis, reversed its rotation, and brought an end to the civilizations of Minoan Crete, Dravidian India, and Middle Kingdom Egypt. Furthermore, Velikovsky went on to assert that the comet had in fact split off from Jupiter and later became the planet Venus, which nearly collided with Mars in the eighth century and then again in the seventh, before stabilizing into its present orbit.

Velikovsky's apocalyptic images, needless to say, earned him a scientific crucifixion, although fellow Princeton resident Albert Einstein found his work fascinating. It was while Abraham was teaching at Princeton that a group of students approached him in regard to Velikovsky's ideas, and Abraham found himself thinking considerably enough about the problem to write his first book, *The Foundations of Mechanics*. Then, in 1972, Abraham migrated to Paris, where he studied with mathematician Rene Thom, whose book *Structural Stability and Morphogenesis* laid the groundwork for a discipline of mathematics called catastrophe theory. Despite its name, catastrophe theory actually focuses on stability in dynamical processes, whereas chaos theory, developing simultaneously in America, emphasizes states of turbulence.

Abraham, meanwhile, had been experimenting with LSD since his first ingestion of it in 1967, which catalyzed a series of visions of radiant mathematical topologies which he later termed "dynamatons." A chance encounter with Ram Dass in a cafe in Amsterdam directed him to a guru in India, where Abraham spent a period of several weeks ingesting LSD, studying Hindu philosophy and practicing yoga. It was during this journey to "the Magic Mountain" that Abraham's various interests began to resonate as a single field of ideas based upon "vibration" research. Proficient in mathematics since childhood, he recognized that the drug-induced visions of luminous dynamatons were similar to the mathematical objects he had been studying in dynamical systems theory, and he recognized that the Hindu vision of the world as a giant series of interlocking waves could provide a larger cosmological paradigm with which to frame his studies. When he returned to California in 1974, he distilled these ideas in a paper which he published the following year, entitled "Vibrations and the Realization of Form." At this time, he was also teaching his theory of vibration research at the University of California at Santa Cruz.

In 1980, he began a four-volume textbook on dynamical systems theory co-authored with Christopher Shaw, called *Dynamics: the Geometry of Behavior*, an eight-year project. The book signals an epoch in the history of mathematics, for it contains not a single equation. It is perhaps part of a larger shift in our culture which Marshall McLuhan was the first to identify as that from the linguistic structures of the left brain to the iconic orientation of the right brain, supported by the post-war rise of electronic technology. In the same year, his conversations with friends Terence McKenna and Rupert Sheldrake were published as *Trialogues at the Edge of the West*. A sequel to this volume entitled *The Evolutionary Mind: Trialogues at the Edge of the Unthinkable* was published in 1998.

In 1994, Abraham's book *Chaos, Gaia, Eros: A Chaos Pioneer Uncovers the Three Great Streams of History* was published. The book explores the historical transformations of myth and science, particularly insofar as the goddess of chaos has been regarded throughout history. Its contents form the axis of the discussion which follows. In 1995, Abraham co-authored *The*

Web Empowerment Book with Frank Jas and Willard Russell. He is currently working on a series of volumes which he terms "The Euclid Project," that traces the roots of Euclidean geometry and the interface of Euclid with chaos theory. He is also co-authoring a book with William Irwin Thompson tentatively entitled *Bolts Out of the Blue: Art, Mathematics and the Evolution of Consciousness.*

> *JE: You mention in your book* Chaos, Gaia, Eros *that when you were teaching in Princeton in 1966 on the stability of the solar system, a group of students who were interested in Immanuel Velikovsky's comet theories came up to you and asked whether it was possible that the earth could be knocked off its course by the impact of a comet, and that this was what inspired the direction of your first book* The Foundations of Mechanics. *I was wondering if you wouldn't mind talking a bit about the relationship between Newton and William Whiston regarding the stability of the solar system.*[1]

RA: Well, Whiston was attracted to Newton's mathematics and Newton was attracted to Whiston for his book about the origin of the earth and the solar system. Of course, Whiston's main theme was this comet theory, which is an interesting thread going back to Giordano Bruno, who also had a comet theory. Descartes had a vortex theory. All these theories were similar kinds of heresy in their time, but now, of course, make a lot more sense — for example, in relation to the Couette-Taylor stirring experiment, in which it is shown that vortices create form. They are the main mechanisms for form to emerge out of fluid.

So anyway, the comet theory, in the time of Whiston and Newton, was regarded as an exegetical thesis on the *Old Testament*. Whiston and Newton were very serious Christians and believers in the *Old* and *New Testaments*, and interpreted particularly *Genesis*, line by line. There had to be a concordance between classical science as it was emerging in their time — and that was the great creative moment for classical science — and the *Old Testament*. So in Whiston's book, the comet theory entered as a creation myth interpolated between the first two verses of *Genesis:* there might have been a big bang and then a fluid dynamical spinning universe in which vortices developed and coalesced into comets and galaxies. Hence, the earth.[2] Now I think that both Whiston and Newton agreed that the solar system was unstable and required periodic interventions by God in order to keep it on track. So they did not believe that the equations of motion according to Newton had solutions that corresponded exactly to the motion of the solar system.

JE: And of course, Immanuel Velikovsky picked up this old comet heresy for his book Worlds in Collision *in 1950.*

RA: Yes, that book is also about this comet theory, in which various paradoxical statements in traditional histories like the *Old Testament* and in the myths of various countries were interpreted as being true accounts of celestial catastrophes by Velikovsky. That was his idea.

JE: Did his comet theories have anything to do with those that were proposed for the extinction of the dinosaurs?

RA: I'm not sure that Velikovsky touched on that. I think it would have had a negative impact, if any, in that if this theory had been associated with Velikovsky's name, then orthodox scientists would have been more loathe to propose it when they did, although it was controversial. All these things have been controversial upon the moment of their introduction. For example, the theory of continental drift was a very difficult theory for scientists to accept, and that controversy has been studied in great detail in a historical book.

Velikovsky was rather beyond being a scientific heretic in that he particularly attacked the *stability dogma.* If science said the solar system was stable and then Velikovsky said it wasn't, then Velikovsky would be a heretic. But science didn't say the solar system was stable; scientists *thought* that science said that. They hadn't really thought about it. They didn't know, it was just a belief. And Velikovsky attacks their belief as opposed to science itself. As far as the science is concerned, as people understand it today, Velikovsky was *not* heretical. He agreed with the actual understanding of Newton, Laplace and modern astronomers that the solar system is as a matter of fact not stable, it's chaotic. So, it's a heresy in the context of dogma and not a heresy in the context of theory.

That's what really took my attention in 1966 when these students came to me from Velikovsky's living room: from what I heard there was no heretical content. By 1966 Velikovsky had been vindicated by Kolmogorov, Arnold and Moser, the great mathematicians of solar system dynamics, but the astronomers didn't know that. The word wasn't really out until 1970 or so, in the astronomical community. So I could see that this was just dogma at work. And they had attacked him most viciously. *Worlds in Collision* had been attacked even before it was published. There was an unsuccessful attempt of orthodox astronomers of Harvard University and so on to suppress it, by contacting the publisher and insisting that it should not be published.

There was a similar situation in the case of Giordano Bruno, who, when he was led to a pile of firewood on Easter Sunday in the year 1600 was given one last chance to recant his main position, that the universe was infinite. If it was infinite then there was no place for God to reside. So the picture of the universe held by the Pope in 1600 was that the stars occupied a two-dimensional universe: the celestial sphere, inside of which the planets moved and outside of which there was an empty space that was God's domain. There couldn't be any evidence at that time that the universe was two-dimensional or three-dimensional. You couldn't really tell. Telescopes hadn't been used to observe the parallax and establish that the stars were in a 3-D continuum. So it was just dogma. Bruno was offered this deal, a chance to recant his views, as 100,000 people assembled to watch his immolation, and he said, "I don't think I should say that, so I won't," and they burned him.

JE: And Bruno had helped to revive the Hermetic tradition by attempting to carry it on into the scientific mainstream?

RA: Well, he was giving public lectures to groups of interested people in which he participated in the Hermetic revival of the Renaissance. One of the main themes of the Renaissance was the discovery of this literature of late antiquity, *The Chaldean Oracles* and *The Corpus Hermeticum*. These were regarded as so important that when Cosimo de Medici founded the Platonic Academy in Florence in the 1440s he ordered its new director Marsilio Ficino to translate *The Corpus Hermeticum* before beginning on the Platonic corpus.

JE: And these writings had come from Alexandria?

RA: Yes, in the second century C.E. That's what's now believed. But in the time of Cosimo de Medici and Marsilio Ficino it was believed that they were much older and that they derived from the tradition called the *prisci theologi*, the old masters, including both Moses and Hermes. Hermes himself was thought to have written *The Corpus Hermeticum* around 2000 B.C.E. or so. That's why it would precede Plato.[3]

JE: What does this tradition have to do specifically with what you term in your book the Orphic tradition?

RA: Well, *The Corpus Hermeticum*, although written down in 200 C.E. in Alexandria does truly represent an ancient tradition, and I am suggesting that this Hermetic tradition, as it's called — especially since its revival in the Renaissance — is a remnant of the Goddess partnership society which preceded the patriarchal takeover in 4000 B.C.E. The patriarchal takeover began a process of the suppression of that literature, which became more and more complete as the years went on, and after the arrival of Christianity, was eventually almost totally buried, and along with it the Platonic corpus. So the rediscovery in the Renaissance of the Platonic corpus and the Hermetic corpus essentially revived the oral literature of this pre-patriarchal society.

Now in order to understand that this theory makes sense you have to read *The Corpus Hermeticum*. What's it about? And the main idea, I would say, is what we would call a kind of esoteric astrology, or star magic, in which there were influences on earth emanating from the stars and not just from their positions radiated through the gravitational field, but actually a spiritual emanation. So this is one of those emanation theories which have existed in all times and places and cultures. The emanation theory gave rise eventually to optics and therefore to experimental physics in the Middle Ages and to science as we know it today. Alchemy and astrology are remnants of the Hermetic tradition going back to pre-patriarchal times, and therefore part of what I call loosely, the Orphic tradition. The literature and mythology of this peaceful society spanned the entire globe for a long time, so it was a very deeply rooted tradition.

JE: And you see Newton as one of the last bearers of this tradition within the scientific mainstream?

RA: Well, we'd have to regard Newton himself as a kind of hinge person. He was on the cusp. Some people describe him as the last of the Hermetic philosophers because until his death he practiced alchemy on a daily basis with his own furnace.[4] So he was truly a scholar of the Hermetic tradition. But the theory that he gave the world, which is sometimes described as the greatest intellectual contribution ever made by a single person, was very quickly pressed into the service of the law and order mentality of modern science and the so-called Enlightenment.

JE: So if we may shift, then, to Poincaré, who's generally credited with being the father of chaos theory, what role did he play in all of this?

RA: Well, he's the father of chaos due to the discoveries that he made while striving to earn the prize of Oscar II of Sweden, which was offered to anyone who could prove that the solar system was stable. It was thought possible to do so because Dirichlet on his deathbed said that he could prove the stability of the solar system using Newton's equations, but like Fermat's Last Theorem, it wasn't written down, and then he died.

So the efforts of mathematicians struggling to supply this missing proof and being unable to do so created a kind of Mount Everest in pure mathematics at that time, which was fueled by popular interest in the stability of the solar system. This goes back to these early spiritual roots where the original tradition said that the stability of the world was provided by emanations from the stars associated with gods and goddesses. In pagan belief, the stability of appearances was maintained by the *anima mundi*, the spirit of the world, particularly through its various manifestations as gods and goddesses, semi-gods and semi-goddesses, including stars and constellations of stars associated with names of mythological characters that participated in celestial dramas like soap operas in the sky.

Poincaré, then, set out to prove the stability of the solar system, but ended up by actually establishing the inability of Laplace's analytical method to do this. He won Oscar's prize, anyway, and went on to invent new mathematical systems which resulted in the discovery of chaos in the solar system.

JE: Wasn't it true that Newton's theory of universal gravitation originally met with a certain amount of resistance because it reminded people of these emanations from the stars and these nonmaterial forces connecting everything?

RA: Yeah, it still does. I think that the problem of understanding the gravitational field is not yet solved. Einstein gave us a big advance there by saying that the gravitational field is simply the geometry of the underlying space-time continuum of the universe. But that still kind of begs the question because, when you put a large object like a quasar out there, and then the geometry of space all over the entire universe is suddenly changed by the appearance of that mass, how could that be? We have a mathematical model here; the Einstein equations there; and numerical solutions by computer showing exactly what this would look like. But there's no intuitive model. It's still action at a distance. We could, in other words, regard Newton's theory of universal gravitation and Einstein's model for the cosmos simply as modern representations of the old emanation theory.

JE: Now in your book Chaos, Gaia, Eros, *you say that chaos theory retrieves this stream of the Orphic-Hermetic tradition. How does it do this?*

RA: Well, it's one of the main themes of my book, concerning the importance of the chaos concept in the entire span of cultural history. I'm identifying the Orphic tradition with an outgrowth from its roots in pagan society, especially before the patriarchal takeover. That society was characterized by a distinguished role for chaos as a goddess of creativity, so that throughout that time you have the image of the goddess in association with snakes and vortices and water and chaos.[5] After the arrival of the patriarchy, however, then the chaos concept — personified for example as Tiamat in the *Enuma Elish* — is replaced by the god of order, which represents the key to understanding patriarchy — this obsession with order.

Then the chaos revolution comes along and as I say, puts Tiamat back on her throne, reestablishes the importance, the validity, the beneficence of chaos in life as well as in science, in the solar system, in the biosphere and so on. Therefore, it gives new life to the lost goddess tradition along with its chaos concept, with its emanation theory, with its idea of the maintenance of ordinary reality through something more or less supernatural or paranormal. All of that is suddenly restored and revived by the chaos revolution of these past twenty, thirty years.[6]

JE: So chaos theory also in some way rescues catastrophe theory from its place as a scientific heresy as well?

RA: Yes, catastrophe theory was kind of a harbinger of chaos theory. It's kind of a special case of chaos theory, and it was the intellectual product of Rene Thom, who was one of the great pioneers in chaos theory after Poincaré. It's the one little tiny branch on this big tree which happened to make it to the front page of magazines and newspapers. It's the first breaking of the waters as a coming into popular consciousness and it was specifically this popularity and the attraction of public view, I believe, which led mathematicians to attack and kill catastrophe theory just a few years later.

JE: Could you say something then about attractors, basins and bifurcations?

RA: This is the main paradigm that mathematics provides you for all dynamical processes in the sciences. Bifurcation is a loose term denoting a special kind of change in the map of the dynamical behavior of a complex system. By the map, I mean the configuration of the attractors and the basins. In each basin, there is one attractor somewhere down in the center, some diffuse thing like a galaxy of stars: that's the attractor. In between the basins there are boundaries which separate one basin from another. And in this map, the attractors are diffuse and complex fractals, so that when you look at them in the microscope you see a recursive representation that looks the same as the unmagnified view.

Now when the underlying rule of the dynamical system is changed for some reason, for example, by the increase of an external force or temperature or the wind pressure or whatever, then the map changes and sometimes it changes in an insignificant way and sometimes it does a sort of snap and settles into a recognizably different map. That's a bifurcation. It's when the dynamical system is changed by external forces and something significant happens. Bifurcations generally are classified into three different sorts, called catastrophic, subtle and explosive bifurcations. The catastrophic bifurcations are also known by the pop name "catastrophes."

All of this picture — how it can be applied in the sciences, and why it's important — is a way of thinking which is now called dynamical literacy. And the way of thinking is more important than the mathematical theory or the specific models in which it's applied, as for example, fluid dynamical turbulence, or the origin of the universe or whatever. Rene Thom popularized this way of thinking in the special case of chaos theory called catastrophe theory. He made it understandable. He drew into dynamical literacy people from every branch of the sciences through his writings and exemplary applications to biology, linguistics, the social sciences, and so on.

JE: And his book is Structural Stability and Morphogenesis?[27]

RA: That's right.

JE: Now in your book you introduce a concept called "dynamical historiography," where you create this model of history based on these phase changes with three different kinds of attractors. Can you explain that?

RA: This is based on an idea of Thom or perhaps Christopher Zeeman, his main popularizer. The idea has to do with relating the history of mathematics to cultural history. As a culture evolves, through the practice of what they already know, people become more and more prepared to know more. So there is eventually a critical moment in which a new idea can come into the group mind of the culture because the culture has in its evolution arrived at the first moment in which it is capable of having that idea. In primitive times people would be unable to conceive such a thing as the cusp catastrophe. It wouldn't even fit into the mind because the connectivity of the neural net was too simple to envision such a complex mathematical object.

I have expanded this idea into what I call dynamical historiography in my book *Chaos, Gaia, Eros,* and also in various articles published earlier, in the last decade or so. I particularly applied this idea that certain mathematical objects come into the mind of a culture as soon as they can. I apply this idea to these three basic attractors of chaos theory: the static attractor — which is just an isolated point, obviously much simpler than a circle — came into the culture through fixation of nature in the form of gardens during the agricultural revolution; and the circular attractor, in which a sequence of states is repeated over and over again, each cycle being completed in exactly the same span of time, hence periodic attractor, came in when the wheel was discovered 6000 years ago, as a toy wheel, then a pottery wheel, and then a cart wheel, and a model for the zodiacal belt and the solar system and the paths followed by the planets. All of this occurred suddenly in the period of 3500-4000 B.C.E. This is a much more complicated idea than a point attractor and yet it doesn't seem too complicated to us because we've had circles in our culture for 6000 years.

And now we're in a similar phase change, or paradigm shift, as Thomas Kuhn would say, with the chaotic attractor having just appeared. During my lifetime, I saw the complete process though which the chaotic attractor passed through a period of transition from heretical idea to orthodox science. This occurred during the span of my professional career. I personally experienced it in the context of my relationships with many different friends. I could feel the essence of it and I could imagine therefore very vividly how this paradigm shift happened. So that's my idea of dynamical historiography. These transformations happened on two sides, on one side as a mathematical model and on the other as a cultural manifestation that swung history on its axis.

JE: You often mention in your writings the work of William Irwin Thompson who also sees a series of these phase changes throughout history. Would you say that your theories are isomorphic for the most part with Thompson's?

RA: Yes. In one of his earlier works, *Pacific Shift*, he had already presented a model of cultural history in four phases which he traced back to ancient Mesopotamia.[8] So on the level of the big ones only there was, as you say, an isomorphism between my model and Bill Thompson's. In fact, my book was fairly complete when I sent a copy of the manuscript to Bill Thompson and he immediately fired back a letter saying, "look here, look there, look on this other page," and so on in his book. I already knew him and had two or three of his books on my shelf, and hadn't really noticed this. But when he called my attention to it I looked back and, yes, indeed, he had anticipated my view of history in almost exactly the same bifurcations and paradigm shifts on the largest level. However, when he saw my book he realized for the first time I think, that his view of history must be mathematical and on that basis was formed our friendship, which goes on to this day.

He and I are engaged now in an interesting exercise which is a further working out of this mathematical view of cultural history. And that is a new curriculum for elementary schools, grades K through 12.[9] The major bifurcations in culture history are mapped onto the major bifurcations in psychological development in the sense of Piaget, so that in kindergarten you're in the early Paleolithic culture; and in the first grade you're in the Epipaleolithic; in the second grade, you experience the agricultural revolution; in the third grade comes the wheel, the first cities: Sumer, Egypt, Babylon, Canaan and so on; in the sixth grade you're in ancient Greece; and in the seventh grade comes late antiquity and medieval Islam and so on.

JE: You've also worked with Rupert Sheldrake.[10] Would you say that his morphogenetic fields are similar in any way to attractors, bifurcations and so forth?

RA: Well, his theory is very consistent with chaos theory. Sheldrake has a slightly larger view than any of the views we've discussed so far in our conversation except possibly what I've described as the pre-patriarchal or the Orphic view about the emanations of the stars, the *anima mundi* and so on. Rupert Sheldrake's idea could be seen in this way: that when we have been talking about concordance between mathematical evolution and cultural evolution, Rupert Sheldrake would have put in here a third thing, which is the soul of the world or the morphogenetic field. He would see mathematical evolution and cultural evolution as manifestations of an evolution which is going on in the morphogenetic field. It's a slightly bigger picture than we've talked about and I think it is compatible with Giordano Bruno, Marsilio Ficino and Renaissance hermetical philosophy but his idea also breaks with the perennial philosophy of the *prisci theologi* in that he sees the field as evolving in a coevolutionary process with culture, the human mind, the biosphere, and so on. So that in having this talk, we are giving nutritional support to the growth of the morphogenetic field; and the morphogenetic field is giving a certain guidance to the form of our conversation and the evolution of our thoughts and relationship. All of this is evolving together. It seems to me that this is an essentially novel and original contribution to our model of the universe by Sheldrake.[11]

> *JE: Chaos theory has a lot to do with pattern recognition in the processes of nature. A great deal of Carl Jung's work involved the recognition of patterns structuring processes in the psyche, and he termed these patterns "archetypes of the collective unconscious." Do you see any relationship here between chaos theory and the work of Jung?*

RA: Oh, absolutely. For example, myth and ritual — as remnants of archetypal processes in the minds of earlier peoples — can be regarded as the most stable and long lasting mental cycles or trajectories of the historical past, and in dynamical theory we would translate these states into mathematical models, such as these attractors.

Now, mathematics is not everything, there's a lot more to an archetype than simply its mathematical model so I don't want to imply here that understanding the mathematics would complete an understanding of all and everything. The insights of Jung and people of that sort are ultimately transcendent of mathematics.

However, mathematics as we understand it today involves space-time patterns and a space-time pattern is an ordinary pattern that's moving, and therefore a model for a process. There are certain special kinds of process models which can be recognized in processes occurring in nature and even in the collective unconscious, so in terms of Jung's theory we would have to say that the mathematics is suggesting that we look at myths transforming into other myths. In other words, the mythogenetic process itself might be an archetypal object in the collective unconscious, and if we understand these archetypes correctly, then the past and the present are simply stages on the way to the future and the whole thing is an archetype in space-time. So it could be that a development in mathematics would enable us to see more deeply into the collective unconscious.

> *JE: So you see myths as dynamical models for morphological processes in the psyche as well as in patterns of culture?*

RA: Well, the transformation myth is a manifestation of an archetypal process in the psyche, yes. Even within a generation we can see the myth of Jesus Christ for example, being completely transformed, and that transformation is archetypal, and as a mathematical object it's had many manifestations in the past. Or say, the birth of Christ or the arrival of Mohammed and his vision of the angel Gabriel: these are different manifestations of a special kind of movement, a bifurcation in the collective unconscious, which as a mathematical model is manifest through history many times over. So understanding the process of transformation is possibly a step toward understanding the myth itself.

JE: Do you see the possibility of all the various domains of the sciences ever fusing together into a single internally consistent paradigm?

RA: Well, yes, it's possible. You see, all of the sciences are fine in themselves. What's missing is a general systems theory, a synthesis of the sciences into a single understanding. Over the years, as everybody knows, science has been afflicted by a disease of reductionism that manifests as an actual repression of synthesis. For example, if a scientist or a professor in a university gets too involved in interdisciplinary work, and let's say, makes a bridge between physical astronomy and botany, then his reputation will suffer and he will be punished or dissuaded from continuing in this way. What is necessary to synthesize the sciences in a significant way, to develop a synthetic scientific view that would actually be taught successfully in universities, high schools and elementary schools, is some kind of sea change in the dogma of science which gave more credit to the synthesis function, and therefore encouraged more synthesis. One way that synthesis could regain its prestige is through the acceptance of chaos theory and complexity theory into universities. That hasn't happened yet: universities are still abusing chaos theorists and excluding them.

JE: Speaking in terms, then of synthesis, you've mentioned that you see the Internet as a material manifestation of a synthesis of all the minds on the planet?

RA: A lot of people are really excited about the World Wide Web and a lot of other people are really petrified because of some wild fantasy of child porn or something. This polarization is taking place and so far I'm still optimistic because of its commercial utility, that the Web will persevere. Within it there are many synthetic activities ongoing in which science, philosophy, religion, history and so on are being strung together by amateur intellectuals who have no restraint. There's no censorship and no pressure for them to abandon what they're doing and so there's a fantastic synthesis of the sciences, of mythology and so on. How long that will continue I don't know, but it looks good. I think we're up to about 30 million browsers participating in the Web and some of the access providers, America Online for example, encourage people to have their own web pages, so there's something like 10 or 20 million people about to put up their own web pages and any idea they think is important will go there and other people can browse it with the aid of these brilliant indexing engines, web crawlers and robots. It still looks to me that the World Wide Web could actually be an occasion for the synthesis of knowledge on a world-wide scale in which minds are not connected so they become one mind exactly, but there's a very strong coupling between all these minds.

JE: You've also mentioned that you're studying the history of Indian philosophy.[12] *Is that what you're engaged in now?*

RA: Well, this is still for the future. I have projects in which I'm trying to trace the Orphic tradition through the arrival of the Aryans in India carrying the *Rig Veda* and so on. But my latest book is a high-level math text on chaos theory, *Chaos in Discrete Dynamical Systems*.

I'm largely focused on one project now called the *Euclid Project*, which involves many volumes and CD-ROMs. Its aim is to revolutionize the teaching of mathematics in the schools. It would include *The Roots of Euclid* on sacred geometry and a volume on the connection between Euclid and chaos theory, *Euclid's Voyage Into Chaos*.

LYNN MARGULIS

AND

THE EVOLUTION

OF GAIA

In his book *The Universe Story*, Brian Swimme invents a mythical theogony in order to describe the genesis and evolution of living forms during the first two billion years of life.[1] The earth spun itself into being along with the other planets about 4.6 billion years ago from out of a swirling vortex of dust, gas and elements, and over time this "Hadean" tension between radioactive heat and gravitational pressures produced molten, glowing crusts of land which began to solidify and cool as huge strips of lightning burst like snapshots over turbulent, foaming seas.

As in Mary Shelley's *Frankenstein*, the emergence of life was catalyzed by flowing streams of electricity, and the annunciation of the Archean epoch was signified by the appearance of tiny, dot-sized living cells, which Swimme names "Aries," after the sign of the zodiac which marks the spring equinox. The duration of this epoch was nearly two billion years, and during that time the foundations were laid for all five kingdoms of the living world by these prokaryotic cells better known as "bacteria."

Borrowing once again from the iconic language of mythology, Swimme distinguishes two more generations of bacteria that followed "Aries" during the Archean epoch as "Promethio" and "Prospero," the ancestral progenitors of the plant and animal kingdoms, respectively. It was the innovation of the former to develop a kind of molecular net with which to capture light and thereby create the type of metabolism known as photosynthesis, whereas the latter developed the oxygen-respiring capabilities with which we have come to associate the animal kingdom.

But as Lynn Margulis points out, the earliest beings are neither plants nor animals but members of the most important kingdom of life: Bacteria. These omnipresent microbes are sharply differentiated from the familiar kinds of life that compose the other two kingdoms, plants and animals, which are made of eukaryotic, or nucleated cells, whereas bacterial cells lack nuclei. It is Margulis's symbiotic theory of the origins of nucleated cells with which we are concerned here. In the drama which Swimme describes in his mythic theogony, the birth of the nucleated cell was the inevitable outcome of a number of cellular fusions.[2]

With the invention of photosynthesis by "Promethio," the levels of carbon dioxide in this early oxygen-poor atmosphere — substantially different from the oxygen-rich one which we inhabit now — were reduced dramatically, since carbon dioxide is essential for photosynthesis and oxygen is its waste by-product. Prior to the evolution of oxygen-releasing bacteria, very little free oxygen was in the earth's atmosphere. But by 2.3 billion years ago, these little beings had created an apocalypse for themselves. Oxygen gradually poisoned their world, turning the skies from a dusty brown to their present azure, and causing an early Ice Age, since carbon dioxide is a greenhouse gas, the reduction of which would have brought down the global temperature. The response to the impending doom of all life during the end of the Archean eon — as oxygen destroyed cell membranes, ripped electrons from stable molecules and created free radicals which began scavenging other molecules for their amputated electrons — was the birth of aerobic bacteria, the generation which Swimme terms "Prospero," after the magician in Shakespeare's play The Tempest.

But a certain type of bacterium known as a spirochete — microbes with long, thin, serpent-like tails, which always squiggle, never resting or sleeping, and which swim until they die or reproduce by division — created the first symbiosis by attaching itself to one of the fermenters ("Aries"), thereby conferring on itself a fast-paced motility to quest more rapidly for its nutrients.[3] The generation of "Prospero," meanwhile — the aerobes which were capable of oxygen respiration — began mass campaigns of pillaging the insides of earlier generations of cells like the fermenters, who had been thrust down into anoxic regions where they shunned oxygen and produced methane and carbon dioxide.[4] As Margulis has made clear for us, over time, these Viking-like aerobes took up their permanent abodes *within* larger cells like the fermenters, where, protected against high temperatures and acidic conditions, they provided their host with fresh reserves of energy in the form of oxygen respiration. Eventually, this new kind of being swallowed but did not digest a photosynthetic bacterium, and the second kingdom, that of the Protists, and along with them, the nucleated cell, was born.

Thus, in Margulis's vision of symbiosis, the aerobes became the mitochondria of the protist ancestors to both plant and animal cells. The photosynthesizers became the chloroplasts of protists, and then later the organelles in plant cells which confer on them their photosynthetic abilities. The spirochete with its whip-like tail, according to Margulis, would go on to become other things within our bodies, like the tails of our sperm, the cilia which line the esophagus, and maybe even parts of the axons and dendrites in the nerve cells of our brains.

Much of what we know of the earth's early history as described above is due to the work of Lynn Margulis, whose doctoral dissertation in 1965 focused on chloroplast autonomy in *Euglena*, a type of protist containing both chloroplasts and mitochondria, as well as a whip-like tail. Because of this microorganism's photosynthetic ability, botanists traditionally classified it as a plant, whereas zoologists claim it as an animal; but according to Margulis it is neither, for the problem lies in the oversimplification of life into just two kingdoms. Expanding Whittaker's 1959 classification of the five kingdoms of Monera, Protists, Fungi, Plants and Animals, the problem is resolved by stepping back from the botanical-zoological dichotomy and seeing life from a larger, multi-tiered perspective.

In 1957, at the age of nineteen, Margulis was married to Carl Sagan and had already begun to study the science of genetics. In the post-Watson-and-Crick era of the discovery of DNA in 1953, it was thought that genes were centralized in the nucleus of the cell, but Margulis, "no more constitutionally inclined to focus monomaniacally on the cell nucleus than [she] was to be a satellite wife in a nuclear family," became fascinated with the possibility of cytoplasmic genes, and so her career, as she puts it, began "off-center."[5]

The cytoplasm is the liquid portion of the cell which contains organelles such as mitochondria, chloroplasts and centrioles, and some scientists at the beginning of the twenties had inferred from genetic crosses that both mitochondria and chloroplasts contained their own genes. But these genes were considered of trivial importance in determining the characteristics of offspring. Margulis thought otherwise, and over time, it became clear to her that the genes of these extra-nuclear organelles were actually the key to their ancestral lineage. Margulis hypothesized that these organelles had different genetic lineages from the genes in the cell's nucleus because both mitochondria and chloroplasts had descended from once free-living bacteria like the aerobes and photosynthesizers which, at the dawn of life, had sculpted the entire architecture of the planet to suit their own ends.

In 1967, Margulis published her paper on "The Origin of Mitosing Cells" in *The Journal of Theoretical Biology* after enduring a gauntlet of fifteen rejections from other journals. But when the paper was finally published, stating her symbiotic theory of the origin of nucleated cells from symbiotic mergers between once independent bacteria, it became an immediate "citation classic," for which over eight hundred reprints were requested. The biologist J.D. Bernal declared that Margulis had solved one of biology's ten unsolved problems, and Margulis followed this long article with her first book, *The Origin of the Eukaryotic Cell* (1970). The rewritten and revised book appeared with a new publisher in 1981 as *Symbiosis in Cell Evolution*, her most important book and perhaps one of the classics of twentieth century biology. This was followed by later works sounding out various aspects of her theory, such as *Early Life* (1982), *Origins of Sex* (1986), *The Garden of Microbial Delights* (1988), *What is Life?* (1995), and the recent *Slanted Truths* (1997) and *Symbiotic Planet* (1998), many of which were written in collaboration with her son Dorion Sagan.

At about the same time as the publication of her first book, the atmospheric chemist James Lovelock had proposed his Gaia hypothesis in a 1969 paper. Both he and Margulis were fascinated by their awareness that most of the gases of the atmosphere — hydrogen, oxygen, methane, dimethyl sulfide — had been put there by living beings. Lovelock wanted to know what was understood by gases produced by live organisms and he sketched out his Gaia idea in conversations with Margulis over a number of days. In 1974, they co-authored a paper on the Gaia idea which was published in Carl Sagan's journal *Tellus*.[6]

As Margulis points out, "Gaia is symbiosis seen from space," and indeed, the idea itself is a product of the space age. The theory was born out of research funded by NASA for investigating the possibility of life on other planets — Mars, in particular — and Lovelock was hired to think about the problem of life detection. He reasoned that if Mars contained life, then its atmosphere should reflect that fact, for its gases would be different from any atmosphere maintained by chemistry and physics alone. But in fact, the atmosphere of Mars is much like the burned exhaust of automobile engines, for it is composed of 98 percent carbon dioxide with only traces of oxygen, nitrogen and argon. The earth's atmosphere, however, exists in a constant state of thermodynamic *dis*equilibrium, since its concentrations of oxygen and methane, for example, coexist; whereas, thermodynamically, they should chemically react in the presence of sunlight to form water vapor and carbon dioxide. Yet the traces of methane in the atmosphere remain because they are put there by methanogenic bacteria, cattle, rice paddies and water-logged soil.

The Gaia theory, in short, proposes that the earth is a self-maintaining system analogous to the homeostatic properties of a living being; that is to say, the earth's surface maintains fairly constant ratios of oxygen and other gases in its atmosphere, salinity in the seas, and global mean temperature somewhere between freezing and boiling. These aspects of the surface are regulated as a consequence of the growth and reproduction of a diversity of organisms.

The fact that this holistic theory bears a mythic appellation is no mere coincidence, nor is it just a matter of convenience, as Lovelock implies when he tells the story of naming his theory on a stroll one day with the novelist William Golding. He told Golding that he needed a good four-letter word that would describe "a cybernetic system with homeostatic tendencies as detected by chemical anomalies in the earth's atmosphere." Golding suggested the name "Gaia," and as William Irwin Thompson remarks, "had the scientists named their hypothesis 'The Homeorhetic Mechanism of Planetary Dynamics,' no one would have taken much notice.'" For it is a thesis of this book that one of the ways in which science is benefiting from its dialogue with mythology is in the creation of a kind of iconic language with which to render its new theories. As Margulis comments, "When you're paradigm shifting, you don't have the language. Whatever you say, people take the words in the context of *their* paradigm, which makes your scientific life difficult. You don't want to create neologisms. But you are not saying what they think you are saying." The Gaia hypothesis and Chaos theory are both examples of densely textured, extremely rich visions of the world which can only be adequately encapsulated in the picture language of mythology, for the words by which these theories are conveyed compress entire cosmologies within them.

So the influx of images from mythology is actually changing the language of science because the way science imagines the cosmos is changing from that of a reductionist, analytical, perspectival point of view, to a holistic, synthetic, aperspectival one that is entirely consonant with the way in which the lens of mythology brings the world into focus with huge shapes, patterns and forms, like mountainous islands looming out of a fog.

The two concepts of symbiosis and Gaia as articulated by Lynn Margulis perfectly capture the sort of interface between myth and science that we are exploring in this book. This vision of the earth, which has "the organized, self-contained look of a live creature, full of information, marvelously skilled in handling the sun," as Lewis Thomas puts it, is part of the same ecology of ideas as the self-organizing dynamics of chaos theory. The earth as envisioned in Gaia is self-making, not designed from the blueprint of a cosmic architect like Yahweh or Plato's Demiurge. It is less like a building, and more like a tree that has sprung up from out of the dark soils of Mother Space.

JE: How do you think that life originated out of the prebiotic soup, as it's called?

LM: I've never directly studied that problem. The simple answer for purposes of this discussion is that whatever the chemistry was on the early earth — and not just chemistry of course, the geology, meteorology and environmental science as well, whatever it was — it led to the origin of cells on earth. The first cells probably were very small, tiny spheres a quarter of a micron or smaller. And they were membrane-bounded bags with distinctive individuality. Any other assumptions will get us into a long and silly discussion.

Everything I work on assumes the origins of such a minimal cell, and that the size and functioning of the cell has already evolved in some way. So that when people say I've made contributions to the origin of life, they don't know anything about my work. I let the prebiotic chemistry boys argue about origins.

By 3.5 billion years ago, life on earth has already evolved. There's no doubt about that. As soon as we see sedimentary rocks capable of preserving fossils we have direct evidence for life, not prebiotic chemistry. The oldest rocks that permit the preservation of microbial fossils already harbor them. Evidence for life is in those rocks. Older rocks exist, but they are too deformed, too heated, too metamorphosed. In principle, fossils could not remain in them. The earth as a solid object is 4.6 billion years old and yet no single place has survived melting. Certain meteorites collected from the Antarctic, and lunar rocks, are that old, but no rock on earth *in situ* is that old, since none survived from this early date on the earth's surface.

When I was a student we were taught that it took all that time to evolve fossil animals such as trilobites[7] because they were so complicated and all of that huge period of time was involved with the low probability emergence of life. The Precambrian (the time before Cambrian animals) was basically void of life and that's what Darwin thought, too. But we know now the idea that life did not appear until the Cambrian is completely incorrect.

JE: You don't give any credence then to the panspermist hypothesis, do you?

LM: None. Except as an incentive to study. Svante Arrhenius proposed the idea, which became a wonderful incentive to test such things as the viability of spores in space. But panspermia says *live beings*, living propagules, traveled through space and seeded the earth. To that kind of panspermia notion, I give absolutely no credence.

Let us distinguish between life and organic matter. Organic matter is abundant in certain kinds of meteorites. Since the Japanese began collecting meteorites on the ice fields, the percentage of organic-rich meteorites to the stony irons has increased. Organic meteorites preserve least when they fall on substances other than ice. Two or three percent organic matter is in some of these meteorites. But this is not panspermia. It is influx of organic matter from space. Both organic matter and water do enter the earth's surface from meteorites, but life does not. Organic matter, not life, comes in from space.

JE: At what point in this early history of the earth did Gaia awaken?

LM: That's a really interesting question. Life may have originated in some localized place in the beginning, but at what point in the history of life did a Gaian system begin? I suspect Gaia began as soon as not just a living form originated but when an ecosystem started. An ecosystem differs from a community or a population. The members of a population are of the same species living at the same time in the same place. In communities, members of different populations of species live at the same time in the same place. Examples include a forest, a pond, a mountain top or a coral reef community. Ecosystems are larger than communities. To be an ecosystem, the component communities must entirely recycle the elements: carbon, nitrogen, sulfur, etc. Carbon dioxide must be fixed into organic matter, and the organic matter converted eventually back to carbon dioxide. In any ecosystem, the biologically important elements must be completely recycled: Phosphorus, carbon, hydrogen, sulfur, nitrogen. An ecosystem recycles within its boundaries. So as soon as functional ecosystems were in place, as soon as carbon, nitrogen and the rest were recycled in interacting communities and groups of organisms at the same time and place, then a rudimentary Gaian system was operating. Probably smaller, slower and less efficient, it was a Gaian system nevertheless.

No one doubts that the environment of the early earth far more resembled the inside of cells today than it did the environment of today's earth. Today's earth differs from the inside of cells, markedly such that today far more has to be regulated than in the early days of Gaia. Early ecosystems had less need for complex regulation than extant ones.

Organic compounds inside of cells resemble those in early environments. Watery conditions in shallow, sunlit, organic-rich waters lacking free oxygen are much like Archean earth environments. The tops of today's mountains and deserts are very different. Therefore organisms that live on the tops of mountains and in deserts require much more environmental regulation than those that live in the mud and shallow water, organic-rich anoxic environments.

Regulation is not a single, monolithic phenomenon; rather, environmental or Gaian regulation is quite complicated. Whatever factors are regulated change; they hover around varying set points for many variables. Gaia has changed through time. I suspect that Gaian regulation in the early days was more lax and easier since the insides of organisms were so much like their outside environment in the Archean and Proterozoic eons. As our planet became more and more oxygen-rich, the requirements for regulation stiffened. I suspect the Gaian system regulated loosely in the beginning, analogous to how temperature regulation occurs in reptiles. Over time, regulation of acidity, atmospheric composition, water and temperature became tighter and more complex.

JE: So about 2.3 billion years ago, by the time we have oxygen being released up into the air by these cyanobacteria, we're getting a Gaian system?

LM: No, cyanobacteria produced oxygen much earlier than that. As soon as carbon dioxide was fixed into organic matter (body chemistry), released as methane and oxidized back to carbon dioxide, the carbon cycle existed and we had a Gaian system.

JE: Lovelock mentions in his book Healing Gaia *the possibility that Gaia may be growing old because it has been oscillating back and forth between Ice Ages and what he calls "Gaian fevers" for the past two million years, whereas, before that, Ice Ages were less frequent. Do you see signs of Gaia aging?*

LM: Lovelock is fond of saying that the fluctuations resemble feedback systems just before they succumb and go out of control. And when you draw it that way it sure looks like that. The cutting down of our forests changes the cloud cover over them. Moreover, clouds over the forests reflect light and tend to cool the world. Another major mechanism to cool the earth's surface is to remove carbon dioxide, a greenhouse gas. So when the forests are cut down and the removal of carbon dioxide is drastically reduced and evapotranspiration of water that forms clouds that reflect solar radiation off the top of the trees, the trouble compounds. I do not believe that Gaia is coming to her untimely death, but I think that the kind of ecology in which humans evolved is under severe threat. It is an issue of timescale. Probably not developing in the next ten years, but certainly in the next thousand years.

JE: Brian Swimme, in his book The Universe Story *makes the statement that the first Ice Age 2.3 billion years ago might have been caused by the photosynthetic activities of bacteria at that time. What do you think about that?*

LM: It certainly is possible that he's correct. Ice Ages are not just caused by photosynthetic CO_2 removal; many astronomical factors are also at work, such as the precession of the equinoxes or the Milankovitch effect.[8] But it is true that the cyanobacteria from this period would have removed carbon dioxide, a greenhouse gas, in massive quantities. Of course, atmospheric CO_2 tends to heat up the earth's surface. There's no doubt that Swimme is correct about the coevolution between the planet and life. He may not be right about many things, but I think it very likely that he's right about the importance of CO_2 removal.[9]

JE: Much of your work describes how these bacteria lived for two billion years without aging, sex, or death. At what point did sex and death come in and why?

LM: Sex is the biological phenomenon that produces a new live individual cell or organism with genes from more than a single parent. Sex is not necessary whatsoever except in the development of animals. But since we are animals, we delude ourselves that sex is necessary. Most organisms, if you look at the world's diversity, do not require sex for reproduction. But all the animals do because sex is an intrinsic part of the life history of animals. Animals develop from a sperm that fertilizes an egg. This in itself is a sexual act. So, since ours is the animal lineage, we are mammalocentric, specifically anthropocentric. And zoologists, who know very little about biology as a rule, are especially mammalocentric. They tend to know only paramedical stuff.

JE: What about aging, then? Is it true that these bacteria don't age?

LM: The kind of aging that we see in mammals and in plants (more so in animals than in plants), is connected with their sexuality. Aging is deeply embedded in mammalian sexuality. And this sort of sexuality was and is absolutely intrinsic to the evolution of animals. But the fact is that the whole world is not just animals and plants.

One way to think about this is that if a sperm fertilizes an egg, it forms a double cell — two sets of genes. The two sets of genes making up the two chromosome sets — one from each parent — is called "diploid." A programmed release of that diploidy must eventually occur in the life history of an animal to prevent the recurrence of the doubling unit. Doubling must be followed by singling. Double, double, double, will just kill the potential animal. In order to develop the animal with only two sets of chromosomes, and one proper set of organelles, programmed death of the extra stuff must occur. And once that programmed death begins in the system, it becomes required. Like electricity, for example. Is electricity necessary for the survival of the ancestors of New Yorkers? Well, this question requires a funny answer. Yes electricity is necessary because of historical contingency. What we know of as New York would die if all electricity was removed. On the other hand, electricity is not intrinsically necessary to human survival. This is analogous to cell death. After programmed cell death evolved, it became fixed because of doubleness accumulation in animal sex. Death becomes inextricably linked with sex. The death of individuals familiar to us is a consequence of the accumulation of a lot of historical contingencies that are related to observations that animals — their muscles, their nerves, sense organs, etc. — do not develop unless the intricate sexual system makes animal embryos.

JE: Your symbiotic theory involves a vision of the human body as a kind of walking collection of bacteria which have given up their various individual freedoms to perform specialized roles within the larger architecture of the body itself. You suggest, for example, that the tails of sperm, the cilia that line the esophagus and even the rods and cones in our eyes evolved from once free-living motile bacteria and spirochetes. Your theory also entails a more controversial notion that the axons and dendrites of the nerve cells in our spinal cords and brains are remnants of spirochetes who have traded in their physical motility for the motility of thought. Have you found any evidence supporting this?

LM: Brain cells — except in syphilitic patients — are not made up of spirochetes. The idea is that remnant motile bacteria (perhaps spirochetes) are present in all animal cells, just as remnant chloroplasts are present in all plant cells — even the white ones of nonphotsynthetic plants. A spirochete is no more a brain cell or a nerve cell than a computer is a basket of silica sand and five percent iron fillings. All component percentages may be present in proper proportion but you still would not have a computer. If mine is the correct view, a swimming bacterium similar in size and behavior to today's spirochetes was one of the players in the microbial mergers that became so totally genetically fused that evidence is difficult to find. The cell's microctubule structures are no longer spirochetes any more than the chloroplasts are still cyanobacteria. There is lots of evidence, but it is so arcane I can't tell you about it without sounding unconscionably pedantic.

Just yesterday, I received a paper from a former student of mine, called "Karyotypic Fissioning and Lemur Evolution," unless she changes the title. The theory of lemur evolution enables us to see that the centromeres (kinetochores) of the chromosomes are *remnants* of motile bacteria, perhaps spirochetes. They have properties of reproducing bacteria because, in my view, they once were bacteria that entered the mergers that formed the first protist ancestors to the animals. But the centromeres are not spirochetes at all. Once this simple concept is understood, incredibly accurate phylogenies ("family trees") like this one for the lemur can be generated.

So, in other words, there's a lot of evidence that's not direct but becomes clear by inference. You can't observe a nerve cell and see the spirochete wriggle or anything like that. My detractors oversimplify what I say and they attack their own oversimplification. They do not know about life in anoxic environments, symbioses and much other relevant work. The reason they don't is because this work is not of any economic importance for anybody to know.

> *JE: When you published your paper on Gaia with James Lovelock in Stewart Brand's* Coevolution Quarterly *back in 1975, the New Agers picked up the term, and turned it into a buzzword. Do you think their adoption of Gaia has hindered the concept being taken seriously by scientists?*

LM: Not really. The Gaia stuff has been embraced entirely by many in the scientific community who just don't use the four-letter word. Gaia is still rejected by biologists, and zoologists especially despise it because it forces them to learn something besides the muscle system of animals. One cannot do Gaia sciences without chemistry, since it is basically an idea based on inorganic and atmospheric chemistry. One needs to understand aspects of microbiological metabolism, which again is a form of chemistry. This kind of chemical thinking is rejected *en masse* by the zoologists because they tend to use probabilistic mathematics which, in my opinion, is the wrong language for describing life. To understand Gaia, they would be forced to learn areas that they have arbitrarily declared to be out of their field, like chemistry, microbial metabolism or geology. So that's why they're apoplectic. Gaia, as a scientific idea, has developed and been embraced by the people who know that it is a concept useful to them. They just don't use the name. They use another name. Money is flowing in all sorts of directions towards the other name, which is called Earth Systems Science. "ESS" is legitimate but "Gaia" is not. When some colleagues wanted to form a scientific Gaia society and name it 'Geo-physiology,' I said I would never join. I reject hyphenated names for sciences. The world isn't hyphenated, it's just that people's budgets are.

A community of scholars now is quite excited about Gaia because geologists with physics and chemistry alone cannot explain the earth's surface processes. They've been taught that geology is basically applied physics and chemistry and life is just a passenger on spaceship earth. The idea is that life sits on the planet because the earth is in a perfect position in the solar system, probably because God made it that way. And the Gaia view rejects this myth. Life constantly modifies the environment on a planetary scale. Life changes what earth would be if it were just molded by simple interpolation between Mars and Venus. Life is very active in planetary modulation. This kind of thinking resonates perfectly with those who are really out there studying planetary modulation. The zoologists are most vocal against Gaia thinking. The geologists do not go to Washington D.C. and ask for the NSF money to work on Gaia. So they call it "Earth Systems Science" and there's no problem.

JE: Is it accurate to say that your characterization of Gaia differs from the way Lovelock describes it as this giant living organism, whereas you describe it as a huge ecosystem?

LM: Yes, I claim it is a huge ecosystem made up of interacting ecosystems. I think Lovelock basically agrees with me but he also believes that the personification is useful for people; it helps them to understand. To me the personification is nefarious and mischievous and I don't like it at all. It's very simple to see why: a single organism — and it doesn't matter what it is, animal, plant, fungus, protoctist, bacterium, it doesn't matter — any single organism cannot cycle its own waste. It can't eat its excrement, nor drink its liquid waste. All individuals require appropriate delivery of food, water and gas. All live organisms produce and remove some gas. They all become food or remove food or mineral nutrients or other material substances from the others. Any single organism is limited with respect to carbon, nitrogen and other element cycling. Gaia as an organism is an utterly inept analogy because no single organism can cycle elements. The definition of an ecosystem is the minimal unit that cycles all the carbon, from carbon dioxide to organic fixed carbon to protein carbon back to carbon dioxide. Gaian regulation requires a minimal ecosystem. The system cycles, therefore it's obvious to me that Gaia is at least a set of interlocking ecosystems made of smaller ecosystems. It is far greater than an individual organism. To me Gaia is not an organism.[10]

JE: I know that you've stated that you're fundamentally an atheist, but do you see any place at all for spirituality as opposed to orthodox religious systems within science?

LM: Perhaps it would be better to describe me as an agnostic. I certainly do not believe in any Judeo-Christian gods, but I do see spirituality as a human physiological need. If I don't get out in nature and smell the water lilies, I feel something's missing. I love nature as such with feelings that are probably not directly related to science.

I think humans crave reassuring spirituality just as race horses need to run and eagles must fly. These needs, evolutionary legacies, are intrinsic to our biology and must be fulfilled for our lives to be healthy. Crowd-surfing at football games, rock concerts and parade marches are religious practices that fulfill, at least in part, spiritual needs for young people in the United

States. The religious unit requires a minimal number of like-minded people. At least a set of nuclear families, more or less fifteen, twenty people to bond together with identifying symbols is absolutely minimal. Often much larger groups satisfy more completely. The minimal is the number of people that it takes to bring down the mammoth or the bison, the number that can economically support and handle the big game. This is what people function in, groups with structure where their individual place in that group is comfortable for the people. Spirituality is reinforced by drum-beating or loud music or swaying or ritual costumes. Religious practice is what's going on at football games. The details of any religion differ enormously, but the details inform the group members about his or her tribe: the Jewish tribe or the African-American tribe or whatever. Everyone must feel a part of the tribe or experience a sense of spiritual deprivation. The details differ but the fact of reinforcement of symbols that develop the identity and cohesiveness of the tribe, the physically-connected human group, is absolutely essential. If you remove the physical connection from people, it causes the same physical deprivation as food or water scarcity.

I don't at all deny spirituality. I see it as a phenomenon that can be identified by heart rate and sweating and rhythmic swaying, chanting and the like. The details of any peculiar form of spirituality can be deduced by the emotional response to the symbols. If you show an Arab a Jewish star, or show Christ with nails through his hands to an adolescent who suffered anti-Semitism, his heart beat increases, he begins to sweat, his adrenalin flows — for good reason.

I suspect the physical deprivation of the spiritual is crucial to understanding our weird dysfunctional society. Many of us are without a tribal group. Is it not ironic that in order to do anything at all in science one must hold the rest of the world constant and concentrate intensely on some tiny detail? One must control the variables one at a time. Science as a practice is very disciplined and slow. Scientists tend to just ignore everything except their object of attention. To do science is lonely. Scientific practice is not religious or spiritual, but scientists require tribal reinforced physical religious practice, as does everyone else.

JE: I know that you're probably familiar with Rupert Sheldrake's morphogenetic fields. What do you think about his work?

LM: I think he's wrong. I have read only a part of one of his books, *A New Science of Life*. I'm very sympathetic to the criticism he raises against scientific oversimplification. He is a charming, and very nice person. He has a good background in traditional anglophone biology that claims to understand evolution by a mechanism of random mutation and natural selection. The biologists gave him these answers as if they are absolute truths, which they are not. His criticisms are accurate. However, he lacks the chemistry, the microbiology, the environmental science, the geology, and details in other fields of science that could help him understand what he wants to know. Instead he makes up "theories." That's the way I see it.

His is a kind of a generic problem in science. One learns a subject and the implicit assumption is that the answers to your questions are obtainable in the same field of science. For example, a really profound and serious problem in 1950 was, how does cell and organismal reproduction work? How is heredity to be explained? How does one organism give rise to two others? This is the fundamental problem that faced biological science in 1953 when Watson and Crick discovered the complementary structure of DNA. But this biological problem was answered by work in an arcane, apparently unrelated subfield of inorganic chemistry called crystallography. The people interested in solving the problem of the physical basis of biological reproduction found that the answer was to be obtained by study of an entirely different scientific field. Most scientists assume that if the problem is in one field, then the answer is in their field as well. This is a stupid assumption. And most people don't respond like Watson did. When they said, "why don't you mind your own business and go work on your own field?" Watson refused. He said he wanted to solve a scientific problem. He hated having to learn crystallography, but he wanted the answer to his question. So, as soon as he realized that he would have to study some crystallography because that was the domain in which the answer lay, he did it. But Sheldrake did not venture out of his field. I did. I was interested in a scientific problem, not in getting ahead in some academic field with arbitrary boundaries. I wanted to know the answer, so I would buck my professors and colleagues and read what I thought interesting and relevant, never mind that it was not on the reading list. The problem is one of specialization, basically.

JE: What do you think about William Irwin Thompson's amplifications of your work in his book Imaginary Landscape *where he talks about how myths and fairy tales conceal a sort of coded memory of the evolutionary record of the history of the universe? He draws parallels with dwarves and goblins to fermenting bacteria and elves and beings of light to photosynthetic cyanobacteria and so forth.*

LM: I think his work is marvelous. He draws, of course, with sweeping brushes, there's no doubt about that. He paints with large strokes. I have tried for twenty-some years to obtain a MacArthur fellowship for him. I believe he is the most deserving person I know. Every time the MacArthur Foundation asks me to nominate somebody I renominate him. He still doesn't have one and he probably never will win one. They want younger people but I consider him a magnificently original scholar. He certainly is correct about the power of unstated preconceptions that one might call myths. Scientists of course share legends or qualities of mind under which we labor. Those "thought styles" are probably of critical importance to how people accomplish scientific activity, which is very limited, by definition.

I feel there is little comparison between a sincere Christian like Rupert Sheldrake and a profound intellectual like William Irwin Thompson. Yes, Bill Thompson is sometimes sloppy. But he has the biggest vocabulary of anyone I've ever read. I have to look up every five of his words. When you read him you think he is a very bitter and critical person. His strident criticism, however, especially of so-called "Western civilization," is exact. In person, he's not at all bitter. He's a sweet, verbose, articulate and kind guy. His personal qualities are very much like those of Sheldrake. But his criticism of our "culture" is devastating. And with respect to academic specialization, although he is a cultural historian who has written enough to be qualified for tenure in any English department or in a history department, he is *persona non grata* because he criticizes the hand that feeds him. So, he doesn't get fed. One of my favorite essays by him is called "Walking Out on the University." But he's a man of great integrity, and you don't find people of integrity anymore. They all sell out.

Some colleagues of ours say Thompson needs a podium from which to preach, and in a way, that's true. He lectured a few years ago at Hampshire College and drew a huge, appreciative audience; people were just hanging out of the windows, sitting on the floor and just lapping up every word. Most academics don't even know his work, but those who read books love him. He can't get a job here because he does not conform to some academic authority's preconceptions or to the "departmental rules."

JE: Are you familiar with Evelyn Fox Keller?

LM: Yes. She wrote a biographical piece on me called "One Lady and Her Theory." Perhaps it appeared in *New Scientist.* I don't remember.

JE: Her book Reflections on Gender and Science *raises the issue of how the masculinist rhetoric of science was designed to enforce the Biblical world view of domination over women and that this has infected the so-called "objectivity" of scientists with a gender-biased viewpoint that renders their paradigms far from "objective." Have you yourself found it difficult being a woman and practicing science?*

LM: Not at all, I find pleasure in it. The ratio, until relatively recently, was about nine men to one woman, or eight to one, or ten to two, in any conference, meeting or advanced class in which I participated. Even in biology, it was usually way outnumbered in favor of men. And I'm one of the people who love that.

JE: Can I ask why?

LM: Because I love men. I first became acquainted with Evelyn Keller through a book with a chapter about her, "Women at Work." It contained interviews with women very active in different areas of study or performance and Evelyn Fox Keller was the scientist in this book. I was absolutely horrified by what she wrote. She talks about her experience as a first-year graduate student at Harvard and some fellow student leaned back in his chair smoking his pipe, blew smoke at her and said, "There's no place for women in physics," or something like that. Obviously, her experiences were negative, and she was discouraged in her science. She clearly faced a lot of prejudice. I do not deny that such prejudice exists. Many people, especially young women, have extremely discouraging experiences. Much depends on their looks, their age, their backgrounds and how willingly they accept victimization.

The first time I ever knew about any kind of discouraging experience among women science students was at Cal Tech, long after I had become a faculty member, where I was invited to a session with a women's science group. I couldn't *believe* their horror stories of discouragement. Mary Catherine Bateson, when she was the dean at Amherst College — and no one fools with Mary Catherine Bateson — describes *ridiculous* prejudice against her and fellow women in her best-selling book *Composing A Life*. I do not deny prejudice exists. But I've been fortunate. I can't suffer prejudicial people; I consider them assholes. Let's put it bluntly. I don't care whether they're men or women, I just don't suffer them. So I don't stay in the presence of people who I feel are likely to be prejudicial or repressive. In the first five or ten minutes I recognize the type and I stay away from it. As a result, since attaining adulthood, I've had no problem whatsoever. My problem has always been with people protected by their little intellectual specialty. Often my critics simply don't know obscure facts and literature that I do so their arguments are not valid and they tend not to criticize me in person. They just reject without knowing. I consider that gender independent.

JE: I'm curious what you thought about the film version of Contact.

LM: My beloved grandson, Tonio Sagan, had the greatest comment. He said, "Gee, it's a shame Grandpa died halfway through." I think that is probably what happened. The scenes with the religious fanatic were awful and the ending was weak. I thought the film started quite strong, with the intensity of Jodie Foster's excellent acting as this young girl and the SETI (Search for Extraterrestrial Intelligence) technical stuff.

JE: Yeah, I thought it lost it right exactly halfway through with the religious nut coming in.

LM: Did you know that that's when Sagan died?

JE: I did not. So he was involved with the project — ?

LM: Sure. He and his wife were involved for years with the project. For years, they tried to raise the money to make the film. And they wrote and rewrote it, but they just didn't have Sagan's firm hand directing the intellectual content at the end. And Tonio, who is an incipient film director, realized that right away.

JE: Yeah, the ending was a real disappointment. But then I never read the novel so I'm not sure how different it was.

LM: I couldn't read the novel. I read a bit of it but I found the people so monodimensional. They lack subtlety. Sagan was notoriously bad at any kind of human interaction unless he was pontificating at everyone else. But he was a great talent. He did wonderful things for the space program, for science education and popularization. But he was always on the side of the angels.

Part Two:

THE

RETURN

TO

THE

SOURCE

"Our birth," wrote the poet William Wordsworth, "is but a sleep and a forgetting: / The Soul that rises with us, our life's Star, / Hath had elsewhere its setting / and cometh from afar." For whether we are considering the cosmologies of *The Tibetan Book of the Dead* — in which the soul drops from the overwhelming radiance of the Primary Clear Light through galaxies swarming with luminous bodhisattvas and fiery demons, to the karmic heat generated by the lovemaking of a specific couple — or that of the ancient Greeks — in which the soul's descent through celestial spheres to the sublunary realm of the earth imprints it with a map of the entire structure of the cosmos — we can say that the traditional cosmologies dismissed by mainstream science tend to agree that at the moment of birth, the soul is already very ancient, indeed. In the Platonic view, it was the aim of education to reawaken that knowledge of the archetypal universals by which the Demiurge had constructed the universe. Socrates' demonstration in the *Meno* elaborates the point as he questions Meno's untutored slave boy in such a way as to elicit from him the length of the side of a square whose area is twice that of one given.

But, as Wordsworth goes on, "Shades of the prison house begin to close / Upon the growing boy," for the moment we are born society begins to shape the neural structures of our brains in accordance with a particular image of the world, and a corresponding set of sentiments to guide our behavior within it. The mind very early on makes certain cognitive commitments to this world-image, which, however, may drown out the soul's memory of its cosmic journey altogether.

And so, like his intellectual forebear Rousseau, Terence McKenna distrusts civilization, for he believes that its trivialities are just so much "noise" drowning out the visions, dreams and intuitive wonders sent to us by Nature's mighty and ancient intelligence. His solution to this problem is a communion with the Gaian Overmind through hallucinogenic plants and mushrooms. McKenna's botanical sacraments resemble the blissful sojourn of the Lotus Eaters in the *Odyssey* who become so entranced by their reveries that they refuse to return to civilization.

With Stanislav Grof, we return to the source of creation through an involution of consciousness that replays the sequences of Bardo from *The Tibetan Book of the Dead* in reverse. Beginning with a re-experience of the trauma of birth, we journey back through the collective unconscious of our ancestral past, encountering modes of being cast aside by the human mind's evolutionary descent through time and space. Recovery of past lives, identification with plant and animal consciousness, or even encounters with spiritual beings form the road signs and landmarks along this highway through the astral plane.

With Deepak Chopra, we arrive at the source of our own innermost Being, and reach the point where, paradoxically, the end of the cycle flips over like a Mobius strip into its beginning. For *Brahman* is the ground of origin from out of which all things have precipitated and back into which they dissolve. When the human mind fuses with this plane of Being during the trance states of meditation and yoga, it sees through all things as though with the Eye of God.

Finally, the vision of William Irwin Thompson provides us with the Landsaat map of the whole cultural landscape we have left behind. In a way, Thompson exists from a vantage point outside the cycle, like Markandeya, the legendary Hindu counterpart of Noah who, in the *Puranas*, accidentally slips outside of the mouth of the dreaming god Vishnu, and is afforded a vision of the universe between cycles of destruction and creation. Thompson, like Markandeya, has been privileged the vision of the whole, and stands outside the evolution and involution of the universe, from which vantage point he can see where the bridges connect Valhalla to the heavens and the earth.

TERENCE MCKENNA

AND THE

GARDEN OF

PSYCHEDELIC DELIGHTS

In what amounts to a kind of psychedelic in-joke, authors William Gibson and Bruce Sterling resurrect T.H. Huxley, grandfather of the famous Aldous, for a scene in their novel *The Difference Engine*. A paleontologist who has just returned from America gives to Huxley a few buttons of peyote which he has received from a Native American shaman. Huxley, receiving the gift, says, "Certain vegetable toxins have the quality of producing visions." Then he places the buttons in a desk drawer and remarks, " . . . I'll see they're properly catalogued later."[1]

The joke is, of course, that Huxley will do precisely nothing with the peyote buttons and not until the mescalin experiments of his grandson Aldous in the middle of the twentieth century will their value be discovered. For it was in 1955 that Aldous Huxley ingested four tenths of a gram of mescalin — the psychoactive content of peyote — and discovered that, in the words of James Joyce, "any object, intensely regarded, may be a gate of access to the incorruptible eon of the gods." Huxley's book *The Doors of Perception*, in which he writes of this experience, would eventually drift into the hands of 14-year-old Terence McKenna, for whom it would provide the impetus for a lifetime of exploration in the unsounded depths of human consciousness.

T.H. Huxley's attitude, however — as Gibson and Sterling have imagined it — typifies that of the scholar toward such matters: knowledge fit for the yellowed pages of decaying volumes on library shelves, but unrelated to the world of *lived* experience. It is most ironic that the scientific method envisioned by such men as Leonardo da Vinci and Francis Bacon emphasizes precisely the validity of individual experience. Western civilization, in fact, was shaped by the mythology of individual experience, in opposition to the outdated Oriental notion of trust in the authority of others, and owes its present magnificence to those of its great explorers who have had the courage to visit lands thought to be swarming with strange Boschian creatures guarding their gates. It is this Western mythology of personal experience which, for example, impelled Vesalius to reject the authority of Galen and cut open human bodies himself, in order to verify once and for all the structure of human anatomy; or the Promethean courage of Galileo in defying that Renaissance incarnation of Zeus — the Catholic Church itself — to peer through the telescope at what none had dared to look at with such intensity before; or the trans-Atlantic migrations of Columbus (from *"columba,"* the dove) intent upon discovering *for himself* whether the Indies could be reached by sailing beyond the sunset. Right down to the Apollo space flights and our current explorations of Mars, the myth has remained essentially unchanged, to the present.

That "transcendent country of the mind," however, which Aldous Huxley described — the dark and unknown labyrinths of human consciousness — still remains, for the most part, unexplored by Westerners. The investigation of the unconscious mind only began with Freud and his German Romantic predecessors during the nineteenth century.

Terence McKenna is one such Magellan of consciousness, and his journey began with a trip to Asia in 1967 to study the pre-Buddhist iconography of Tibetan thangkas. He discovered instead that the roots of Tibetan Buddhism lay in the native shamanism of Bon-Po, some of whose practitioners use hashish and the hallucinogen datura to catalyze their shamanic journeys.

In 1971, Terence and his brother Dennis journeyed to the Amazon basin in quest of an authentic shamanic experience, and in the process encountered a species of psilocybin-containing mushroom (*Stropharia cubensis*) which, McKenna claims, is second only to DMT (dimethyltryptamine) for its power to induce a hallucinogenic voyage to the realm of the Ancestors. And it is this realm which shamans normally contact in order to learn knowledge and valuable information capable of healing the afflictions of their community, or the disorders of a specific person. Such interior cosmonauts may, in the words of Aldous Huxley, "become conduits through which some beneficent influence can flow out of that other country into a world of darkened selves, chronically dying for lack of it." The McKenna brothers' experiences with telepathy, synchronicity and UFO encounters are described in vivid detail in McKenna's *True Hallucinations* (1993).

The major task before them upon their return from the Amazonian shamanic underworld was, in the words of Joseph Campbell, "how to render back into lightworld language the speech-defying pronouncements of the dark." To which challenge they responded with a book entitled *The Invisible Landscape* (1975). In this strange and poetic work, the authors attempt through a synthesis of science, philosophy, and history to fathom the implications of their experiences in the Amazon. In the general resonance theory of nature which they spin out like some exotic helix of cultural DNA, the microcosm of the shamanic journey to the interiors of human and cosmic consciousness is mapped onto the macrocosm of time and space through a philosophy of history which McKenna terms "The Timewave." In this theory, the events of history are described as a non-linear fractal wave in which distant epochs influence epochs separated by time and space through resonances in their structural similarity.

In 1976, the authors followed this work with *Psilocybin: the Magic Mushroom Grower's Guide*, and in 1991, McKenna gathered up a decade and a half of essays and interviews in *The Archaic Revival*.

In 1992, Terence McKenna's book *Food of the Gods* appeared, in which he describes his theory of the origins of human consciousness as having been precipitated by the ingestion of psychoactive mushrooms. The book then chronicles the long decline of mushroom usage and its unsatisfying history of such replacements as opium, sugar, coffee, and heroin throughout the evolution of human culture.

In the same year, McKenna's longtime acquaintance with biologist Rupert Sheldrake and chaos theoretician Ralph Abraham culminated with the appearance of their *Trialogues at the Edge of the West*, to which a sequel,

The Evolutionary Mind: Trialogues at the Edge of the Unthinkable, was added in 1998.

McKenna is currently co-authoring a book with Philippe DeVosjoli, to be entitled *Casting Nets Into the Sea of Mind*. McKenna promises a further sounding out of his theories of the evolution of human consciousness and its relation to language and technology.

> *JE: In your first book,* The Invisible Landscape, *you and your brother Dennis evolve what seems to be a kind of general resonance theory of nature that encompasses the visionary experience of shamanism as well as the larger epochs of historical time. I wonder if you wouldn't mind discussing how this theory grew out of your reflections on the nature of time after your journey to the Amazon in 1971.*

TM: Well, I think probably the central perception in all of that was the idea that time is really, when you analyze it, metabolism, which is the unique quality that associates itself with organic life, by which life creates an open system far from equilibrium and by that means sustains itself in and through time. So the structure of organic life, specifically the structure of DNA, is, I think, a unique evolutionary response to this thermodynamic drive toward nonequilibrium that seems to characterize biology. By studying metabolism — which, in practical terms means by looking inside our cells — we can actually not only understand what time is, but make generalizations about it that we can effectively extend to other domains of the universe.

> *JE: It's interesting the way you connect the microcosm with the macrocosm. In* True Hallucinations, *for example, you talk about how you built up this whole resonance theory around the number 64, which you claim is significant for both DNA — in which there are 64 possible sequences of codons — as well as for the* I Ching, *in which there are 64 hexagrams.[2] Could you talk a little bit about how you constructed that out of a meditation on that number?*

TM: Sixty-four is an interesting number. It is two to the sixth and arises out of four, which according to Jung and others, is a primary division of space, time, and reality. We live in a four-dimensional universe. My notion about the *I Ching* was that if we take it seriously — and we certainly did — and by take it seriously I mean if we recognize that it does seem to have an uncanny ability to function as advertised, then it seems reasonable to ask, how does it do that? I think the way it must do it is by being, as you mentioned, somehow a microcosm of the larger macrocosm. And the realization that it was directly analogous to the structure of the DNA, seemed to be the clue. The *I Ching* is a primary insight into the structure not only of the universe we live in, but of the Mind that we are embedded in that looks out at that universe.

JE: Your resonance theory of time suggests that distant events in history can have an effect or an influence on present events through a kind of resonance of their structural similarity. For example, you compare the end of the Roman Empire with the events of the present day. Can you discuss how that resonance works?

TM: Sure. First of all recall what ordinary historical theory assumes: that the most important moment in terms of shaping this moment is the moment which immediately preceded it. I took a different view, and felt that a given historical moment in time is a kind of standing wave of interference patterns set up by other moments in time which may or may not have immediately preceded it. So, for example, the Greek Golden Age, though it lies now 2500 years in the past, nevertheless continues to shape our ideas about law and society. And in any given situation there are many of these influences impinging, some of them trivially, to give us clawed bathtub legs and things like this; and some very profoundly, to give us the endurability of democracy or something like that.   .

JE: Do you think the fact that your model ends in the same year —
2012 C.E. — as that of the Mayan calendar suggests some kind of a resonance between our culture and the Mayans?[3]

TM: I'm not sure what it means. I think all cultures which look deeply into time, if they reach correct conclusions, their models will be in some sense congruent. Even if you look at Western civilization and its calendars, we go through a millennial turning just twelve years before the end of the Mayan calendar. On a scale of a thousand years, that's a difference of point-one-two percent.

So, oddly enough, the unconscious life of cultures seems to fall into synchronization with these very large cosmic rhythms, whether the culture recognizes these rhythms or not. It's just the lay of the temporal landscape, if you will.

JE: On the microcosmic side, in your book The Invisible Landscape, *you and your brother evolve a theory that the visionary experiences of shamanism are activated when psilocybin bonds chemically with neural DNA. I wonder if you wouldn't mind discussing this theory.*

TM: Well, in ordinary metabolism, psilocybin is an antagonist, meaning a competitor, with serotonin, which is an ordinary brain transmitter at the synapse. However, a very small percentage of psilocybin actually finds its way into the nucleus of the cell. There are very striking structural affinities between DNA and many of these naturally occurring psychedelic molecules. As you know, DNA can be visualized as a ladder-like structure while many of these drug molecules are called planar, meaning simply flat, and are of the precise size and geometry to allow themselves to fit in and out of the spaces between the nucleotides of DNA. This process is called intercalation. It's well studied, but no one knows what the purpose or consequences of this lock and key fit between the structures of DNA and these drug molecules may be.[4]

JE: Karl Pribram talks about the holographic paradigm of memory storage, but he seems to be concerned with it on an individual basis, whereas you and your brother expand it to suggest that something like the world soul or the collective unconscious is also somehow hologramatically accessible in the psilocybin experience?

TM: Yes, if we accept the Jungian model of a collective unconscious — a shared set of archetypal images that are not culturally imparted — then we have, as you mentioned, not only the problem of individual memory to account for, but the larger problem of these racial or archetypal memories. I think that we have made it very difficult for ourselves in this area by putting so much phobia and stress on doing psychedelic research. Our fear dictates that anyone who chooses in pharmacology or molecular biology to concentrate in these areas, is choosing a life of pure marginalization. It's very difficult to obtain funding, and there's very little institutional support.

JE: I'm curious what you think about Stanislav Grof's work with LSD and his theory that it reactivates the birth trauma.

TM: Well, Stan's a personal friend of mine, and he did very courageous work with LSD, and then when LSD was made illegal, he developed a model of breathing techniques to move people into the same areas. Having said that, my own personal exploration of the psyche has not tended to support his theory of the various perinatal matrices. I would call it a neo-Freudian theory. I'm open-minded about this, but I don't think most people who have not heard of Grof's theory would have experiences that could really be mapped onto that system.

JE: Can you discuss, then, what in your experience, are the differences in the visionary contents of the LSD versus the psilocybin experience?

TM: Well, yes, to some degree. Each one of these things, being chemically unique, is like a lens made of a slightly different colored glass. LSD goes directly to the structure of the personality, the structures that have arisen through the experiences in the life of the individual, so that it's very good for working through what I think of as normal psychoanalytical issues. It is reluctantly a hallucinogen. In other words, it transforms the quality of thought, but it doesn't transform the input in the visual cortex as dramatically as some of these other things do.

Those compounds which are plant-based, on the other hand — psilocybin or DMT — seem to be full of their *own* information which they wish to impart. So that often one does not come away with deep insight into one's relationship or one's parental situation, but instead comes away with a much deeper sense of connection to the dynamics of nature or, you could almost say, the world of spirit or magical energy. Now, why this difference should obtain between psilocybin and LSD. . . . It may be structural or it may be something deeper.

For example, it may involve something like the Sheldrakian notion of morphogenetic fields. LSD, after all, was invented in the twentieth century, in the late thirties, and is entirely characterized by twentieth century Europeans and Americans. Compounds like psilocybin, on the other hand, used for millennia by tribal peoples in the mountains of Mexico, would then, of course, have a completely different kind of morphogenetic field.

JE: You've mentioned that psilocybin facilitates contact with what appears to be an alien Mind or intelligence of some sort. You have a theory about UFO's which suggests that they might somehow be projections of this intelligence out of the psyche. Could you discuss that?

TM: Psyche, or consciousness, is a very slippery concept. One researcher, Julian Jaynes, has suggested that human consciousness has changed its character even in historical times. Jaynes felt that in Homeric times, the ego as we know it was really not in existence, except under extreme stress. And then it presented itself almost as an exterior intrusion into consciousness, like the voice of a god.[5] I think that the major difference between modern materialistic consciousness and archaic shamanic consciousness, is that the archaic shamanic consciousness interprets much of its perception as coming from an organized and intelligent Other. And I, after having gone through the extraterrestrial interpretation for a number of years, have come to the opinion that this Other that we contact through these things is nothing more or less than a kind of integrated intelligence that pervades the entire planet. For want of a better tag, let's just call it the Gaian Overmind.

I think for a long time through history, people were fully conscious, fully at home with language and theater and ritual and magic, but they were cradled, if you like, or embedded in an almost continuous dialogue with the rest of reality, experienced as of a seamless consciousness which they called the Great Spirit or the Ancestors or simply God. The Western cultural and linguistic heritage has been largely a building of defenses against this Other and a replacement of it with the politically expressed mass ego of humanity.

So when we go into the wilderness and take psychedelic plants and perform ancient paradigmatic rituals, if we are successful in dissolving the conditioning and the expectations of modernity and materialism, we discover that this mystery is still there, still alive, still capable of dialoguing with us. And it's absolutely confounding to people. They react to it either with ecstasy or fear, or tales of religious conversion or alien abduction. It entirely depends upon how it hits you. In this case, one man's revelation is another man's nightmare. But the thing that lies behind all of this, is a living intelligent natural mind of some sort that is simply an extension of the biosphere, of Gaia.

JE: In your book Food of the Gods, *you deal with some of the historical dimensions of the use of hallucinogens. You envision the history of culture as a steady decline in the use of plant-based hallucinogens and their gradual replacement with such unsatisfying substitutes as alcohol, opium, tobacco, cocaine and so forth. Is it possible that if people used hallucinogens in a more ritualized and controlled way, such as, say, twice a month, that it might significantly reduce the abuse of some of these other drugs?*

TM: God, twice a month! That *would* be a revolution, wouldn't it? I think people without this helping hand from this Gaian intelligence that we were talking about are simply clueless. They have Marxism, and modern advertising, and whatever cultural values they're born into to guide them, but inevitably, as Freud pointed out in *Civilization and its Discontents*, these things lead to neurosis.

I think that the key thing to understand about the psychedelic experience, whether you love it or hate it, is that it dissolves boundaries. It dissolves cultural programming and replaces it with a much more basic kind of programming that is in the human animal. All culture steers us away from this original source of self-authentication. And in that sense, Freud was right; all culture is neurotic. So in the book you mentioned, and also in another book of mine called *The Archaic Revival*, I simply pointed out that when civilizations become massively neurotic, they seem to have an instinctual reflex to go back in time looking for a model. This is why the Renaissance created Classicism as a response to the failure of the Medieval church. It's why in the twentieth century we've seen outbreaks of phenomena that range from Cubism and Surrealism to Rock and Roll. These are impulses toward an archaic state of mind. At the center of this impulse toward the archaic state of mind is the boundary dissolution of cultural values that takes place under psychedelics. Certainly if we could find some way to bring this to people — and I think twice a month sounds massively more frequent than is necessary — on a yearly basis and in a powerful manner, that would be sufficient to keep people operating in the light of the certain knowledge that there are value structures larger than that of the knowledge being handed down to them through the mass media and cultural conventions.

People are being absolutely *starved* for authenticity, and in the meantime they're offered an endless selection of German automobiles and hair-care products and ice cream flavors and witless entertainment, and none of it satisfies because what people really feel deprived of is an authentic sense of their own being and their own importance in the natural scheme of things. Culture cannot respond to that unless it makes a place for the transcendence of itself.

JE: In Food of the Gods *you suggest that human consciousness may have evolved from that of its hominid forebears as a result of hominids having incorporated hallucinogenic mushrooms into their diet. What is the earliest evidence that we have for the use of mushrooms in human history?*

TM: I think probably the earliest evidence that I would consider having any weight is a group of rock-chipped images in the Tassili Plateau of southern Algeria. They keep dating these things older and older, and I think they've got them pushed back now to about 12,000 years ago. There we see shamans with mushrooms sprouting out of their bodies and fistfuls of mushrooms.[6] This kind of evidence, though, has never been sought, and in the areas where I think you're most likely to find this no digging has ever been done — specifically, in southern Algeria. You could do pollenological studies looking for mushroom spores. You could try to find yet more remote and older rock art representations of these mushroom-using shamans.

The great embarrassment of ordinary evolutionary theory, you see, is the very dramatic explosion in human brain size over a very short period of evolutionary time. One evolutionary biologist, Lumholtz, calls it the most dramatic transformation of a major organ of a higher animal in the entire fossil record. Well, it's a great embarrassment to evolution because notice that the brain is the organ which created the theory of evolution. So if we can't account for *its* origin we've run up a ladder that has no resting place.

Something extraordinary was impinging on the hominid situation, let's say from 125,000 to 25,000 years ago. All other theories have failed. I've concentrated on psilocybin but really when I talk to my peers in this field, what I'm saying is that what we need to look at is diet. Diet is one of the major factors affecting rates of mutation in any species. The reason most species of animals have very defined and specialized diets is that it's a conservative evolutionary strategy to limit exposure to mutagenic compounds, and hence to mutation. When a species gets under nutritional pressure and starts trying food previously considered marginal or unacceptable, why naturally that means the genome is going to be exposed to new chemical stress through the food chain, and you're going to get more birth deformities, blindness, low IQ, low birth rate. But you're also going to get the very rare positive mutation, and the rate of those positive mutations will also be concomitantly kicked upward a little.

So I think that the place to look to understand the break-out in human evolution is that period when we changed from a canopy-dwelling grassland creature. The subsequent shift in diet and the upheavals in the exposure to various chemicals made many changes in human beings. Psilocybin is simply one of the most dramatic. We can construct a scenario with psilocybin that I think is very appealing to evolutionary biologists because it shows how psilocybin, by incrementally contributing slight advantages, could have worked its way toward being a major chemical influence on the evolution of brain architecture and consciousness.

JE: In Food of the Gods *you trace an arc of historical diffusion of an originally mushroom-using goddess society — the Tassili people in Paleolithic North Africa — and follow it across Asia Minor as it travels into Anatolian Catal Huyuk, from which it migrates to Minoan Crete. Finally, the Greeks take up this Goddess culture in the much reduced form of the Eleusinian mysteries, in which the hallucinogenic ergot may have been used, just as the Cretans used opium. My question, then, is, do you have any idea exactly where along this path, or why it was that mushroom usage died out?*

TM: Yes, I link it entirely to slow changes in climate. In other words, probably 100,000 to 125,000 years ago was the optimum in terms of size and extent of rainfall, and the optimum over-lap, as well, of mushroom ecosystems and human habitats. All of North Africa was vast grassland with evolving ungulate animals and many streams flowing out of the highlands. And that grassland had itself arisen out of a climatic change. Before that, at an even earlier time, there had been forest. But as the grassland over millennia gave way to desert, the mushrooms — their range, availability, and potency — all underwent retraction and diminution. As that process continued, the human population either went without or began to seek substitutes. And no substitute really has the same effect as the original, and so you get beer cults, the fermenting of fruit juices into wine, experimentation with hemp and opium. But it was simply a series of climatological disasters, and the thing which put the kibosh on the whole thing — which was also a response to this climatological change — was the invention of agriculture. I think Frazer in *The Golden Bough* says something about when the gods turned into food the great orgies and celebrations became marginalized, because the cultural values that became important at that time were the ability to get up early in the morning and pick up your hoe and go to work.

JE: Some scholars have said that the consumption of hallucinogens is a poor substitute for the long hard road of spiritual discipline that it takes, they claim, to become truly enlightened. How do you respond to this point of view?[7]

TM: Well, I don't know, I guess they're truly enlightened. That's a tough thing to knock. This is an ongoing and endless argument at every level in anthropology. The great proponent of it that I'm familiar with is Mircea Eliade, who took the position that what he called "narcotic shamanism" was somehow decadent, and that the real shamanism was running on ordeals and wilderness abandonment and that sort of thing. I don't think aboriginal people were any more fond of discomfort and unpleasantness than we are. Faced with a number of methods to get to the same goal, most of us would choose the most effective and non-destructive method. I really think that when direct access to the mystery or to the spirit becomes problematic for any reason, then that's when you get codification of dogma, appointment of special classes of people to interpret for the rest of us the wishes of the invisible world. Then you get moral laundry lists of do's and don'ts. And the whole thing turns into organized religion. The phobia that most of these organized religions exhibit toward the psychedelic experience is simply that they sense in it a very powerful competitor for their customers.

JE: You mentioned that you traveled around in Asia for a while trying out these various yogic disciplines and they didn't work for you?

TM: Well, it's not that they don't work; they do not deliver the psychedelic experience. They deliver very interesting and very useful experiences, and they certainly teach self-discipline and all of that. But I think with organized religion there is a tension within it because religion is *in* the moment and seeks to address man's yearning beyond this world, and yet inevitably religion becomes about its investment schemes, its own self-aggrandizement, its wish to pull more people and more territory under its sway. So I've always felt that the authentic religious journey was something that was going to happen between a single human being and the Spirits. I think it's a pity that religion is so fearful of direct experience that it inevitably places an elite class between the ordinary speaker and the mystery.

JE: Have you ever taken psilocybin in conjunction with an isolation tank?

TM: I've never done it actually in a tank. I don't think that you have to go that far, but that the best environment for these things is what I call comfortable silent darkness. Some people want to listen to music and that certainly will sweep you away. But we can't do anything with the news that Bach is God; we already know that. I think that when people have to have music or art books stacked up around them, they're already selling themselves short. The inner riches of the silent human mind is beyond anything we have ever created in any courtly situation or in any splendorous society that we've ever put together on this planet. And really that news is tremendously existentially empowering. The whole consumer society that we're embedded in is really a system for delivering marvels. Toys, clothing, games and entertainment: it's all to astonish you and sweep you away. Well, if you were growing mushrooms in the cow manure in your backyard, you would quickly gain a completely different relationship to such wonders. You would realize that of course, there's an infinitude of such wonders, and most of them lie within me.

So, again I see culture offering cheap substitutes for authentic experience. Culture wants you to regret the past, anticipate the future, and barely notice the felt presence of immediate experience. To my mind, this is the most toxic value that we tolerate; the devaluation of our feelings as they occur to us *in* the act of living *in* the moment *in* a defined locus of space and time. That's who we are, that's all we will ever be, and a world made out of hope and regret is a very pale substitute for that feeling of being vitally connected and present in the living world.

JE: Your ideas about resonance through time have much in common with Rupert Sheldrake's morphic resonance and Ralph Abraham's vibration research. Other than the Trialogues, *do you think the three of you would ever consider collaborating on a book together?*

TM: We're tight, and in fact we've done a whole second set of *Trialogues*. All we need is a publisher crazy enough to publish them, although I don't think the first book did terribly well in English, but it was very well received in Germany. But yeah, I feel very close to those guys. I think Rupert's theory of the morphogenetic field and my timewave are basically two sides of one coin. And then Ralph's chaos dynamics offers the larger intellectual environment in which those ideas have to be contextualized.

JE: Are you working on a new book?

TM: Yes, I have a book I'm working on with co-author Phillipe De Vosjoli. We're doing a book called *Casting Nets Into the Sea of Mind*. A lot of it is talk about technology and where it's taking us, and then a lot of trying to firm up this whole thing about early evolution and all that. Since I wrote *Food of the Gods* there have been a number of very interesting developments. The key thing that I think is misunderstood, and that is blocking progress in understanding the human condition, is that we really need to re-think our relationship to language and what it is. What I mean by that is that language is something very deep and general in nature. I think all of nature seeks to communicate and that information is moved around on many levels. What is new and unique about human beings is speech. In standard English, speech and language are used almost interchangeably. I would like to see that change.

Language is something very old and very general, and I think speech is a much more technologically recent phenomenon. It's something someone invented. People were communicating on many levels and in great detail long before the invention of speech. There was some fascinating research revealed just in the past few months in *Science News*. Researchers discovered that with a group of newborn infants they could teach them standard

American Sign Language months before they became verbal. The argument for the ancientness of language is that we learn it so young that we must therefore be biologically programmed for it. Well, this new research shows that we must be even more biologically programmed for ASL. I think what it suggests is that we are programmed for language and that we can acquire it in many ways, and that speech is not the primary or most easily acquired method of communication. It's something that people learn to do. And reading is something that we learn to do much later than that, which is also an astonishing phenomenon. Yet, it's a technological innovation. So, the new book will go into speech as technology and the future history of technology as we move toward quasi-telepathic drug and machine-assisted communication environments.

JE: Do you think virtual reality technology will play an important part in all this, or will it just turn out to be a novelty?

TM: I think it has a tremendous potential because it's really a technology that will allow us to show each other the inside of our heads. This is something we have never been able to do. You and I are having this conversation and the polite assumption is that we have identical dictionaries open in front of us, and therefore you understand what I mean. But nothing brings conversation to a more screeching halt than for somebody to say to someone else, "could you explain to me what I just said?" And you know, in the face of that challenge, the assumption of communication is exposed as pretty thin stuff.[8]

If we could actually show each other what we mean by building 3-D sculptural environments of our intentionality, we would be able to eliminate the maddening ambiguity that attends low bandwidth small mouth noise style conversation. It's amazing to me that we can have a global civilization based on small mouth noise communication, given that there are 500 languages and nobody has the same dictionary and nobody has had the same education and everybody has a different set of experiences. So, I think we've done an amazing job with the blunt instrument we've been given, but the future of communication is the future of the evolution of the human soul, and as we communicate with each other with greater facility, the boundaries and the illusion of difference will just evanesce and disappear.

BIRTH, DEATH AND THE BEYOND:

STANISLAV GROF AND

THE TRANSFORMATION

OF CONSCIOUSNESS

The genius of Sigmund Freud was not his discovery of the unconscious. As Thomas Mann pointed out in a speech delivered on the occasion of Freud's eightieth birthday, Freud's ideas were actually the culmination of a long stream of cultural discourse on "the primacy of instinct over the mind and reason" which had nourished the unfolding of Romanticism throughout the nineteenth century, and in Germany, in particular. From the publication in 1819 of *The World as Will and Idea* — Arthur Schopenhauer's rapturous synthesis of Kant, Plato and *The Upanishads* — to the operas of Wagner, the dramas of Ibsen, and the publication of Eduard von Hartmann's *Philosophy of the Unconscious* in 1869, the existence of an unconscious mind was already clearly sketched out. What remained for Freud was the translation of this idea into the language of scientific parlance.[1]

Of course, the essence of that language had been epitomized by Isaac Newton in the seventeenth century in terms of the mechanics of forces and masses. Biology, consequently, was not even regarded as a formal science until the publication of Darwin's *Origin of Species* in the mid-nineteenth century. For just as Newton had resolved all motion into the tension between the two forces of inertia (which all matter possessed innately) and gravitation (which acted upon matter from without) so too, Darwin saw that the evolution of species could be translated into the language of mechanics: all species possessed an innate force of mutation while natural selection acted upon these mutations by way of environmental pressures exerted in the struggle for survival.

Freud, likewise, saw that the idea of the unconscious was susceptible to a mechanical model: the innate forces of the id were held strongly in check by the outer forces of society, and the ego was evolved with almost geologic pressure between them. But just as the limits of Newton's laws were sharply circumscribed by Einstein, so too, the validity of Freud's theories were restricted by the genius of his disciple Carl Jung, who had spent his Sundays in medical school absorbing ideas from Kant, Schopenhauer, Nietzsche and von Hartmann — all of whom Freud completely ignored. With this philosophical immune system built into him, Jung rapidly outgrew Freud's limitations. For Jung, the foundations of the psyche were cosmic and the soul came equipped at birth with the knowledge of its lost evolutionary journey through the cosmos. This wisdom was only forgotten, and the psyche each night instructed the mind in the form of dreams, and entire civilizations through the language of myth. As Thomas Mann has written, "Very deep is the well of the past. Should we not call it bottomless?"

In a way, the life and career of Stanislav Grof are a recapitulation of the history of psychoanalysis. Born in Czechoslovakia in 1931, Grof happened to chance upon Freud's *Introductory Lectures in Psychoanalysis* just as he was preparing for a career in the film industry. He decided instead to become a psychoanalyst, and enrolled in Prague's Charles University School of Medicine. Although his atheistic upbringing was congenial to Freud's mechanistic theories, he soon realized the limitations of Freud's exclusively verbal approach to psychoanalysis, which could involve a patient in years of therapy with only minimal improvement. Eventually, he found himself regretting how little his imagination was called upon as an analyst.

Several years earlier, meanwhile, an echo from Grof's future had already materialized in a laboratory in Switzerland. For it was in 1938, that the now famous chemist Albert Hofmann had unknowingly synthesized a new hallucinogen, LSD-25, for what he thought would be either obstetric purposes or the treatment of migraine headaches. Instead he had created "a telescope for the psyche,"[2] although it wasn't until one day in 1943 as he was riding his bicycle home from work that he began to realize what he had accidentally ingested. As he describes it, "I kept pedaling harder and harder and I thought I was locked in one spot. Finally I got home and everything had changed, had become terrifying. My neighbor came in and looked like a horrible witch; my assistant's features grew twisted."[3] Hofmann had discovered a living analog to the paintings of Salvador Dali.

When a package of LSD arrived at the research center in Prague from Sandoz Pharmaceuticals, Grof immediately volunteered to test it, as Sandoz had suggested that it might produce states which mimicked schizophrenia and could, therefore, be of great clinical value. But for Grof, it dilated Freud's model of the psyche to reveal the vast new landscape of the collective unconscious which Jung had described. Studying the effects of the drug upon hundreds of patients — including himself — Grof concluded that it was indeed a useful tool for bypassing the psyche's obstacles in order to access the most emotionally relevant problems, which might otherwise take years through conventional verbal therapy. In the late sixties Grof transferred his studies to the Maryland Psychiatric Research Center.

His first book, *Realms of the Human Unconscious* (1975) not only crystallized his years of research on the effects of LSD, but also the structure of his own synthesis of Freud, Jung, Otto Rank and Wilhelm Reich. While Grof's model of the psyche accepts the theories of both Freud and Jung, he makes substantial expansions of both, for in addition to Freud's biographical unconscious, he adds the "perinatal," while Jung's collective unconscious is comprised under a broader spectrum of phenomena which Grof terms "the transpersonal."

The perinatal unconscious is a record of the traumatic experience of birth that begins each of our biographical lives (unless one is born Caesarian) and which functions in the unconscious as a sort of gateway between the Freudian unconscious — which begins with one's infancy — and the Jungian collective unconscious, which contains the evolutionary record of the entire universe. For what Grof observed in many of his patients upon administration of LSD was that their strange behavior of contorting into fetal postures and exhibiting various degrees of suffocation seemed to indicate that they were reliving the birth process, to which Grof attributes four distinct phases, or matrices.

The first such perinatal matrix is the state of blissful, vegetative consciousness experienced by the embryo in the final stages of its life within the womb. The memory of peace and serenity in this matrix can become the unconscious goal behind much of an individual's frustrated activities in later life when, through drugs or alcohol, an attempt is made to recapture and sustain this experience. The second matrix actually begins the dynamics of birth itself, as the walls of the uterus contract around the infant, though the cervix has not yet opened. The trauma of this suffocating, "no-exit" condition is the exact inverse of the preceding state, and the imprint of this unconscious memory can poison an individual's attitude throughout life with a pessimistic outlook. In this view, one is and will always be, the archetypal "victim." The third matrix refers to the infant's actual passage through the birth canal itself, which involves a life and death struggle. This trauma has the potential to create a much more aggressive, quarrelsome disposition, for life is viewed here as a struggle which can only be won by fighting, no matter what the situation. Such individuals are driven by a lust for power over others and can even attract situations of violence or bizarre forms of sexuality, such as sadomasochism, bondage or coprophilia. The fourth matrix is the explosion into the world of light and life, and is symptomatic of all states of expanded consciousness after the soul's long journey through "the dark night." This state is the goal of somatic, as well as, psychological birth.[4]

Beyond these four matrices, there lies the realm of Jung's collective unconscious, a vast repository of cosmic and evolutionary memories, wisdom, and instincts. But Grof's studies have indicated additions to this realm, as well. He terms these experiences "transpersonal," meaning that they transcend the limitations of individual experience. They can include anything from memories of past lives to visionary encounters with alien beings, to identifications with animal or plant consciousness, or even planetary or cosmic consciousness.[5] Visions of gods and deities are common, as are out of body experiences, travels in the astral plane, and so forth. The psyche, in Grof's work, is a holographic microcosm of the entire universe. There is no dimension of it that cannot be experienced through the proper means.

And these means are not only psychedelic. After LSD was made illegal, Grof and his wife Christina developed what they call "Holotropic Breathwork," which involves a mixture of sustained hyperventilation, musical accompaniment and a specific form of bodily intervention. This form of breathwork acts as a catalyst to many of the same realms facilitated by LSD, and is what Grof currently uses as he tours the country with his workshops.

The books which followed *Realms of the Human Unconscious* were largely elaborations on themes laid down there: *LSD Psychotherapy* (1980) is a more detailed version of his case studies; *Beyond the Brain* (1985), his magnum opus, is a complete treatment of the theoretical implications of his paradigm, including what his findings imply for classical mechanistic science; *The Adventure of Self-Discovery* (1988) articulates the theory and practice of Holotropic Breathwork; and *The Holotropic Mind* (1992) is a popular presentation of his ideas.

His most recent book *The Cosmic Game* (1998) is concerned with such transpersonal themes as the nature of God, evil, space and time, the origin of the universe, and the destiny of the soul.

JE: You have said that you began your career as a Freudian analyst with a basically atheistic upbringing. Could you describe how your early clinical work with LSD transformed your perspective from a materialistic one to that of a more spiritual orientation?

SG: Yes, I actually became a physician after I read Freud's *Introductory Lectures in Psychoanalysis*. This was for me the incentive to study medicine in the first place. And after I read Freud, I enrolled in medical school and joined a group of psychoanalysts who were at that time operating in Prague. I also started my own analysis. As I was getting more deeply involved in it I developed a conflict concerning the theory and practice of psychoanalysis. I was fascinated by the theoretical conclusions, how many different areas psychoanalysis penetrated and gave seemingly brilliant interpretations for things like the symbolism of dreams, neurotic symptoms, religion, culture and so on.

But when I became aware of the clinical efficacy of psychoanalysis, I was very disappointed because of the enormous amount of time and energy and money that it required and the relatively meager results it produced, sometimes even after years of therapy. So I was in a very difficult situation; I actually started regretting that I ever became a psychiatrist. Originally I wanted to work in animated movies and was deeply interested in art. Ever since childhood, I liked to paint and draw. Before I read Freud, I had already had an interview and I was supposed to start working in the film studios in Prague.

At the time I was experiencing this conflict about psychoanalysis, we were doing some research for the Sandoz pharmaceutical company in Switzerland. Since we had a very good relationship, they kept sending us samples of various substances that they had developed. And so one day we got a supply of LSD, which was discovered more or less by accident by Dr. Hofmann in the Sandoz laboratories. They asked us if we would like to experiment with this substance and give them some feedback; let them know if we saw any uses for LSD in psychiatry.

They gave us two preliminary suggestions: they felt that the experiences one can have after the administration of LSD are very similar to what we find in psychotic patients, and that this state could be used as a kind of experimental model of psychosis. One could study various psychological, physiological and biochemical parameters of these states and get valuable insights into naturally occurring mental disorders. The second suggestion was that LSD could be a very unconventional training tool for psychologists and psychiatrists, nurses, students and so on. They could spend a few hours in the world of their patients, and as a result come back with a deeper understanding of these conditions, be able to communicate better with psychotic patients and hopefully be able to treat them more effectively.

So I became one of the early volunteers; this was an opportunity I didn't want to miss. This experience generated in me a lifelong interest in non-ordinary states of consciousness, which now has extended over a period of more than 40 years. I came into this LSD experimentation equipped with traditional psychiatry and Freudian psychoanalysis. My initial idea was that LSD was a catalyst that can take one into the unconscious faster and deeper than free association. And as a result this could accelerate and intensify therapy. So I started a study where patients who did not respond to any other traditional treatment were given a series of LSD sessions in a psychotherapeutic context. What we saw in this work was that typically the patients would not stay in the domain defined by Freudian psychoanalysis as the psyche, which basically would be postnatal biography and the individual unconscious. Although some of the early sessions, particularly with lower dosages, had a lot of biographical material in them, typically, when we either increased the dose or continued with the sessions, every single person that we worked with would sooner or later transcend the Freudian framework. And then we would see all kinds of experiences that simply were not accounted for in the Freudian model.

As I was doing this work with other people, I would occasionally have additional experiences myself. It was an extremely powerful confrontation with my unconscious that overshadowed everything I knew about or experienced in psychoanalysis. I was comparing what was happening with others to what was happening to me and, for a while, I found it very confusing. The phenomena that were emerging in the LSD sessions simply were not described in the Freudian literature and I had no reasonable explanation for them. So I was almost on the verge of giving up this research because I found it disturbing and scary.

But I became fascinated by this world that was opening here and decided to continue. I spent about three years conducting sessions with people and having occasional sessions myself, keeping detailed records and mapping this new territory. And after these three years, when I finally had sketched a cartography of the psyche which accounted for all the categories of experiences that we were seeing, I became increasingly aware that this was not a new cartography at all. I was making connections to everything from shamanism and rites of passage to the ancient mysteries of death and rebirth, and Eastern spiritual philosophies like various schools of yoga, Buddhism, the Taoist teachings, and Sufism. I became aware of the fact that we were rediscovering very, very ancient knowledge about the psyche.

JE: How would you characterize then the differences between shamanism and the states that these LSD experiences induce?

SG: Well, LSD phenomena covers a much larger realm. The shamanic domain is just one small part of it, one direction that the LSD experiences can take. So we see many people in whom the sessions would repeatedly entail shamanic symbolism. Sometimes it could be one session, two sessions or even several that would take that form. But the experiences can also take the direction of some other ancient systems, such as tantra, cabala, alchemy, or even African, Egyptian or pre-Columbian religions. So the full spectrum is very large. And the fascinating thing is that this is completely independent of the racial, cultural, educational or religious backgrounds of the people who have these experiences.

JE: How do these states differ from schizophrenia?

SG: When you ask about schizophrenia we have to discuss first the problem of diagnosis. There is a narrow definition of schizophrenia which I was brought up with: to be diagnosed according to this European definition, where we talk about core schizophrenia, the patient has to show the so-called primary symptoms as defined by Eugen Bleuler. In the United States the definition of schizophrenia is usually much broader and looser. So you would find very little similarity between the LSD experience and some of the classical forms of schizophrenia like hebephrenia or schizophrenia simplex or even the paranoid persecutory syndrome with voices. But you would see many similarities with states which would be diagnosed as paranoid reactions.

As a result of these observations, first in psychedelic sessions but now also in the Holotropic Breathwork where no drugs are used, my wife and I came to the conclusion that there is a substantial subgroup of the states that these days are diagnosed as psychotic which can be seen as crises of spiritual opening, or "spiritual emergencies." In these states people simply start experiencing for unknown reasons deeper dynamics of their psyches. This process, if properly understood and supported can be healing, transformative or even evolutionary.

JE: Can you describe what you mean by a spiritual emergency?

SG: Well, it's a concept that's based on our observations, both from the psychedelic work and particularly from the breathwork. We see in the breathwork that people after half an hour, 45 minutes of faster breathing show many of the kinds of experiences that you find in people who are currently hospitalized and treated by tranquilizers. In the breathwork, the same kinds of experiences, with proper guidance, can be healing and transformative. We then apply the same principles to people in whom these experiences happen spontaneously. So instead of giving them tranquilizers, we encourage them to go through the experiences and give them the support they need to accomplish that. We find that even the spontaneously occurring experiences, when supported this way, can be very beneficial in the long run, like the breathwork sessions or the psychedelic experiences.

JE: What would you say to the criticism of those who maintain that you can't equate spirituality with the chemical properties of LSD?[6]

SG: From the very beginning of LSD research until this day there has been a heated discussion on exactly what these phenomena are and how they are related to the kind of experiences that we find described in the mystical and spiritual literature. Basically, there have been three groups of experts with very different opinions: the first group are materialistic scientists who say, "Well, what this shows is that mystical and spiritual experiences are not authentic phenomena. They are manifestations of biochemical disturbances in the brain." If we can induce them chemically, that means what we find described in the books on mysticism is just a misinterpretation of brain pathology and biochemistry.

There is another group of people who see it differently: "No, what this means is that there is a subgroup of chemical substances that can induce mystical experiences and this makes them very special. These are not ordinary chemical substances, these are sacraments." They basically take the perspective of the shamans of psychedelic cultures, like the Mazatec Indians, the Native American Church, the Huichol Indians in Mexico, or the South American Indians who use *ayahausca* as a sacrament.

And then the third group is aware of the deep phenomenological similarity that cannot be denied. You cannot really distinguish spiritual experiences from the ones described in the mystical literature. But this group takes a kind of moral attitude. They insist that these are pseudo-mystical experiences, that there is no way you can force a genuine mystical experience. It has to come as a result of ascetic practices or prayers or spiritual disciplines. Or it has to come as a divine grace.

But there is basic disagreement among spiritual teachers concerning this issue. For example, I had a lot of contact with Tibetans who have taken LSD and generally see psychedelics as being accelerators of spiritual practice. But they warn that these are very powerful tools and that they have to be used with tremendous caution. There are other people like Meher Baba or Dr. Zahner from Boston, who vehemently denied that these experiences should be considered true mystical experiences. In my own sessions, I couldn't tell the difference. For me, that whole journey with psychedelics has been one of self-discovery, of serious spiritual questing. I didn't find anything artificial in it.

JE: Can you describe how your Holotropic Breathwork sessions differ from those of the more traditional verbally oriented psychoanalysis?

SG: There exist many differences that we can talk about. One is that Holotropic Breathwork is absolutely non-verbal. We do the talking before and after the sessions. The talking during the session is minimal. Another major difference is that people don't just remember past phenomena, they relive them in total age regression. So when you're experiencing something from infancy, for all practical purposes you become the infant. You have the body image of the infant, experience primitive emotions, and have a naive perception of the world. In verbal therapies you're trying to remember past things or reconstruct them from, let's say, dream symbolism, neurotic symptoms or slips of the tongue. So that's one major difference.

Also the experiential spectrum of holotropic therapy is much larger. We see not just the biographical material, but also the perinatal phenomena, and the whole spectrum of transpersonal experiences. Holotropic breathwork engages the mind, the emotions, the body and the spirit. It covers the whole spectrum of the psyche.

JE: You suggest in your work that a person can get psychologically stuck in one of these matrices and that this can then determine the kind of experiences that the person might have in life. How is it that though the body goes through all these matrices as it moves through the birth canal, the mind can get stuck in one of them?

SG: All of us who were born vaginally have a record of all those stages with their problematic emotions and physical feelings. How close to the surface this perinatal material will be and how significant it will be in the person's life depends not just on the nature of the birth process itself, but on the whole postnatal development. So, your postnatal history as it is described in psychoanalysis determines how close to the surface this material will be and which facet of it will be the one that's most relevant.

For example, you can be born to a very loving mother and have a fairly nourishing infancy and childhood. In this case, the perinatal material will sink deep into the unconscious, and you might not know that you carry it until you take LSD or do some other intense experiential work. For somebody else the postnatal life might be full of additional traumas, insecurity, anxiety and dissatisfaction. And in that case, the whole perinatal area remains open and very close to the surface. So, for example, you can grow up in a family which is like a closed system, where you experience a lot of traumatic situations in which you play the role of a victim. That would make the second matrix much more relevant in your life than the other matrices.

JE: So it's your biographical experiences that determine which of the four matrices becomes most relevant?

SG: Yes, they seem to have a significant influence on how relevant that material will be. So for example, you could experience a lot of sexual abuse which would accentuate the sexual aspect of the third matrix. Or you can have very heavy toilet training or experiences in that area which would emphasize what I call the "scatological aspect" of the third matrix and so on.

JE: One of the most intriguing aspects of your model is how it seems to make sense out of why people choose to commit suicide in particular ways. Could you talk about how these matrices can determine whether a person might choose a particular type of suicide?

SG: I've found that the perinatal memories represent a reservoir of difficult emotional and physical experiences, a kind of universal pool out of which various forms of psychopathology can develop in connection with postnatal material. And what is most relevant in relation to suicide, of course, is depression. If you include the perinatal roots in the understanding of depression you get a much deeper and more refined understanding of its dynamics.

The current theories don't account for the fact that we have two very different categories of depression. One we call inhibited depression, the other agitated depression. As long as we explain depression by some kind of simple biochemical change or as a result of traumatization in the oral period, we have no clue why we would have these two different kinds of depression. In deep experiential work, we find out that inhibited depression seems to be specifically linked to what I call the second matrix, which is the stage of birth where the uterus is contracting but the cervix is not open. And what you find typically in people who are in this form of depression is that they tend to precipitate towards nonviolent suicide, like an overdose of tranquilizers or barbiturates, drowning, or walking in the snow and freezing. When you analyze this, you find that what's behind it is an unconscious need to undo the discomfort of the second matrix and create a situation that has the characteristics of the prenatal state.

Those people who are in agitated depression seem to be under selective influence of the third matrix, where there is a sense of tremendous tension and a fight for control. There is a fear that one might lose control of one's impulses and hurt others or oneself. People in this state describe themselves as time bombs. They generally contemplate violent suicide by driving over a cliff, causing a car accident or jumping under a train or out the window. Or blowing one's brain's out.

When we analyze it, we find that what's behind this is a fantasy of biological birth, where at the time the child comes out of the birth canal, there's a build-up of tension to an explosive release, and it happens in the context of a lot of biological material: blood, fetal fluid, and even urine and feces. The main idea here is that at the time of our biological birth we were born anatomically but we were not born emotionally. We still carry within ourselves an incomplete emotional gestalt of birth. And people who are in a suicidal state under the influence of the emerging third matrix use the anatomical liberation, which happens during birth, as a model for emotional liberation. As a result, they seek a situation in which the tension builds to a catastrophic explosive ending and there has to be biological mess associated with it.

So generally people who experientially complete the birth process, move either to the first matrix or to the fourth matrix and retrospectively realize that they didn't want to kill themselves. They wanted to move out of this perinatal discomfort to a situation which is more like what it felt before birth or after birth. But they didn't know they were trying to create a situation which had the characteristics of these perinatal memories.

JE: Have you seen the film Crash?

SG: Yes, that had many perinatal elements to it.

JE: Could you elaborate on how it is that car crashes can become an aphrodisiac? What is the connection there?

SG: The third matrix, when the child is struggling through the birth canal, is related to a situation where there is physical confinement, pain and at the same time, a type of sexual arousal, which comes from the suffocation and the pain. This is the kind of mechanism that underlies sadomasochism, for example, the bondage syndrome. I don't know if you saw the movie *In the Realm of the Senses*.[7] It was a Japanese movie where the lovers at the end strangle each other during intercourse.

When people are reliving birth, with this strange mixture of pain, choking and sexual arousal, they typically have these kinds of sadomasochistic images of bondage. And towards the end of the birth process there often occurs imagery related to falling and fast speeds, as the pent-up energies are being released at a very high rate. For example, I have a friend who got stuck in this third matrix in a psychedelic session and then the next day took a job as a tester of parachutes. This meant going up fifteen times in a small airplane and jumping with an untested parachute. Do you know the story of Mishima?

JE: No.

SG: Mishima was a writer and a political figure in Japan who was actually nominated at one point for the Nobel prize in literature. After a stormy life, he committed *hara-kiri*. His favorite pastime was to take a four-seater plane to a very high altitude and then take off his oxygen mask and lose consciousness. Then he would let himself fall until he came to an area where there was enough air. He would come to and then level off the plane and go up for more. And then he ended up with the *hara-kiri*.[8]

JE: You mention in The Adventure of Self-Discovery *certain similarities between the phenomenology described in UFO abduction experiences and the birth trauma. And in films like* A Fire in the Sky *you do see a lot of womb and fetal imagery. There's also a kind of medieval torture chamber atmosphere in a lot of these abductee accounts. What do you think might be the relationship, or is there a relationship between the birth trauma and these experiences?*

SG: Well, there's a guy named Alvin Lawson from Los Angeles who had a hotline for UFO's. He wrote a paper in which he used my material trying to explain the UFO phenomena. According to him, they were not authentic experiences; they were all derivatives of the perinatal. I don't think that's an adequate explanation. The question is, why would people make up these kinds of stories by not hundreds but thousands? There are conferences where many hundreds of abductees would come and share their stories. So I now see the UFO phenomena as a manifestation from the collective unconscious, the way Jung was talking about it. When you deal with archetypes, there is one general form of the archetype and then you find specific variations. I think the perinatal and UFO abductions are variations of the same basic archetype, but I don't think the UFO phenomena can be explained from the perinatal matrices.

JE: In Beyond the Brain *you contrast your approach to transpersonal psychology with the spectrum approach of Ken Wilber, who in his book* The Eye of Spirit *devotes an entire chapter to criticisms of your work.[9] Although both of you recognize vast areas of agreement in your models, there are some significant differences. Could you describe some of those differences?*

SG: The major difference is that I find the perinatal area of the unconscious to be very clinically important, whereas until quite recently that whole dimension was absolutely left out in Ken Wilber's work. His evolution of consciousness starts from the pleromatic stage of the newborn and then goes through the stages of the uroboric, typhonic and verbal-membership to the egoic level and the centaur, and from there to the subtle and causal levels, to the Absolute. And when he talks about cosmogenesis, he takes it from the Absolute downwards, using the *Tibetan Book of the Dead* and that journey ends with conception. So his system leaves out everything between conception and the moment of birth. That was my original objection. But then I also pointed out the fact that Otto Rank is the only one of the classical psychoanalysts that's left out of his synthesis. So he basically uses Freudian analysis and ego psychology when he is trying to create a synthetic model.

I also disagree with his linear model of spiritual development where one has to reach the centauric level of consciousness before spiritual development begins. From there one continues straight on towards the Absolute. What we see is that the spiritual development much more frequently happens through regression: one brings full consciousness into childhood and infancy and then into birth and the prenatal period. This leads to psychospiritual rebirth, which is a critical step on the spiritual journey. And then the regressive process reaches ever farther into the collective unconscious and one discovers the karmic realm, the reincarnation dimension. In this way, the spiritual development has the form of a spiral. Ken sees the perinatal consciousness as being simply the primitive embryonal fetal consciousness, whereas I see it as something that is much more complex. It includes a dormant transpersonal dimension that becomes manifest when one regresses back to birth. His understanding of the spiritual process is really linear.

> *JE: When I interviewed him, Terence McKenna said that his own personal exploration of the psyche has not tended to support your theory of the perinatal matrices and that most people who have not heard of your theory would probably not have experiences that could be mapped onto your system while taking LSD.[10] How would you characterize the differences between LSD and psilocybin? Is one more effective than the other?*

SG: No, I think they basically generate the same spectrum of experiences. We've worked with both of them clinically and observed birth experiences in both. I don't know what would account for Terence's position, since the perinatal domain is a very important part of the psyche that is obvious even outside of the realm of psychedelic experimentation. After we shifted to Holotropic Breathwork we still see the perinatal experiences daily in people. If you look at the history of spirituality, the death-rebirth phenomenon is an extremely significant one. Take the shamanic crisis, for example: the journey into the underworld where the initiate is subjected to ordeals and annihilated and returns back to life in a new form. You also see the same experiences in the puberty rites of aboriginal cultures, where the idea is that boys and girls die and men and women are born. You read about it in the Christian literature, as well. There's a discussion between Nicodemus and Jesus in the New Testament where Jesus talks about the need to be born again and Nicodemus doesn't understand it. He says, "Look at me — I am a big man and my mother's pelvis is small. How can I be born again?" And Jesus says, "Well, we're not talking about being born from the flesh. We're talking about being born from spirit and water." And in Hinduism you have the concept *dvija*, being twice-born. And in the whole history of Jungian psychology, there is this tremendous emphasis on death and rebirth, the night-sea journey of the soul and so on. So I don't know how he can say that.

JE: In Beyond the Brain *you briefly mention the work of L. Ron Hubbard, the founder of Scientology, and you say that there are some similarities in his work with yours. Isn't this man's work just a parody of psychotherapy designed to make money?*

SG: Well, it has two different aspects for me. Unlike the other verbal psychotherapies, Scientology has something that guides the process objectively. He uses the galvanoscope, that measures objectively the intensity of the emotional arousal. So when the Scientologists do the so-called auditing, the clients are holding the galvanoscope. When they start talking about something that's emotionally relevant, the auditing person gets a reading. So they don't spend a lot of time on issues that are emotionally irrelevant. They have an objective guidance, and using this guidance they've found, for example, that physical traumas are extremely important psychotraumas. This is something one does not find in any of the other systems except Scientology and my own work. In the same way, Scientologists also stress the importance of the birth trauma, because the auditing took them to the birth trauma directly. They also include past life experiences. This is similar to the work with non-ordinary states because non-ordinary states of consciousness have this very peculiar characteristic, namely, that they activate material that has a strong emotional charge. So they automatically sort out the relevant from the irrelevant.

Whereas if you work with verbal therapies, we have many different schools, and each school has a different focus, a different idea about how the psyche works and why the symptoms are there. And each school gives you a different therapeutic technique. So that what is to be considered relevant and what's considered irrelevant depends on the emphasis of the different school. For Freudians it's sexuality, for Adler it's inferiority feelings, for Karen Horney it's social factors, for Reich it's the conflict between biology and society and so on. These different systems have theoretical biases and even if the therapist is trying to be indirect there is a subtle indoctrination and guidance by the philosophy of the school. Whereas, with a galvanoscope there is simply an objective guidance, as in non-ordinary states of consciousness. What Scientology does as an organization, how it uses its system is another matter.

JE: You mention that people undergoing these holotropic sessions occasionally remember what seem to be past lives. Is it possible that when they claim to have memories of past lives during these sessions that they're just using their imaginations to invent these scenarios?

SG: No, I don't think so. You know, this was my original attitude as a Freudian. I was always trying to see these past life experiences as fantasies that were somehow elaborations of something in postnatal biography. But now I see these past life phenomena as a very authentic kind of phenomena *sui generis*. But I would separate the phenomenology of these experiences from the problem of whether we lived before as separate units of consciousness.

It is a very important category of experiences that you will see even in people who don't believe in reincarnation. These experiences take them to another century, another country, where they find themselves suddenly identified with a protagonist, and they have a personal sense of remembering: "I once was that person; this is not the first time this is happening to me." If you study these kinds of experiences, you'll find out that people frequently come up with very esoteric information about the time and the culture they are experiencing in terms of understanding a lot about costumes, architecture, weapons, social structure and so on — and sometimes even details of historical events. Once in a while you can actually verify this information by independent study of archives.[11]

Another thing that's quite extraordinary is that they find, typically, certain aspects of these experiences that explain various emotional and psychosomatic disorders that they have at present. And when they complete the experience, these emotional and psychosomatic problems disappear. There can also be correction of some problems in interpersonal relations.

Sometimes people find that the other protagonists in that experience are people from their current life with whom they have some kind of difficult issues. And when they complete the experience the relationship seems to clear on both sides, which is fascinating. Sometimes synchronistically powerful things happen at the same time in the life of the other people, so that when they meet it's on a completely new platform.

So those are all facts concerning past life experiences. Now this does not necessarily prove that we lived before as separate units of consciousness. For example, the high Hindu teaching has the idea that believing in the continuity of the individual over many lifetimes is a very low level popular interpretation of these kinds of karmic phenomena. The highest teaching says that there is only one entity that incarnates, which is *Brahman*. There are no absolute boundaries in the universe whatsoever. If we have a story that has more than one protagonist, we are still under the influence of *maya*, the world illusion.

There's an approach from another direction which you've probably heard about. It's the study of past life memories of children between the ages of three and five. Ian Stevenson published several books on it, and his last one just came out. It discusses specifically the problem of tell-tale birthmarks. He found many cases in which the child remembers a past life in another town and describes the circumstances of the death. The child carries the birthmarks in the places where the person in the previous lifetime was wounded. And when they find the town and the person that the child is talking about, they find out that person actually was killed in the way reflected by the birth marks on the child.[12]

JE: You've done a lot of work with the astrologer Richard Tarnas over the years, who suggests that the archetypology of the planets Neptune, Saturn, Pluto and Uranus correspond to the four perinatal matrices. What sort of relationship do you think these planets might have to the matrices?

SG: These correlations are truly astonishing. I think that the reason why so many people have difficulty in taking astrology seriously is that they are trying to approach it using causal thinking which is characteristic of materialistic science. What they think astrologers are saying is that the planets are *causing* something, having a material influence on our psyches and the events in the external world. I remember talking about it with Carl Sagan and he said, "This is nonsense. As I'm standing here by you, I have more influence on you than Pluto." You know, thinking in terms of gravitational pull and similar mechanisms. This is not the way this should be understood.

What we found out empirically, is that when people have experiences of the four consecutive matrices, the experiences are identical to what's described in handbooks of astrology as the planetary archetypes. So the first matrix carries Neptunian characteristics, the second one is Saturnian, the third one Plutonian and the fourth one, Uranian. But what was absolutely astounding was that we found that people actually have experiences of those matrices when they have important transits of these corresponding planets. These are simply facts of observation.

If good astrologers are trying to formulate a conceptual framework that would account for it, the interpretation would be synchronistic not causal. It would point to a universe permeated with superior intelligence, built on a kind of grand plan or blueprint in which events on the material plane are correlated with events in the archetypal world. And the dynamics of the archetypal world is correlated with the movements of the planets. Because the planets are kind of visible signs, we can use them to infer what's happening in the archetypal world and from that, what's happening in our world.

You would have to make a very radical shift in your understanding of the universe. Rather than seeing it as a mechanical system that created itself out of bouncing particles, it is a system that is in a sense alive and conscious, based on a master plan designed by absolute consciousness or universal intelligence. A kind of understanding that's very similar to the Eastern spiritual systems of the great mystical traditions. It's basically impossible to simply add astrology to what Fritjof Capra called "the Cartesian-Newtonian materialistic world view."

JE: Do you think that the current visions of apocalyptic imagery in our contemporary arts and culture — including phenomena like Waco and Heaven's Gate and so forth — might indicate that we are undergoing a birth process, that some new phase of culture or mythology is coming into being? [13]

SG: I have heard this repeatedly from people that I have worked with, and I have experienced it myself. There seems to be a tremendous parallel between the kinds of phenomena that one encounters, particularly in the context of the third matrix, in the individual process of transformation and the phenomena that we see today manifested in the world. For example, we certainly see a tremendous increase in aggression. If you look at the rapidly deteriorating situation in the American cities, the rise of crime and terrorism in the world, there is no doubt that we are witnessing a major unleashing of the aggressive impulse. We also see the release of the sexual impulse, both in its positive and negative aspects, in terms of sexual freedom, adolescent sexuality, gay liberation and so on, as well as sexual slave markets, sadomasochistic parlors, and all kinds of sexual extremes. The same applies to the satanic element. There's also the pollution, both industrial and a kind of moral pollution, if you look at the political scene, business practices and so on.

Many of these phenomena that we see manifested in the world are something that we typically encounter in the process of inner transformation. Many people feel that we are in a kind of critical race. If we continue acting out all these dangerous impulses we will undoubtedly destroy ourselves. On the other hand, if we manage to internalize them on a large scale, we can move to a level of consciousness evolution which would be unprecedented. Terence McKenna has this interesting sentence in one of his books, "The history of the funny monkey is over, one way or another." We are either going to change into something different or we're not going to make it. When you look at the history of humanity, it's full of malignant aggression, violence, and insatiable greed. And these tendencies have now become incompatible with life. The weapons of mass destruction are simply too powerful. In a similar way, the insatiable greed has become incompatible with life. We cannot continue plundering nonrenewable energy resources and turning them into pollution. So all those tendencies have to change should life continue on the planet.

JE: Your new book The Cosmic Game *seems to be almost entirely focused on transpersonal themes. Could you describe what this book is about and what impelled you to write it?*

SG: It was in the late sixties when I looked at the frequent occurrence of mystical and spiritual phenomena in psychedelic sessions. I spent some time analyzing over 5,000 protocols from LSD sessions, specifically looking at the episodes where people were dealing with some basic philosophical, ontological, cosmological problems. Asking such questions as: Is there a God? What is God like? What is the supreme principle in the universe? How am I related to God? What is Time? What is Space? What is causality? How was the universe created? Is there karma? What about good and evil? Those are the kinds of questions.

At that time I wrote a paper which was called, "LSD and the Cosmic Game: Outline of Psychedelic Ontology and Cosmology." I was astounded when I analyzed this material and found that all the people who had these kinds of deep metaphysical experiences basically agreed on one kind of overarching cosmology. It was not just a jungle of some kind of idiosyncratic psychotic fantasies about the universe, but it was a really comprehensive alternative vision of reality that emerged out of this research. I became aware how similar this was to what Aldous Huxley called "the perennial philosophy." And then I gradually realized that this vision was increasingly compatible with the new paradigm description of the universe. And so the new book basically describes the philosophical and metaphysical insights from non-ordinary states, comparing them to perennial philosophy on the one hand and to new paradigm science on the other.

MEDICINE

DEEPAK CHOPRA

AND

THE YOGA

OF DESIRE

The East has become something of a mecca for Westerners in whom the soul's hunger for spiritual protein is neither assuaged by the legends and fables of the Bible nor satisfied by the equations of Newton's *Principia*. T.S. Eliot, in his 1922 masterpiece "The Waste Land," had in mind for the metaphor of his title the atheistic landscape of industrialized Europe, where the steel pistons and clockwork planet gears of its gigantic factories were darkening the skies and poisoning the trees of its great forests. Eliot's grail quest took him to India, where he found in the pages of the *Brihadharanyaka Upanishad* a spiritual ethos of cooperation with the almighty powers of the universe as an alternative to the Western motto of "putting her to the rack and torturing her secrets from her." In the subsequent decades, a significant portion of the Western intelligentsia — including Carl Jung, Mircea Eliade, Arthur Koestler and others — followed Eliot's lead by traveling to the East. And as we have seen in the pages of this book, at least three of its protagonists, Ralph Abraham, Rupert Sheldrake and Terence McKenna, have undergone transformative experiences while sojourning there.

In fact, this romance with the East has been going on in the Occident since Alexander the Great invaded India in 327 B.C.E. Having just conquered the Persians and added Egypt to his collection, the story goes that he and his troops marched into the Indus valley, where they encountered a group of naked old yogis roasting themselves in the hot sun. When word reached them that the Greeks were interested in discussing philosophy, they let it be known that no one dressed in battle gear could learn anything from them, unless the Greeks were willing to strip naked and sit on broiling rocks. But a yogi named Kalanos took a liking to the Greeks and traveled with them for a time, personally instructing Alexander in the points of Hindu philosophy, until they had returned to Persia, where Kalanos surprised them by announcing his intention to burn himself alive as a demonstration of his teachings. And so the Greeks built for him an enormous pyre which he climbed onto with great ceremony and as they watched, ignited himself and sat burning peacefully. Thus began the West's dialogue with the East.

And although the dialogue was reduced to a virtual monologue during the Middle Ages, it was renewed with especial force in the eighteenth century when the British, following in the footsteps of Alexander, extended their empire to include India. As in the time of the Hellenistic epoch following the decay of Alexander's empire, a period of vigorous commerce in ideas was initiated. The British supervision of translations of Indian classics was received with delight by portions of the Western intelligentsia. Goethe praised the work of Kalidasa while Thoreau retired to Walden Pond with Homer and the *Bhagavad-Gita*. And when the great German philosopher Arthur Schopenhauer picked up a French translation of the *Upanishads*, the masterpiece resulting from his pen, *The World as Will and Idea*, was a grand synthesis of Plato, Kant and Hindu philosophy. This brought a new thrust into the Western academic mainstream, which was instantly seized upon by Schopenhauer's two most famous disciples, Wagner and Nietzsche,[1] from whence the torch was passed along to Carl Jung, James Joyce and the illustrious scholars of Europe's Eranos conferences.

The story of Deepak Chopra's contribution to this dialogue is quite unique. As he recounts in his autobiography, *Return of the Rishi*, his career as a medical doctor began when his uncle explained to him the mystery of death. To his family's horror, it had been discovered that his uncle was a communist, and although this tarnished Chopra's image of his favorite childhood uncle, he was nevertheless fascinated by his uncle's atheistic explanation for death. Pointing to the rusty skeleton of an old automobile, he explained that death was no more mysterious than what happened to that automobile as time wore it away with oxidation. So likewise with the body, and there was no need for any conception of a soul or an afterlife to make sense of what science could explain rather easily, given enough study and ambition. It has been said that such ideas as the immortality of the soul and eternity are invented to mollify anxieties about life's inevitable end, but in Chopra's case, the idea of death seems to have motivated him to spend his life doing what he could to lengthen it the only way science will allow: through the study and practice of Western medicine.

Indeed, the India in which Chopra grew up was one of turbulent transition from the colony of an empire to a modern nation state, with its industry and politics traced largely through Western stencils, while its own traditions were fading into the murky darkness of folklore and superstition. Chopra's father, for instance, who was trained as a medical doctor under British supervision, regarded the Hindu medical tradition of Ayurveda practiced by Chopra's grandmother as mere folk remedy and part of India's superstitious past.

So Chopra decided to become a doctor and underwent training in India as an endocrinologist. He took advantage of the Vietnam war shortage of doctors to come to the United States and work in Boston hospitals. By 35, he was chief of staff of New England Memorial hospital, but his lifestyle was centered around alcohol, cigarettes and coffee, addictions he had picked up as coping strategies in the high tension atmosphere of Boston emergency rooms. But then a chance encounter with a book on Transcendental Meditation began to point him back in the direction of his native traditions. Chopra had always thought of meditation as something strictly for yogis ready to renounce the world, but Transcendental Meditation spoke instead of stress and relaxation, and so he began to practice it every day and soon was relieved of his bad habits. On a visit back to India with a friend, he encountered an Ayurvedic physician who impressed him with the ability to make diagnoses just by touching the wrists of those who came to him. His capacity to do this is actually based on a very old tradition of thinking common to both East and West, which Aristotle termed "physiognomy," meaning that a person's inner character or spiritual essence is made visible in their physical makeup and biorhythms.

The classical paradigm for this was Greek medicine, which was based on a theory of four humors, or bodily substances, that were physiological analogies of the four elements, earth, air, fire and water. The predominance of one or another of these humors in an individual produced a type of psychological disposition, either phlegmatic (water), choleric (fire), sanguine (air), or melancholic (earth). The four humors, black bile (earth), yellow bile (fire), phlegm (water) and blood (air) made up the physical composition of the body, and when these humors fell out of balance, either somatic or psychological illness resulted. Thus, health was defined as maintaining a perfect balance of humors, just as the whole world was constantly trying to balance itself via the four elements: the cold of winter was nature's attempt to redress the heat of summer, and so on.

Ayurveda, likewise, is based on a similar conception: there are three *doshas* instead of four humors, and the predominance of one or the other creates a specific body type. The three doshas — *vata, kapha and pitta* — are microcosmic analogs of the three *gunas* which compose the substance of all things in differing proportions: *tamas,* or "inertia," corresponds to *kapha,* a slow-moving metabolic type; *rajas,* its opposite, is "energy," the analog of a *vata,* or rapid-metabolic type; while *sattva,* "pure clarity" is loosely analogous to *pitta,* which tends to produce clarity of judgment, and hence *pitta* types are generally born leaders. Health is defined as a state of balance, sickness as an imbalance of the *doshas,* which can be influenced by specific diets, since all foods are made up of these *doshas* (in their form as *gunas*).

In 1987, Chopra published his first book, *Creating Health,* which presented his synthesis of Ayurveda and Western medicine. This was followed in 1988 by his personal memoirs, *Return of the Rishi* and in 1989 by his finest book, *Quantum Healing,* which addresses the larger problems of fusing Western science and medicine with Eastern metaphysics. It is still the best introduction to his ideas.

In 1991, Chopra and Maharishi Mahesh had a falling out over controversy surrounding an article which Chopra and two other *Ayurvedic* physicians published in the *Journal of the American Medical Association.* Chopra then wrote his bestseller, *Ageless Body, Timeless Mind,* which elaborates his theory that aging is to a large extent shaped by cultural preconceptions and can therefore be reprogrammed when these preconceptions are shed. Following a guest appearance on The Oprah Winfrey Show, his book sold 137,000 copies the next day.

According to *Newsweek*, Chopra's enterprises bring in about 15 million dollars a year, making him the wealthiest guru of all time.[2] He has become perhaps the first true multimedia guru, having saturated the market with nineteen books, a monthly newsletter, videotapes, cassettes, CD-ROMs and herbal products. He also travels the world giving lectures and seminars at $25,000 a talk. He has opened a new clinic in La Jolla, California and plans to open several more. He has a novel to his credit, *The Return of Merlin*, and is presently working on another about the Jewish mystical tradition of Kabbala. Two screenplays have also been optioned. *The Path to Love* is his most recent bestseller, but there are more on the way. Chopra has become something of a one-man corporation.

Indeed, it must be said that the value of Chopra's contribution to the East-West dialogue is controversial. Articles in *Newsweek* and *What is Enlightenment?* magazine, for example, have portrayed him as a greedy snake oil salesman out to make a buck by hustling spiritually-starved Westerners with a consumer-tailored version of Hindu spirituality. [3] The problem with these caricatures is that they not only misrepresent Chopra's sincerity and the hard work that has led him to his profound insights, but they also vastly oversimplify the enormous heterogeneity of doctrine that is the legacy of Hindu spirituality. It should be evident to anyone who bothers to read through, say, Henrich Zimmer's *Philosophies of India*, that Hindu philosophy can no more be reduced to a single point of view than can that of the West. It is composed of various schools, contending sects, and differing doctrines with quite specific emphases, not all of which are based upon renunciation of the world. In fact, Chopra's translation of *Vedanta* into a philosophy based upon the gratification of desire is far from unspiritual; it constitutes, rather, an updating of the life affirming — *not* renouncing — traditions of such Eastern schools of thought embodied by Mahayana Buddhism, Karma yoga, or Tantra. Indeed, the dictum of the latter school, "*bhoga* ('physical enjoyment') is yoga," means that delightful participation in the pleasures of the world can involve spiritual consciousness since *everything* is a manifestation of *Brahman*, the Absolute. Immersion in the realm of the senses is spiritual if the consciousness of the person participating in it is *aware* of this metaphysical dimension.[4] And the central insight of Mahayana Buddhism is that the distinction postulated by the Buddha himself, that nirvana is *opposed* to samsara as release is to bondage, is false, since the ultimate realization of the highest consciousness transcends *all* dualities, including that postulated by renunciation *versus* desire. As is written in the Tibetan Buddhist text, the *Madhyamika Sastra*:

The bound of nirvana is the bound of samsara.

Between the two, there is not the slightest difference.[5]

And so, we may judge for ourselves the value of Chopra's contributions in the following interview.

JE: In your book Return of the Rishi *you describe how you were trained in India as a medical doctor although you didn't become acquainted with traditional Eastern approaches to medicine until you came to America. Can you describe how this journey from East to West and then back again transformed your materialistic world view to a spiritual one?*

DC: I trained in Boston in internal medicine and neuro-endocrinology, which is the study of brain chemicals. This was in the 1970s. And it became obvious to me as I was doing my studies that there was this very exciting new frontier that interfaced both consciousness and material reality: the study of neuropeptides, these material messengers from inner space, if you want to call them that. Then I became aware that there was a whole body of knowledge in the East that regarded material reality as the by-product or epiphenomenon of non-material reality, which is consciousness. And there was the possibility that the understanding of this non-material reality could have a role in healing and transformation, so I began to embark on my own personal journey through studying Ayurveda and meditation.

At the same time, I was perfectly well grounded in the very sophisticated understanding of brain chemistry — neurochemicals — and brain physiology. So I also started to study the physiology of meditation and I went back to India many times to study with Ayurvedic physicians. Ayurveda is part of a larger body of knowledge called *Vedanta*, which is all about spiritual transformation. Once I became familiar with the whole theoretical framework of healing as it has been articulated in a very sound body of knowledge for several thousand years in India, I also realized that this was just a stepping stone to knowing and exploring an even deeper reality and consciousness which we call Spirit. So it was a very gradual transformation over many years.

JE: You've mentioned that the scientific world view of the West surprisingly supports the vision of the ancient sages of India. Could you describe some of the ways that Western science supports Eastern spirituality?

DC: I would say, it depends on how you interpret Western science, because there are a lot of scientists in the West who are pure materialists and may not agree with what I have to say. And yet, as we go into the most recent explorations of quantum physics, I think we are unable to escape the conclusion that the essential nature of the material world is that it's not material, that the essential stuff of the universe is non-stuff. But this non-stuff is not just ordinary non-stuff. It's a void that isn't a void at all, but the fullness of information and energy. And if we go beyond the information and energy, it's more than that, it's intelligence. And if it's intelligence, then it must be consciousness.

So consciousness becomes the raw material of creation. Consciousness conceives and governs and constructs and ultimately becomes physical reality. If you look at anything that's material, whether it's my body or the table that is here before me or the chair that I'm sitting on, you can break it down to its essential components, which are atoms; the atoms in turn are particles that are moving at lightning speed through huge empty spaces; and in turn, those particles are not material things, they are fluctuations of energy and information in a huge void. Seen through the eyes of a physicist, this chair and this table and this body are proportionately as void as intergalactic space. Even those particles which we call fluctuations of energy and information are actually intersections of fields. They are mathematical ghosts, probability amplitudes.

So, in reality, we are being fooled by our senses. The senses tell us that there's a material world out there. But what is really out there is a radically ambiguous and ceaselessly flowing quantum soup. And the magic occurs in our perception. Somehow, through our sensory apparatus, we decode that field of information and energy into trees and stars and physical bodies and thoughts. But in fact, that is the same way a radio traps a field of information and energy and creates a symphony out of it, or a television traps the field of information and energy and creates a soap opera out of it. Right now, the space around me has all this infinite amount of energy and information: there's every radio program and every television program, every cosmic ray, every microwave, every radio wave, all this huge immensity of information and energy is present in every cubic millimeter of space in the entire universe.

There's so much activity in what we see as nothingness. Actually, what we see as a material world is less than one billionth of a billionth of a billionth of it and we think that's where the activity is. Most of the activity is in the unmanifest, and the unmanifest is not just information and energy, it has self-referral feedback loops. It feeds back upon its own self and as it does, it creates loops. And that's what intelligence is. The only difference between intelligence and ordinary information is that intelligence is information which has the ability to evolve, to learn from its own experience, to actually create more abstract, more flexible and therefore more creative expressions of its own self. So we begin with chaos, and then out of that chaotic soup of intelligence there emerges order and then chaos again and then order again. This is the way consciousness behaves. So I think the quantum vision of scientists and the sacred vision of *rishis* is essentially getting us to the same place.

JE: Would you equate the quantum field with the Hindu conception of Brahman *or does* Brahman *transcend even that?*[6]

DC: *Brahman* transcends the quantum field because *Brahman* is intelligence and the quantum field right now as we understand it is defined as a continuum of probability amplitudes for space-time events. So there are probabilities built into the field. And *Brahman* is beyond that, it's even beyond the probability field of pure potentiality.

JE: You have articulated a kind of philosophy of wish fulfillment throughout your work. For example, you say that "when we have a desire, our slightest intentions are rippling across the universe at the quantum level." Can you explain how our desires are fulfilled or frustrated through their relationship to the quantum field?

DC: Yes. I look at desire, or intention, as a force in nature, just like gravity is a force in nature or electromagnetism is a force in nature. Around the time of Darwin, there was a scientist by the name of Lamarck who was discredited by his contemporaries, but he was probably the first to suggest that biological organisms organize their behavior around intent. To make it simple: a giraffe has a long neck because it intends to reach that tree up there to eat that leaf. A camel has a hump because the quantum field or the consciousness that we experience as the material expression called "camel" really has the intent to navigate the desert for seven days without water, so it develops a hump. Or a bird knows how to fly because it intends that. The biological organism creates wings. A parrot has a brain which is less than one third of my fingernail and it has hardly any vocal chords and a beak for a mouth, but it can simulate human language and be taught to speak. How does it do that? If I was a scientist trying to study the mechanics of that, it could take me a lifetime and yet with intent, the biology will organize that. And you can study many other things: the migration habits of monarch butterflies, how homing pigeons go back to their breeding grounds, etc.

So it seems like the principle behind intent is that if it is structured from the most basic level in the field — and the field is *Brahman*, or you can call it the unified field or what is beyond the quantum field — then intent organizes its own fulfillment. There's an expression that I learned as a child in India that's from the *Vedas*: "intent, structured in *Brahman*, has infinite organizing power." The teaching of that is also in the *Bhagavad-Gita* when Lord Krishna says to Arjuna, "established in yoga, perform in action." What he's saying is, if your intent is from that level — which means it's not overshadowed by the ego and you're also detached from the result — then that intent assumes the power of the field itself because it's not so much a personal intent as it is a universal intent.

So, when applied to our own personal life, intent — or desire — becomes very powerful: first, when it comes from a level of deep silence; second, when there is no ego involved; third, when there is surrender to the mystery of the universe; fourth, when there is detachment from the outcome; fifth, when there is communion with the intelligence of the universe; and sixth, when there is an attitude of defenselessness. Now, these are basically the attributes of intent in the field, but it's not an ego-motivated, ambition-driven intent. If our personal goals arise from this dynamic, they will be fulfilled with much more ease and much less anxiety. We think that the fulfillment of desire is always through ambition and exacting plans and hard work and discipline, which does, of course, result in its fulfillment, but also brings about hypertension and heart attacks and strokes and malignancy and divorce and addictive behavior, etc., etc. Once you're on the spiritual path, though, what happens is that because the spirit is a domain of awareness where we are experiencing our universality, then automatically, your intent becomes less personal and more universal, so that your inner dialogue shifts from "what's in it for me?" to "how can I help?"

JE: A lot of people have the understanding in the West that Eastern philosophy involves a renunciation of desire. Are we misunderstanding Eastern ideas in the West?

DC: Not necessarily. It depends on who's interpreting. If you read the writings of Gautama Buddha, he basically says, "in the path to enlightenment, nothing should be clung to as me or mine." Now it depends on how you interpret that. You can interpret that as renunciation. But I know a lot of monks who live in monasteries and they haven't relinquished anything. They're reading *Playboy* magazine. So true detachment has nothing to do with whether you live in a monastery or you live in a castle. True detachment is in consciousness. Your attitude of renunciation is that you're detached from outcome, that you've surrendered to the mystery of the universe. And I also believe that as one understands this, then renunciation is a by-product and not a means.

You see, if I am on the spiritual path and I'm experiencing my universality and my joy and my capacity to experience joy and spread it to others, then I'm experiencing my ability to love and have compassion. I'm experiencing the security of knowing that I have a sense of connection to the creative power of the universe. If I'm experiencing at some deep level that my life has meaning and purpose, and at the same time, my desires are getting spontaneously fulfilled, then I'm automatically ready for renunciation. It's a by-product of that. But if I start out with renunciation I'm just going to be frustrated. There's a prayer of Saint Augustine's: "Lord, give me chastity. Give me continence. But not just now."

JE: You say that we make things happen although it appears as though they are happening to us. Now does this also apply to getting sick? Do we make ourselves sick?

DC: We participate in everything that happens to us, including our sickness, including our wellness. We can't have one without the other. The word "responsibility" literally means "the ability to have a response." And my definition of responsibility, the one I was taught as a child, is the ability to have a creative response to a challenge. Although most of us in any situation respond with a fight-flight response, or a reactive response, we have other responses built into our nervous system: the intuitive response, the creative response, the visionary response and the sacred response. So that in any moment of our lives, we have the ability to make these choices. And it is these choices that ultimately lead to the experience of health or sickness.

So when we get sick, or when something happens to us, it's important to ask ourselves, "What is my contribution to this process?" That's the only thing I can change. If I smoke cigarettes, that's something I can change in my sickness. On the other hand, I may be getting the cancer not because I smoke cigarettes, but because everybody else around me does and the environment is completely contaminated. Well, even there, I have some degree of participation. I have the choice to be in that environment or not. You might say, what about this child that's born and two years into childhood gets leukemia? Well, in the Vedic scheme, life is not squeezed into the volume of a body or the span of a lifetime. It spans eternity. And if you understand that, then you're willing to reconcile with some of the confusion and distress that comes from not fully understanding the mystery of karma. There's an expression in the *Upanishads* that says, "unfathomable are the mysteries of karma." So we don't really know what the true answers are. But as we have more awareness and we stop looking at life as just a temporary sexually transmitted incurable disease, but something much bigger, then we have a sense of peace about some things that we don't understand.

JE: You've described the approach of the medical industry to the treatment of disease as the "magic bullet approach." Can you characterize this approach and what's wrong with it?

DC: I think the medical approach is very effective. If I have pneumonia, then the appropriate antibiotic can save my life. If I have a broken leg, I don't think I would be immediately resorting to some herbal treatment. Medicine has saved millions of lives and continues to do so and yet medicine has made physicians superb technicians who know everything about the human body and nothing about the human soul.

So medicine has lost its soul. That's the major problem with the technical approach of modern medicine. The magic bullet interferes with mechanisms of disease, but it does not address the origin of disease, or for that matter, the origins of health. So the mechanism of disease can be interfered with and you can get rid of the disease in the short term. If you know the mechanism of how bacteria multiply and you interfere with that, you can get rid of the infection. But then if you continue to use these antibiotics and especially if you do that indiscriminately, then you end up with an antibiotic-resistant infection. And right now, that's the biggest problem in medicine: dangerous infections that are being acquired only in hospitals and literally over a hundred thousand people dying from these infections. It's so devastating, nobody knows how to treat them. In fact, there is a deep concern in medicine that we have created these monstrous organisms that are killers and we don't know how to deal with them. The number one cause of drug addiction in the world is not street drugs but medical prescriptions that are prescribed by doctors. Thirty to forty percent of people in hospitals suffer from medically induced illness contracted in the hospital or as the result of a prescription.

I read an article in the *Journal of the American Medical Association* which revealed that if you counted all the deaths in hospitals from medical accidents, it would be the equivalent of three jumbo jet crashes every two days. Now, that's very scary. But on the other hand, medicine is useful, too. You can't say that it's not. But what we've forgotten is that there's a difference between treatment and healing. The word "healing" is related to the word "holy," which means "whole." It means that if you really want to heal somebody, you have to heal their whole environment. You have to heal their physical body. You have to heal their emotional life. You have to give them a spiritual experience, otherwise, you're not addressing the whole being. There's a context to everything. Ten people can be exposed to a virus and not everybody gets the infection. A hundred people are exposed to a carcinogen; not everybody gets cancer. So, we have a very mechanistic approach to both illness and its treatment, and it's based on an incomplete picture of the world.

JE: In Ageless Body Timeless Mind, *you see aging not as a biological constant, but as a function of social conditioning. Can you explain that?*

DC: First of all, we should realize that the whole dynamic of aging has changed over the centuries. In the Roman Empire, the average age of a human being was 28 years. In the early part of this century, the average age of a human being was 49 years. Today, the fastest growing segment of the American population is over the age of 90. So we are seeing a completely different expression of aging. Today's 70- and 80-year-olds are not the same as a generation ago, otherwise John Glenn wouldn't have been able to return to space, as he did. So we are seeing a different biological expression of aging.

There's one elegant study by Ellen Langer from Harvard University, who showed that our expectations of what happens to us influence the biology of aging. She did an experiment in the eighties where she took people to a monastery outside of Boston and had them play-act that they were living 30 years ago. And all the sensory stimuli replicated the experience of 30 years ago, including the music, with Elvis Presley, rock and roll, Chevy Impalas, Alfred Hitchcock movies. They wore name tags with pictures from 30 years ago, and she said, "be as you were thirty years ago," and then measured biological markings and found they had quite dramatically reversed in three weeks. So if your expectation is that you retire at 65 and become useless, and therefore, only spend all your time in Florida languishing in a nursing home, it becomes a self-fulfilling prophecy.

Other people, including Alexander Lee from Harvard, have looked at aging populations in other cultures, in Abkhasia and Georgia in Russia, and found that in these cultures it is considered almost glamorous to grow old. So if you ask somebody how old they are, they'll exaggerate their age because to grow old is considered glamorous. You're honored, you're venerated, you're respected, you're given more responsibility, so you're the most important person in society. And all that affection and adulation and respect and attention somehow influences your biology so that you have a completely different biological response. I think it was Nietzsche who said that we live under the presumption that we think, but most of the time we are being thought. So if the collective mind says, "this is how you age," then this is how you age. If the collective mind says, "no, this is not how you age," then you age in a different way.

JE: You're not saying, are you, that it's possible for us to become physically immortal?

DC: I don't know the answer to that question. I would definitely say that it's not *desirable* to become physically immortal. We might be doomed to eternal senility. But I don't know what the limits of human aging are. As I said, today, the fastest growing segment of the population is 90. Current science says that you can live to 120 in the absence of disease and in fact, there are documented cases of people living as long as 121.[7] Disease is not necessarily an accompaniment of aging. You can be 90 years old and have arthritis, while others won't. Some people will have coronary artery disease and others won't. So you may be more frequently predisposed to disease as you grow older, but it's not necessarily an accompaniment. That's what is happening now, given the nutritional status and the environmental conditions. But if you told me fifty years ago that people would be living to 90 or 100 quite frequently in the 1990s, I would have said, "you're crazy." So I don't know what the future is going to bring us.

JE: In another interview, you said once that if we could remove religion from the face of the earth we would all be much happier people and really become spiritual in the true sense. Could you clarify that for me?

DC: God gave humans the truth and the Devil came and said, "I'll organize it for you and we'll call it religion." In the organization of spirituality we have the loss of it. If you count the number of wars and all the people that have been killed in the name of God. . . . It's been happening from before the Crusades; today in Bosnia, in Sri Lanka, even Buddhists and Hindus, who are supposed to be nonviolent people, become extremely violent when they become religious in the fundamental sense — because that kind of religion breeds the notion that my view of God and my view of the divine is the only true point of view. And that is the contradiction right there: true spirituality is a domain of awareness which is universal.

I spent my Christmas vacation in Islamic country in Morocco and it's a very peaceful and beautiful country with beautiful mosques and very spiritual people. Then I spent months studying the *Koran*, which is all about the *Old Testament* and it's all about Christ. Mohammed is a later prophet. Ninety percent of the *Koran* talks about Abraham and Isaac and Ishmael and Jesus Christ. It talks about resurrection. So, where is the fight? Where is the conflict? It's all a family feud. It's been said that man was created in the image of God; I think it's the other way around, God is created in the image of man. And we all have our own version of Him or Her. On the other hand, spirituality is a domain of awareness. It has nothing to do with even philosophy or a point of view. It's *all* points of view. It's tolerance, it's forgiveness, it's love, it's compassion. It's the ability to connect with the soul of another person.

BRIDGES BETWEEN WORLDS:

WILLIAM IRWIN THOMPSON

AND THE IMAGINATION

OF CULTURE

One of William Irwin Thompson's primary concerns throughout his career has been how the human imagination creates historical "reality." Narratives of human and cosmic evolution are as old as myth itself, and historiography proper at least as ancient as Zoroaster, who imagined the drama of the cosmos unfolding in three acts: the primordial fall of Light into Darkness was followed by the arrival of Zoroaster onto the stage of history itself, and at the end of time, the Great Man, Saoshyant, would come to restore Light to its state of original purity. This tri-fold schema reincarnated itself in the imaginations of Augustine, Joachim of Floris and even the German aesthetician Lessing, but it has played counterpoint to the much older quaternary myth of the Eternal Return, as articulated, for example, in Hesiod's cycle of the Four Ages of Man. It was this Classical species of the cyclical idea that migrated into the imagination of the great eighteenth century Italian philosopher Giambattista Vico in his four-fold cycle of Gods, Heroes, Men, and Chaos. These four great vertebrae, then, evolved into the skeleton of Joyce's Puranic classic *Finnegan's Wake*, which was published in 1939. Goethe had picked up the idea from Vico, and in his 1817 paper entitled "Epochs of the Spirit," had designated the four stages of culture as the Poetic, Theological, Philosophical, and Prosaic.[1] Oswald Spengler, then, in his 1918 masterpiece *The Decline of the West* amplified Goethe's libretto into an operatic magnum opus of culture history, to which Arnold Toynbee, in *A Study of History* responded with his equally brilliant English version of the rise and breakdown of civilizations.

Now, the point at which the trunk of this great tree of historiography bifurcates into the philosophy of the evolution of consciousness is the publication in 1949 of the first volume of Jean Gebser's *Ever Present Origin*.[2] Gebser picks up where Spengler leaves off, seeing in the disintegration of the modern world during the nineteenth century not merely decay, but the genesis of a whole new structure of human consciousness, which Gebser termed the "Aperspectival." But this transformation of consciousness, with its shift from the Renaissance Perspectival Space — in which a world of three dimensions was created by the human eye — to one of Aperspectivity — in which three-dimensional space was relativized to a larger context of multiple spaces, multiple times, multiple points of view — has much in common with Marshall McLuhan's observation of the shift from the Gutenberg Galaxy of print-based literacy and mechanics, to the creation of electronic culture. This new culture, with its sense of "everything all at once" completely shattered the old linear grid system of the Cartesian analytical world view.

It is out of this tradition, then, of grand historical meta-narratives that William Irwin Thompson's vision of human culture draws its inspiration. He is one of those rare minds, like Spengler or Gebser, capable of absorbing the entire spectrum of human cultural activity, and illuminating with X-ray precision the morphology of the human imagination. Thompson's mind inhabits the very Aperspectival Space which Gebser articulated, wherein he shifts around the various ways in which men have imagined the great patterns of history with the apparent effortlessness of moving icons in a MacIntosh. Indeed, already in his undergraduate days, he was freely inhabiting this space, while his professors were still constrained by the myopia of Perspectival Space. As Thompson puts it, "I played my own Vico," and "in a mere two hundred pages of an undergraduate Honors Thesis that my professors derided as my Summa Anthropological-Philosophica . . . I tried to show that the evolution of styles in ancient Greek statuary, Middle American Mayan architecture, and English poetry, all revealed the same structural pattern."[3]

Thompson's first book, *The Imagination of an Insurrection* (1967), in direct counterpoint to his Honors Thesis, specialized by focusing on a single event that took place in "one week in one city." But again, the main theme of the book was "the role of imagination in the construction of historical reality," as Thompson chronicled the unfolding of Irish culture through the restoration of Celtic mythology in the decades preceding the famous uprising.

During this period, Thompson had been teaching English at MIT, but, having become impatient with its cult of technocracy and the paradigm of materialism informing its basic principles, he left and went north, to Canada, where he taught for a time at York University, and in 1971 published *At the Edge of History*. In this book, Thompson's restlessness becomes evident, as he roams from Los Angeles to Esalen to MIT, sifting through the cultural detritus of history's burnt-out civilizations for clues to the creation of his own mythology.

In his next book, *Passages About Earth* (1973), Thompson articulated the vision of that mythology. The creation of the counter-foil institution in the mid-sixties as an alternative to the dismal hi-jacking of the university by the defense industry after World War II, inspired Thompson to undertake a kind of *Volkerwanderung* over the earth, visiting as many of these institutions as he could. The result of this "withdrawal and return" was Thompson's creation of Lindisfarne, an intentional community originally set up in Southampton, New York, where people of all faiths could come to recognize common ground, and in the process, cultivate ecological skills. Lindisfarne was eventually moved to Colorado, where a beautiful chapel was designed by Thompson in collaboration with the geometer Keith Critchlow, based upon the classical principles of Pythagorean geometry. But, as Thompson later wrote in a poem:

> No wife or child could stand
> near the structure's forbidding,
> Platonically absolute tyranny,
> only a constructed crew of single men,
> filled with a lust for masculine abstractions
> that blinded them to the real trash
> that piled up beside their sacred temple.[4]

Thompson's New Age idealism had begun to disintegrate as he realized that Lindisfarne, as a cultural magnet, had attracted too much culture, for a series of ontological conflicts began to be evident to him in the various projects in which he had become involved. The sacred mystery school of Platonic geometry, Thompson realized, was elitist and reactionary, afraid of embracing the transformations of modern culture, though concerned with aesthetic values; meanwhile, the ecological content of the counter-culture, with its concern for energy efficiency and recycling of waste products was intensely democratic, though not much attuned to the soul's need for the harmonious proportions of Pythagorean geometry. This kaleidoscope of cultural overload was resolved when Thompson turned the chapel over to a group of Zen monks and then moved on, taking Lindisfarne with him.

During these years, meanwhile, Thompson produced a pair of books, *Evil and World Order* (1977), a collection of early essays, and *Darkness and Scattered Light: Four Talks on the Future* (1978), a neo-Manichean meditation on the tension between two forces which threaten to undo our society: the one through bureaucratic management — with its obsessive pursuit of power through ever-tightening systems of control — the other through chaos manifesting in various forms of terrorism aimed at blowing apart technocratic systems. Then, in 1981, Thompson published what is regarded by many as his greatest achievement, *The Time Falling Bodies Take to Light*, which was based on a cycle of lectures given at Lindisfarne-in-Manhattan in 1976 on the evolution of consciousness through history.

The epistemological shift in Thompson's imagination — from the static world view of Platonism to the dynamics of "processual morphology," as he terms it — is embodied by two books which he wrote during this period: the novel *Islands Out of Time: A Memoir of the Last Days of Atlantis* (1985) and *Pacific Shift* (1985). In the latter, he invented a new mythos for himself in what is perhaps his best essay, "The Four Cultural Ecologies of the West," in which he imagines that the history of mathematics, literature, and ecology has undergone four basic transformations: from the Riverrine-Arithmetic of the Sumero-Babylonian world to the Mediterranean-Euclidean of Platonic geometry; and from the Atlantic-Cartesian, or dynamical to the post World War II Planetary-Processual. The shift from the Industrial nation state, based on ownership of land — the economic creation of the third mentality — to the Planetary Society, with its emphasis on ecology, the biosphere, the atmosphere, and dynamical systems theory — the creation of the fourth mentality — is the fundamental transformation of culture on which Thompson bases his entire world view.

Thompson at this point refocused Lindisfarne's energies toward healing the schism between "the two cultures" of the sciences and the humanities. Accordingly, Lindisfarne became somewhat of a refuge for maverick scientists interested in amplifying the dimensions of their science with a fresh spiritual resonance. A new group of poets, philosophers and scientists began to migrate to Lindisfarne. Thompson's masterpiece *Imaginary Landscape* (1989) celebrates its rebirth in this period, and expresses his gratitude to scientists James Lovelock, Francisco Varela, Lynn Margulis, and Ralph Abraham, who assisted him in the creation of the new interface between science and spirituality which has become the primary focus of Lindisfarne.

In 1991, Thompson published two of his most important — and entertaining — books, *Reimagination of the World* with co-author David Spangler, and *The American Replacement of Nature*. In the former, Thompson "casts a cold eye" on the New Age, providing a much needed critical look at a movement that purports to be "new" and yet, according to Thompson, contains much that is very, very old; while the latter is an absolutely hysterical, Swiftian critique of the type of American attitude toward nature that is perfectly captured for example, in beer commercials with gigantic Americans playing volleyball over pocket-sized mountains while smooth, silver canisters of beer loom over the events like presiding deities at a Mayan ball game.

Thompson's book *Coming Into Being* (1996), based on a series of talks which he delivered in New York at the Cathedral of Saint John the Divine, is simultaneously an overview of the evolution of human consciousness, and a recapitulation of the main stages in the development of his career as a visionary. It is a "conscious summing up," in which all the strands which have preoccupied his imagination — myth, science, philosophy, anthropology, and literature — are taken up and woven into a tapestry of living ideas. In 1997, he published *Worlds Interpenetrating and Apart*, a collection of the poetry he has written since 1959. He is currently at work on a book with chaos theoretician Ralph Abraham, entitled *Bolts Out of the Blue: Art, Mathematics and the Evolution of Consciousness*.

JE: I wanted to start, if you don't mind, with your first book, The Imagination of an Insurrection. *It seems to be somewhat atypical of your writings in that it's more of a specialized account of a single historical event: the Easter Rebellion in Ireland in 1916. I was wondering if you wouldn't mind talking a bit about how that book evolved in your imagination and what impelled you to write it.*

WT: Well, I've always wanted to go to Ireland, so being American-Irish I had — as many American-Irish have — a kind of desire for a fantasy landscape of returning to the old sod and finding a culture that had tradition and roots and something deeper than the highway strips of America when I was growing up in L.A. So Ireland and the Celtic spirit in general — especially the Celtic writers, like Yeats and Dylan Thomas — were always adolescent heroes of mine.

When I was an undergraduate, I wrote a long honors thesis on a philosophy of history, much to the chagrin of all my professors, who believed that you should just do a specialized thing on one poem or one writer. I did a whole theory of cultural history and played my own Vico and they didn't like that. I had to fight them very hard to do it, as I was majoring simultaneously in anthropology, philosophy and English literature. So the book represented my tying up together all the strands of my three different majors. And then when I went to graduate school — it was even more intensely specialized at Cornell — I became interested in AE and Yeats and the Easter Rebellion and their different poems on it. I wrote a term paper for Robert Martin Adams at Cornell on the Easter Rising, and then suggested that there was enough material there for a doctoral dissertation and they said 'OK,' though there was no one in Irish studies there. Adams was really only a Joyce scholar.

So I said — because I had already published a dissertation-length thesis as an undergraduate, and had published already a couple of articles — that I wanted to skip the whole dissertation exercise and just simply write a book. If it were a scholarly book, you would drag out Chapter 1 for 200 pages and lots of footnotes. Then in your first year as a professor you would have to boil that long 200 pages into just one introductory chapter, and then add on all the other stuff to make it a book. So I said, "Why don't we just skip this exercise, and I'll simply go to Dublin and write a book." So I did that, and so the book was published under the constraints of academe, which is nothing if not specialized. I was interested in combining the anthropological studies of a nativisitic movement, British historical studies, and the literary studies of the Irish Renaissance in ways that no scholar that I knew of combined, or even knew, those areas of discourse. And I found a lot of resistance from academics who were specialists; they have a visceral contempt and suspicion of big ideas. They're primarily postal clerks: they live in a bureaucracy and they receive stamped opinion and then pass it on. And that's their job.

So, even when I was doing the book, the Irish historian at MIT, Emmett Larkin, really disliked my generalizations on imagination and history at the end. He said with scathing contempt, "If I wanted 'Open End,' I would listen to David Susskind" — a television talk show of the sixties.

And I said, "No way, I've done the research to give myself license to make these generalizations about imagination and history. That's what I'm interested in, and I'm going to put it in, anyway." He really didn't like that kind of thing because he was a historian of very detailed studies of the role of the church in nineteenth century Ireland.

But Oxford University Press liked the book and published it as a university press book, so it was not a trade book. It's very much a work of history, not a work of what would now be called trade non-fiction. That was in the old days when I was a professor at MIT, so it was part of that period of time in my life.

JE: In your next book, At the Edge of History, *you talk about your disillusionment with the university. Can you discuss what the intellectual atmosphere was like at MIT in the late sixties?*

WT: It was extremely polarized between World War II warriors who were believers in modernizing the world through American corporations, and believed in high-tech solutions to all things, and were basically captured by the behavioral sciences and a kind of modernizing political science; and then the New Left, who were inspired by Marxism under the leadership of Noam Chomsky and the chair of the Humanities and Literature Division, Louis Kampf. They basically were the mirror opposites of the technocrats. They were technologists who believed in technological rationality, and they believed that philosophy and ideology were just simply the superstructure of the means of production, and that reality was economic and technological. So, either way, you had a choice between a materialism of one variety or another, and there was nothing resembling the tradition that I was attracted to, that was expressed by more mystical poets like Yeats and Blake and Whitman, to the power of mysticism to empower the individual to create a kind of democratic vision, especially with people like Blake and Whitman. Yeats was a little more conservative, so I was attracted more to Yeats's poetry than to his politics.

Basically, there wasn't any room for what I wanted to do. So I just decided to quit and I went off to Canada. McLuhan was in Toronto and Trudeau was just coming into his own, so Canada was no longer the kind of sleepy province of England forgotten by America. It was beginning to be an interesting, exciting place in its own right. And Toronto remains one of my favorite cities.

JE: Did you study with McLuhan for a time?

WT: No, not at all. I was already an associate professor when I went up to Toronto and I think I had already published *At the Edge of History* when I met McLuhan. I had attended a lecture of his when he came to visit MIT, and I had, of course, always read his work in the sixties and used it in all my books. I always liked his free intellectual style because he seemed to be able to live an imaginative intellectual life, even within academe. So he was, in that sense, a positive role model. But I'd never studied under him.

Then, when I went to his Coach House I was a little distressed because it was like a temple in which there were disciples and followers. They were all sort of weak Xeroxes of him, weak clones. They weren't actually taking his ideas imaginatively and individualistically doing original work with them in the way I thought I was doing.

And you couldn't, with people like Bucky Fuller or Joseph Campbell or Marshall McLuhan, actually be around them except in the form of a disciple kissing their rings. I just wasn't comfortable in that mode, so I thought, well, the best way to get the best of these gentlemen was to read them in my study, and integrate what I think is valuable in my writing, and just ignore the personality and the ego, and the ego-dynamics of a cult of followers.

So I went once to the Coach House, and McLuhan was very defensive and threatened by me because a reporter had said the intellectual center of Toronto had shifted from the South with McLuhan at the University of Toronto, to the North of the city, to York University and to me. Of course, that wasn't the way I felt; that was just journalistic packaging. So he felt like I was after his turf.

I went to the Coach House as a way of honoring him and saying, no, this is not the case, this is just an irresponsible journalist, and I respect your work and I'm not after your bishopric. But he basically was a highly autistic individual: he couldn't really listen, he could only recite — *brilliantly* — his aphorisms and insights. He was undoubtedly a genius, and the media tends to exaggerate that in people. Whenever I would meet people like Alan Watts or Bucky Fuller or Joseph Campbell — very much so — the media magnified their egos and put them into a kind of celebrity status and so they didn't have the ability to listen or exchange thought or ideas. They only had the ability to play the tape recording of their ideas. And it's better to get that just by reading a book instead of hanging around the person. So I left and I went elsewhere.

JE: Wasn't it about that time that you founded Lindisfarne?

WT: Yeah, I was getting restless because York was becoming a suburban drive-in university, and was trying to basically duplicate the technocratic vision of post-industrial society that had been pioneered by MIT. So, I took a sabbatical and went around the world — and that was *Passages About Earth* — and went looking at alternatives, because when I was in Canada, I went to a summer conference, and Ivan Illich gave the opening address. He was a *very* charismatic speaker, one of the most charismatic lecturers I've ever heard, actually. He articulated the whole vision of the counter-foil institution, and had set up his own Center for Intercultural Documentation in Cuernavaca.

So I decided to look at these places around the world. I had already gone to Esalen in 1967 and had been very impressed by Michael Murphy, who remains a very close friend.[5] I decided to look at Arcosanti and the Center for Eastern Wisdom and Western Science in Starnberg, Germany, and Auroville in the Sri Aurobindo ashram in India, and Findhorn in Scotland.

So I took off and just went around the world and tried to understand the new planetary culture that was emerging, by talking to people like Aurelio Peccei at the Club of Rome, and people in the World Order Models Project in Tokyo, and the Institute of World Order in New York.

Out of all that wandering I wrote that book, and from the inspiration of Findhorn and my meeting with David Spangler I decided to get up my courage and not go back after the end of my sabbatical. I was promoted to full professor, and thank you very much, but I was not going back; and so I quit and set up Lindisfarne.

JE: Has your vision of Lindisfarne changed any over the years?

WT: Oh, yeah, it has to because Lindisfarne dies every year; it's 24 years old, and it dies every year for lack of money. So, one has to be a *bricoleur* and be flexible. You can only be rigid and inflexible if you have an endowment that makes you into an institution, like Princeton University. Lindisfarne has no endowment, it just has little tactical funds that donors and individuals give from time to time for a program, and that'll do the program, and when the money's gone, you're broke and you have to start all over again. I've done that for 24 years, and so Lindisfarne has changed.

In the first wave, in the seventies, because of the wonderful idealism of the seventies — I miss it in this kind of materialistic nineties — the influence of the intentional community as a way of getting out of the suburbs — since I'd grown up in L.A. — was attractive. And so Findhorn and Auroville and the intentional community dynamic like Zen Center and Tassajara, California, these were interesting. I set it up as a kind of institute that was run by a communal staff. And we were involved with the usual kind of return to nature of organic gardening and alternative medicine, and then a lot of the agenda of the seventies.

Then, as it evolved, it became more of a fellowship of artists and scientists and poets, and it was the fellowship that was really charismatic and dynamic, more than the intentional community. And that began to take us into the interface between spirituality and science. So, in the seventies, it started with Gregory Bateson and the astronaut Rusty Schweickhart, and it just kept growing with Francisco Varela and the physicist David Finkelstein, and then Jim Lovelock in atmospheric chemistry, and Lynn Margulis in biology.[6] Our program in biology and science began to be the strongest and most original thing about Lindisfarne because Findhorn is very heart-centered but is *intensely* anti-intellectual. And Auroville is just a yogic New Age ashram, or community. It has no scientific component.

So, what was unique to Lindisfarne was this fellowship of scientists reimagining a new kind of science, in which art, science, and religion collaborated in a more interesting ecology of consciousness than was the case at MIT. I tried to set up such an interface *at* MIT, but they wouldn't let me do it, so that's why I got restless and quit.

JE: Could you describe what you mean by a shift from an Industrial society to a Planetary society, and what the new social and cultural structures might entail with that?

WT: Well, the Industrial nation state arose in the eighteenth century — England being the charismatic example — and it was a shift away from a feudalistic empire with all value based on land and an aristocracy and a church, to capitalism, with a basis on industrial productivity and a new economic exchange of value. So the Industrial nation state created the international world system we have now and the world economy, which is, of course, creating all the problems that we face now with the industrialization of the biosphere and the green house effect and the ozone hole. Which gives us crazy things like hurricanes in July when they used to come in September, and thirty of them instead of three. And the inability of school children to go out and play in the sun in Australia.

The interface between an industrial economy and the biosphere is what the industrial nation state can't handle. So, the new culture isn't based on nation state turf, it's based more on biological, ecological processes, so the atmosphere is more the model than the land. And the sciences that would describe the processes of the atmosphere are more the new complex dynamical sciences, chaotic systems of clouds, rather than the clods.

The old Romanticism wanted to go back *to* nature and you got a kind of Romantic attempt to achieve the pre-industrial world of folk culture, Romanticism in Germany and England. But I'm more interested in going forward *out* of industrial society, so I use the word "planetary" to distinguish between "international," because "international" is what I had at MIT. That's basically the relationship between the G-7 and commitment to technological modernization and industrial development. And that, of course, just exacerbates the problems we have now.

Also, we're polarizing as we create a new economy in which the rich get richer and the poor get poorer, and the ultimate effect of this new form of post-modern capitalism is the peculiar meltdown of middle-class industrial society, as the middle class is getting pushed back down into the lower class again. So, you're getting a fabulous amount of wealth but with a smaller and smaller group of people. And the lower middle class that used to live in tract houses and had cars and were reasonably well off and had labor unions and could send their kids to college, they're getting forced back into being post-industrial serfs. Industrial society is coming apart at the seams in more ways than one.

My efforts in *Passages About Earth*, and *Darkness and Scattered Light*, and *Evil and World Order* were to try to articulate the shift from economics as the governing science of society to ecology as the governing science. This is a shift away from an ideology in which there is a ruling elite, whether it's a Chomskyesque Leftist elite, or a Jerry Wiesner technocratic elite, to a new diverse ecology of difference in which there is no single elite articulating one simple ideology. That's why Lindisfarne was always a fellowship and not a followership and why we had very diverse people who shared an ethos. But they definitely did not share an ideology, and I was not a leader articulating an ideology seeking followers.

JE: You mention very often in your writings that you see the cultural and social structures of the middle ages reemerging in our new electronic society. Could you describe what those structures are?

WT: Well, part of it is disliterate, in the sense that you're going back to a culture that's not based on the Gutenberg galaxy of the middle classes having access to information through books and paperbacks. You're going through television and channels and cable TV and Internet, and this is creating a kind of disliterate Internet chatter where people certainly don't write Jeffersonian eighteenth century letters on the Internet. So you get a culture which is a meltdown of civilized literacy. You get a meltdown of the nation state and this meltdown of the middle class, and a return to aristocrats and serfs. And you get global noetic polities that are very much like the church and the religious orders in the middle ages — like the Knights Templar — that extend across boundaries and are not wed to any particular nation state ideology, whether these are Microsoft or Pepsi or science, or pop music, or Greenpeace. There are many different versions that are meta-national configurations where identity isn't coming from nationalism.

And also the return to the break-up of religious consensus to religious orders is a medieval thing, where you have fanatical groups like Aryan Nation, or cults, or charismatic leadership or some fanatical saint. That's a very Medieval pattern. All of these come with the breakdown of a civilized literate consensus. You know, there's no *New York Review of Books* and one single intelligentsia, in New York or at Harvard, articulating what civilization is all about for the rest of us. And that's very much a kind of Medieval diversity. So it's a raggle-taggle system of fools and scholars and knights and their electronic capitals, and aristocrats, not in land, but aristocrats in vast resources of money in a kind of Bill Gates way.

The other Medieval thing is the way in which information is being controlled by these vast, what I call, electronic latifundia. Latifundia were these huge colossal slave plantations that came at the end of the Roman Empire before the collapse. And when you have CNN and Capital Industries and Disney and Time Warner and all these vast informational processing units coming together to control books and publishing and Barnes & Noble Bookstores, satellites and software and Internet and all of these things — America Online — you're getting a kind of dumbing-down homogenization where the people are sort of collectivized in these feed lots like cattle and they're just fed this techno-swill. When I had Prime Star on my backyard satellite dish in Colorado I had like fifty channels, and it was all garbage — The Golf Channel, the Faith and Values Channel — and there was no intellectual content whatsoever. And PBS wasn't an alternative because it was an Oklahoma PBS that thought educational television was Lawrence Welk and a concert where you photograph the pianist's hands, which is a travesty of music. So, that kind of dumbing-down of America in creating this techno-swill is very much turning people into serfs. They're not citizens who are reading pamphlets and philosophy and coming to empowerment of philosophical discourse and voting for their representative in Washington, they're just voting for the celebrity of their choice. So that's a Medieval formation, where everybody becomes a techno-peasant.

And that's going to continue. It's very hard for an intellectual such as I to live in this world, because basically it's very hard for anyone to find my books in a bookstore, because in Barnes & Noble the publisher has to be a large rich publisher and he has to bribe and rent the shelf-space. The publisher has to pay a fee if the book is turned out — face out — and if the shelf is in the front close to the window they have to pay more. And so intellectual publishers can't afford to pay those rates and so intellectuals such as I won't be repressed, you just won't find us in Barnes & Noble. You'll find O.J. Simpson or a movie star or some guy who'll pretend to be a philosopher — maybe a human potential sound-biter with the latest gadget on how to fix your life. And that's a Medieval formation, too.

So, it means that literacy — you know, in the time of Kant there were probably about twelve philosophers — it means that intellectuals are going to be very few and far between. The masses are not going to be going to college and becoming smart, they're just going to be . . . they'll probably go to college, but they'll read textbooks that will be produced by Time Warner and will have ads for Nike and Pepsi in the end pages. And you know, they'll be sitting in class with their baseball hats with another commercial on their foreheads. In fact, we're already there.[7]

JE: You see your writings as an example of a new literary genre which you term Wissenskunst. *Could you define what that's all about?*

WT: Well, I tried to find a word for it in English and I couldn't. I guess when I was creating the phrase I had just come back from a meeting with Werner Heisenberg at the Max Planck Institute and I was reading some poetry of Rilke and so my mind was more in the German language. I was thinking of the German word for 'science,' *Wissenschaft*, and thought, well, what I'm looking for is something not quite '*schaft*' but '*kunst*.' So I thought well, why don't I just call it *Wissenskunst*.

But I'm not alone in this. I had lunch once with Lewis Thomas, who won the National Book Award for *Lives of a Cell*, and I said to him, "you know, all your little short essays that you write for the *New England Journal of Medicine* have the structure of Romantic poems of description and meditation," and since I wrote my master's essay on that genre, I was sensitive to it. And he said, "yeah, I love poetry and I write poetry and I consciously tried to make these little essays poetic in that form." So that kind of genre — Tom Wolfe has also raised non-fiction to a novelistic art form — I think it was something that was peculiar to my generation. A lot of us just got bored, and reality was so fascinating as I was running around the world. Trying to invent a make-up reality like a novelist was not as fascinating as just writing about what was coming on down. So I shifted and just tried to make non-fiction an art form.[8]

JE: Your 1981 book The Time Falling Bodies Take to Light *is a meditation on the myth of the Fall. Do you see this as a kind of ur-myth?*

WT: It's certainly a basic myth for the West. I was fascinated with Gnosticism and the repressed Christianity that got excluded from dominant Christianity, from the time of Bishop Irenaeus all the way up. I had been practicing *kriya* yoga and was involved in a kind of Tantric practice and so the mystical approach to philosophy interested me. That book was written in a kind of white-hot seizure of yogic practice. But it's really part of a trilogy because volume two is *Blue Jade from the Morning Star*, which takes up the theme of sinking, falling, capture by focusing on Quetzalcoatl, the avatar of the New World and Mexico. And volume three — *Islands Out of Time* — projects it back into a mythical landscape of Atlantis, but forward into a way in which Atlantis on the turn of a spiral is also a future culture dealing with genetic engineering and trapping people in Bardo, because part of what's happening with the Internet is a kind of return of the astral plane into public space. The qualities of the demonic, shifting identities, pornography; everything that's characteristic of the astral plane is characteristic of the Internet.

In order to capture the complexity of a new planetary electronic culture I couldn't just do three volumes of science fiction. So one volume is a kind of lyrical, rhapsodic scholarship in meta-anthropology; another is the essay and poetic cycle; and the third is the science fiction fantasy novel. I was trying to express the kind of lyrical range I want to have as a writer because I like to have a lot of elbow room. I don't like to get typecast into one discipline or one genre. It gets me into a lot of trouble because in this culture you can't do that in America, because everyone's typecast. You know, you're a poet and you're Robert Bly; you're a philosopher and you're Daniel Dennett; you're a historian and you're Arthur Schlesinger. But if you do what I do then you just fall over the horizon, people don't know what to do with you, where to find you. So they just basically ignore you, because that's easier since they don't know what shelf to put you on in Barnes & Noble.

> *JE: Freud in* Totem and Taboo *saw the origins of religiosity in a primordial murder and a communion meal, but in the* Falling Bodies *book you see culture as having emerged out of the origins of human sexuality, when hominid females shifted from estrus to menstruation and year-round receptivity to intercourse. Could you talk about that?*

WT: Yeah, and also food-sharing in the sense that the female primates would be more likely to babble at the infant and create a bonding through nursing. You know, hunters have to be quiet so as not to scare the animal away. I was seeing the roots of all our culture in female occasions of culture, whereas Lionel Tiger and Fox and Lévi-Strauss were all seeing it as man the hunter, man the killer and there was no female expression of culture. I was rewriting all those myths, including *Totem and Taboo*, which is obviously a myth. It's not science, but a form of active imagination. It deals with Freud's own fantasy structure of the primary father and the brother horde rising up to slay the father, because Freud himself was always terrified that the brother horde of psycho-analysts were going to rise up and slay their father. He was threatened by Jung, and Lacan was kicked out very early on. In the social dynamics of psycho-analysis it became structured as a male-dominant primate band in which there was only one hero, and in order to gain status you had to kill the father and create your own band. So Jung slayed Freud and created his own religion, and Lacan was kicked out and so created his own Lacanian analysis, and that became a cult in Paris and so it goes.

> *JE: During the mid-eighties you seem to have had a kind of epistemological shift from a Platonic New Age world view based on static geometries to more of a post-modern vision of shifting grounds and uncertain horizons. Can you talk about what happened, what was going on in your imagination?*

WT: That was basically coming to the shadow side of the whole European school of sacred geometry and discovering that, unbeknownst to me, Schwaller de Lubicz was an anti-Semitic fascist and had been a member of a fascist group in France. And that Rene Guenon was basically an Islamic fundamentalist who hated the modern world. Keith Critchlow wasn't a fascist, but he was totally in love with rigid geometry and the cult of the leader and the follower and did not like projective geometry or anything that was multi-dimensional. And so what happened was that the school of sacred geometry just became a male-dominant primate band with followers. It was very rigid and there was no place for women or children and it was very esoteric in a kind of nasty, superior anti-democratic spirit.

I just became very restless and unhappy with all that, and at the same time in the complexity of the fellowship of Lindisfarne, separate from all that European group was the scientific circle of Lynn Margulis and Jim Lovelock and Francisco Varela and then later Ralph Abraham and mathematics. I began to understand we were at a critical quantum leap in culture, and we were moving into a new mentality, and that the people like Critchlow were actually regressing to the old one, to the Medieval Platonic one, pre-Galilean. And I wanted, again, to go forward into the post-Galilean and move into the new fourth mentality instead of going back to the second. So that's when I developed the whole theory that there was an evolution of literature and mathematics through history. That it went through the Arithmetic; the Geometric, which is the Platonic, and the Critchlovian; and the Galilean dynamical one, which is the modernist, Cartesian-Galilean; and then the new one, which we're in now, that starts around 1972 with Rene Thom, *Structural Stability and Morphogenesis*, and gets developed into chaos dynamical theory.

I don't like the phrase 'post-modern' because it means different things in different disciplines. I always use 'planetary' to distinguish my approach. I made up this phrase 'planetary culture' 25 years ago, but now it's gotten a little co-opted by the New Age movement so the word seems kind of like a buzz word instead of a technical term, as I would like it to be. But 'post-modern' is an even worse term, because it means one thing in literature and another thing in architecture. So I just don't like the phrase. And it also means nihilistic, amoral, no center, and that's just about the opposite of my own sort of contemplative sensibility.

My 1985 novel *Islands Out of Time* was my effort to write myself free of the charisma and influence of Keith Critchlow, and then redesigning the chapel and moving it away from being a temple to Platonism, and making it a much more post-historic, archaic, simple, Quaker, minimalist architectural form, as it is now. So I had to redesign the building. Only the lattice of the dome is Critchlovian.

JE: How did you become acquainted with Ralph Abraham's work?[9]

WT: The other Lindisfarne fellow who founded Synergy International and publishes *IS Journal*, Andra Akers, the actress, asked me to come out and give a lecture at the L.A. Film Institute on Sunset Blvd. And I did, and she then had a party that evening and introduced me to Ralph Abraham. Then Ralph sent me in Bern a copy of his essay "Mathematics and Evolution" and that was sort of like the seed form of my taking the idea and developing it fully into the chapter, "The Four Cultural Ecologies of the West" in *Pacific Shift*. I developed it further in *Imaginary Landscape*, the theory that there are these four mathematical mentalities. Since then, Ralph and I have lectured together and designed a curriculum for a girls' school, an elementary school K through 12 in East Hampton New York.[10] So we're collaborating all the time.

JE: In your book Reimagination of the World *you talk about cyberpunk fiction — and the works of William Gibson, in particular — as a disguised form of the Gnostic myth of the fall. Can you talk about that?*

WT: Yeah, it's very much about how the body falls and is captured by technology. Gibson is a very interesting writer working in the tradition of film noir and the Raymond Chandler detective novel. It's basically a kind of analysis of the large multi-national corporation as a form of demonic capture, with electronics and cyberspace as a form of capture of consciousness, so it's a kind of *Omni* magazine silicon-embedded-in-flesh farewell to the biological era. I thought Gibson and the television series *Max Headroom* were very sensitive to the kind of biological crisis we were in, from disease and so forth. They focused on silicon rather than the complex of disease in viruses, but I thought it was a brilliant and compelling expression, and I was fascinated.

JE: You've mentioned also David Cronenberg's work, and particularly Videodrome *on the same kind of wavelength.*

WT: That's a great cult film, yeah. That's an *incredible* analysis of McLuhan. It's a work of genius. It scares the shit out of me, but it's an amazing film. And it's a brilliant study of evil and the shadow side of McLuhan in Toronto. Cronenberg as a Toronto artist really picked up on more of the cult that was around McLuhan. The people that sort of lit candles at his shrine were very disturbing. But as a study in evil and how the physiology of television affects us, I thought that was the best analysis, because everybody still gets it wrong that if you have peaceful content on TV, that's OK. Neil Postman and McLuhan were the only ones who understood that television is a system of neurological interruptions generated by massively parallel lines, and as Neil Postman said, brilliantly, "'Sesame Street' didn't teach kids how to read, it taught them how to like television."[11] The only film that ever captured that was Videodrome. So I think Cronenberg and Thomas Pynchon are the most brilliant, penetrating analysts of this contemporary world. *Videodrome* and *The Crying of Lot 49* I think are better than Anton Wilson or Philip K. Dick.[12]

JE: Are there any other artists working in film or books that you admire who are dealing with these themes in an intelligent way?

WT: I like Philip Glass, and though I haven't talked to her in 24 years, I was very impressed with Doris Lessing. She's just a good human being and she's unlike the celebrity cult type of America. She's solid, genuine, and she just keeps turning them out. She just wrote her autobiography, which I haven't read yet.[13] And I don't know if Stanislaw Lem in the original is any good, but certainly I like *Solaris* in the Tarkovsky version and have used it in some of my Lindisfarne symposia.[14] I also like the witty reviews in *A Perfect Vacuum*. Stanislaw Lem predicted artificial life and a few other things. European science fiction tends to be more intellectual and philosophical, and American science fiction tends to be more sort of acid head psychedelic and technological.

JE: In your book Coming Into Being *you compare the work of Jean Gebser with Ken Wilber.*[15] *Can you discuss the differences that you see in the approaches of both of these men to the evolution of consciousness?*

WT: Oh, it's almost classic cultured European versus Midwestern American hick. You know, I think people like Terence McKenna and Ken just grew up in Eastern Colorado and Nebraska in such culturally deprived areas that they get captured by a kind of abstract construction of what they imagine the big European thinker is, or the psychedelic hero in the case of McKenna. And Wilber, as I say in *Coming Into Being*, is just very abstract but Gebser is an artist. He has an incredible insight, for example, into the role of adjectives in Rilke, and what it means when you use language in a particular way to create an imaginative landscape that's more *processive* and less prospective of composed objects nailed down into perspectival space. So there's an amazing sensitivity to art and poetry and painting and the richness of European culture. But when I was teaching temporarily at the California Institute of Integral Studies, all the students didn't like Gebser because they can't remember a painting of Cézanne; they don't read Rilke. They're just into drugs and taking Extasy and going to Raves, and looking for some kind of psychotherapy technique. And so Wilber is their hero because he just gives them all these maps and charts, this Michelin guide. He's a control freak. There's no sense of humor, there's no sense of art, it's all just sterile and masculine in a very dry and abstract way. [16]

I didn't want to be an egomaniac and say, well, my culture history is better than Wilber's. I didn't want to go into that. So I went out of my way to use Ken Wilber's *Up From Eden* as a textbook, and had everybody read it in my Lindisfarne symposium at the cathedral. But when I did that, and went out of my way to give equal time and to really be open to Wilber, and read the book, and underlined it, I just thought, God, the difference between this and *The Time Falling Bodies Take to Light* — they cover exactly the same turf — is the difference between a textbook and a work of art!

And then I went back because I wanted to be fair, because I knew Treya Wilber and was corresponding with her when she was going through her crisis. She was also a friend of my wife's, and I had cancer, and so Treya and I were talking a lot about cancer.[17] I've never met Ken face to face, but I knew Treya before she married Ken, and I wanted to go out of my way to be fair to Ken. So I got the new book,[18] and I thought, God, this is ridiculous! Three-thousand pages that are going to explain everything. You know, that kind of German nineteenth century scholarship, that's over. I don't have the time to read 3000 pages! Then when he kept using this little slogan that his literary agent, John White, put on all his books: "the Einstein of the consciousness movement," I was revolted by the vulgarity of it. And then when he went beyond that to go and put his picture on the front of the book and say, *"A Brief History of Everything!"* Ken Wilber explains the entire universe to you, everything you wanted to know about everything. And I thought, this is just inflation; this is an ego that's just suffering from a hernia.[19]

Conclusion:

THE

TRANSUBSTANTIATION

OF

SCIENCE

The Jains that still survive in modern India are a sort of living religious fossil whose origins lie somewhere in the pre-dawn fog of Indian civilization when its Dravidian society flourished in the Indus river valley before the coming of the Vedic Aryans. Their cosmology is therefore extremely archaic, about contemporary with the building of the pyramids in Egypt or the glorious bull jumpers of Minoan Crete. This was an age when echoes of the Goddess societies of the Neolithic could still be heard in the myths and tales of the world's great civilizations. The Jains were no exception, for they envisioned the cosmos as a single, gigantic Goddess from out of whose protoplasmic substance all of creation had come into being. The earth had grown from her navel, and below her waist were stacked various levels of hell, while the heavens rose above like the tiers of a wedding cake. The inside of her skull was thought to be the world ceiling, within which the souls of the released hovered like bubbles of liquid metal in zero gravity.[1]

For Brian Swimme, the universe is also like a living being, which he compares to the mythopoeic image of Gaia. Swimme sees in the image of a self-regulating earth, capable of adjusting its temperatures and oxygen levels at a mean suitable for life, an analogy to the way in which the universe has expanded at a rate that is just right for the creation of stable structures like stars and galaxies. The appearance of asymmetrical fluctuations in the quantum vacuum at the birth of the universe was fortuitous also, since otherwise the universe would have annihilated itself as the particles and anti-particles paired off to wipe each other out like the gods and titans of the Scandinavian apocalypse.

Both the Jains' image of the cosmos as a Goddess and Swimme's autopoietic universe are quite different from the clocks and steam engines of classical physics, for they envision a universe that is alive and sentient, bursting with creativity. The clock of Newton's solar system had periodically to be rewound by its creator in order to preserve the planets from drifting off into chaotic orbits, and the great steam engine of the thermodynamicists would eventually burn up its own energy through friction and dissipation of the molecules composing its skeleton. In the mechanistic universe, there is nothing new under the sun and no real creativity ever takes place.

The vision of the universe sketched out by the protagonists of this book, on the other hand, is one in which everything is in flux and nothing is predictable. In the dynamical picture of Ralph Abraham, chaos inhabits the solar system, and the possibility of colliding worlds or planets leaping the tracks of prescribed orbits to sail off on erratic vectors is not out of the question. For Rupert Sheldrake, the laws of the universe are not fixed, but themselves subject to creative evolution. Likewise, in Terence McKenna's vision of the Timewave, cosmic and human history is a series of unpredictable Novelties, and for William Irwin Thompson, the creative imagination is the primary conduit to the archaic Mind spoken of in the writings of the ancients. For Lynn Margulis, the individual is holonomically nested within ever larger organic membranes, from the prokaryotic cell to Gaia, whereas, for Deepak Chopra and Stanislav Grof, the human individual is spread throughout creation like a wave rather than one of the classical atoms of Democritus.

The cosmology that we carry around with us in our heads acts like a sort of blueprint for our actions, and so it is important whether that blueprint envisions us situated like cells within the body of a larger superorganism, or like atoms pushed together by the inorganic pressures of some sort of gigantic machine. Without a sense of participation in the body of a cosmic organism, our lives can seem pointless and depressing, and so we end up suffering from what Doris Lessing calls fragmented vision, in which we cannot see the place of our individual lives in the whole of the universe.

Part of the problem is that science and religion are so radically opposed in their methods of approaching the cosmos, and yet, for many, science has usurped the place of religion as the source of our picture of the world and man's place within it. The purpose of religiosity is implied in the very word *religio* itself, which means "to join or link up." The sense of the communion meal, for example, in which we partake of the divine substance by consuming the transubstantiated wine and bread, is that we are absorbed as individual cells within the mystic body of Christ and made one with the universal organism. The method of science, however, is diametrically opposed to religion, for it proceeds by breaking down whole systems into their component parts on the assumption that this will explain how they work. While this might be true for machines, it is not true for the universe; but since the universe was mistaken for a machine during the centuries of the genesis and development of the scientific method, it is no surprise that many of us still think of it that way.

Consequently, for science to have taken the place of religion — as it has for many — is tantamount to a violation of its boundaries. And for those in whom science *is* a religion, there exists an unconscious psychic tension, since the needs of the soul for ever larger and more inclusive images of the cosmos are denied by the very reductionism of science.

Deepak Chopra has described a psychological concept known as "premature cognitive commitment." In India, for example, baby elephants are tied to a tree as part of their training, but as they grow to maturity, their minds retain their early imprinting, for they do not even try to break the flimsy ropes with which they are tied to trees that they could easily rip from the ground. Experiments have been performed with newborn kittens, likewise, in which three different groups were placed in unique environments. The first group was placed in a box painted only with vertical stripes, the second in a box with only horizontal and the third in a completely white box. When they had reached the stage in which their eyesight is fully developed, the kittens were removed from these boxes and it was demonstrated that those who had been raised in a vertical environment could see nothing horizontal. For those in the box painted with horizontal stripes, the reverse was the case, while the group raised in the white box could hardly see anything at all. Once formed, it would seem that their neurological connections cannot be reprogrammed.[2]

And so perhaps we in the West have made a premature cognitive commitment, also. In this case, our fascination with machines would seem to have shaped our whole vision of the world so that we can see nothing else. We are suffering from cosmological myopia because the mechanistic model is what we teach to our children in grade school and that is the way most of them see the world for the rest of their lives.

II. Genesis and the Upanishads

In his 1907 masterpiece *Creative Evolution*, Henri Bergson was one of the first philosophers to begin the process of disentangling the respective spheres of machines and organisms from each other, showing just where and how they differ, and why living things can no more be regarded as automatons than machines can be thought of as alive. The construction of machines, he pointed out, proceeds by way of a *compressive* motion from periphery to center as they are assembled through the *addition* and *association* of their parts, arranged in such a way as to perform a specific function. Organisms, on the other hand, come into being by an exactly opposite process, since they grow by *division* and *dissociation* of their parts as, through cellular mitosis, they develop with an *explosive* motion from center to periphery. More form, that is to say, is derived from less, and the whole is contained in each of its parts, as cloning demonstrates. Yet, this is most definitely *not* the case with machines, which are no more than the sum of their parts and have no ability to self-replicate.[3]

Bergson's distinctions are quite useful here, for his description of organisms is actually much more consistent with what we *know* about the way in which the universe has come into being. The explosion of the Big Bang, with its concomitant process of galaxies dividing and reproducing like cells has more in common with the paradigm of a living universe than it has with a machine.

Einstein, who was acquainted with Lemaître, thought that his friend's version of the creation of the universe from a primordial egg sounded uncomfortably like the first chapter of the *Old Testament*, but there is a Hindu creation myth which actually seems closer to the feel of our Big Bang hypothesis than the latter does to the *Book of Genesis*.

In the beginning, this story goes, there was only a single primordial Being, a sort of bisexual embryo floating in the luminous blue Void of mother space for eternity, like the Starchild at the end of *2001: A Space Odyssey*. It was alone, and in a sudden moment of reverse *satori* it spoke the words: "I am!" With this utterance, the dark wellsprings of existential anguish were uncorked and fear flooded through it and it became unbearably alone. This essential aloneness grew within it until it could stand the tensions no longer, and in an act of cosmic meiosis, abruptly split itself into two halves, a male and a female. The female transformed herself into a mare, he into a stallion, and from their union they produced all the horses in the world. In that manner, they proceeded to fill the Void with all living things. And then, one day, as this Being in its male half was strolling in the garden, *satori* struck and he said: "*I am* all of this that I have poured forth!"[4]

The contrast between this myth and that of the Bible could not be more striking, for here the universe creates itself from out of its own divine substance. The fundamental insight of Hindu metaphysics, consequently, is to realize the divinity inherent in all things, including oneself. The world is a manifestation of *Brahman*, the Absolute ground of being that is the source and root of our origins. Perhaps if there is anything to the idea that the imagery of dreams and visions is rooted in the structures that make up the chemistries, tissues and organs of the body, then it is possible that the myth is a visualization that came to some yogi while in trance of the very process of cellular mitosis itself. In any case, it is certainly more consistent with our Big Bang narrative, in which the universe originated from a sort of primeval atom that spontaneously disintegrated. Everything that *is*, consequently, is consubstantial with that primordial God Particle.

The cosmology of *Genesis*, however, is outdated and I believe it to be pernicious. For there, the world is created by a God who is separate from his creation, which he shapes to his liking the way a potter shapes a clay vessel. We and all things, consequently, are not to be identified with the divine spirit, but with dead matter. The heavens are the only true source of divinity since the earth is fallen. All help comes, therefore, from above, and us fallible mortals down here below are merely degraded Xeroxes of the real thing. Adam is drawn like mud from the earth and Eve is broken off like a twig from his ribcage. The only bridge between us and the Spirit is provided in the Christian mythos of the Savior who is unique in all creation for being simultaneously God *and* Man, spirit *and* matter.

And even though the scientific insights of Galileo, Kepler and Newton fused the laws of the heavens together with those of the earth into a single continuum, the mechanistic picture created therein was really only a secular version of the Christian cosmos. The vision of a gigantic spiritual being pushing dead matter about through empty space is precisely the theological canvas upon which Newton paints his world of forces acting upon stubbornly resistant masses, for matter in the Newtonian universe behaves sort of like the zombies in *Dawn of the Dead*, wandering blindly through space, driven by primordial inertial tendencies until harnessed by external forces.

In the metaphysics of Descartes, these ontological cleavages are miniaturized in his analogy of the soul's relationship with the body to a pair of clocks set to exactly the same time. When one of them points to the hour, the other strikes. There is no causal connection between them, although we might be tempted to say there was if we knew nothing about the function of gears and pinions. The soul and the body, likewise, are set on parallel tracks by God and do not ever really interact with one another.

So the foundations for Western culture's relationship to nature and the environment were laid first by the cosmology of the Bible and secondarily by Newtonian mechanics and Cartesian epistemology, which were its logical outgrowth. Since we do not see the earth as a sacred being — because our traditions have not shaped our minds to see it thus — we feel it is OK to pollute our rivers with industrial sewage, destroy our topsoils, burn our rainforests and send garbage barges floating off into the Hudson. And because we see our bodies as nothing more than concentrated atoms and chemistries that have accidentally joined together and learned to walk around, we are less reticent to pollute them with drugs or chemicals. To make matters worse, the pharmaceutical industries have billions of dollars invested in the simple-minded Cartesian notion that illnesses are a matter of readjusting chemical ratios with pills, for the mind, as far as the medical industry is concerned, has no relationship to the body whatsoever.

And even if they don't take drugs, the majority of people living in industrial societies think nothing of consuming beef and chickens that have been injected with hormones, or fruits and vegetables sprayed with pesticides. It is no wonder that researchers are baffled when faced with tracing the etiology of allergies and diseases like cancer or degenerative neural disorders like Lou Gehrig's or muscular dystrophy. These diseases are functions of *a way of life*; specifically, one lived in an industrial society that is obsessed with controlling nature.

So the Western imagination has developed out of a cultural morphogenetic field in which the Spirit is not resident in matter and our minds do not reside in our bodies. And because so many scientists today remain bound in this outmoded cosmology, it is no wonder that their imaginations are occasionally hi-jacked by a neglected Spirit that whispers to them mythologies of extraterrestrials who live "up there" somewhere and will one day come down and bring us all up to their level of technological or "spiritual" development. The likes of Carl Sagan and Arthur C. Clarke, for instance, spent much of their lives apparently unconscious that they were still living in a medieval cosmology — in spite of their naive pride in their own technocratic sophistication — for they were constantly searching the heavens for spiritual assistance not from angels but from extraterrestrials.

Apparently, what changes in the human imagination is not its *structures* for these remain remarkably persistent whether we are talking about the spirit / nature dichotomy of *Genesis* or external forces pushing dead masses about in Newtonian physics, or even the aliens from "up there" who will come down to those of us still stranded "down here" in technological kindergarten. Rather, it is the particular *content* that is poured into the mold of the human imagination which constantly changes in accordance with whatever imagery the psyche will currently "accept."

Just as the student of comparative anatomy will have trained his eye to identify the *same* organ or bone transformed in different animals for the purpose of adapting to various environments, so too, the mythic imagination is susceptible of a structuralist analysis whereby we can identify the *same* thought pattern as it is adapted to specific functions in differing world views. The idea, for example, that the visible world emanates from an invisible dimension or ground of being that is its source and metaphysical support is one such universal pattern of human thought, for the idea has undergone so many transformations throughout the history of culture that its presence within one or another system of thought may not always be readily apparent. But in fact, it would seem to constitute a sort of a priori category for cosmological thinking, for wherever we encounter myths or narratives of cosmic origins, the idea is almost invariably present in the form of one metaphysical backdrop or another.

Sometimes, its texture is corpuscular, like the radiant monads of Leibniz, or, as in the case of Spinoza, a single, continuous Substance, which he identifies with God. The idea is even present in the shallow empiricism of John Locke, who conceives of it as an ultimate substratum supporting the "scientific" world of objective primary qualities such as motion, extension or shape, upon which depend subjective qualities like taste, smell and color. The Irish philosopher Bishop Berkeley, rightly sensing that Locke's secularization of the idea threatened to do away with God, tried to deny the existence of matter altogether by insisting that even primary qualities are in reality subjective and depend upon human perception. It was not necessary to posit a material substratum to guarantee the stability of appearances, for the physical world derives its objectivity from the mind of God, whose perception of it guarantees that tables and chairs are still there when we aren't looking at them.

Berkeley's cosmology isn't all that far off from the Hindu notion that the world is the dream of a sleeping god named Vishnu, whose dream, however, ends when he enters dreamless sleep, taking the universe down the drain along with him in the form of floods and fires. In India, even the gods themselves are a manifestation of *Brahman*, which is intrinsically without form, since all forms derive from it. Arthur Schopenhauer, recognizing the equivalence of this idea with the Kantian "thing-in-itself," rechristened the invisible dimension simply as Will, the primordial Desire of the world simply to be which is the root not only of the struggle for survival amongst living things, but also, as he describes it, the conflict between Platonic Ideas to incarnate themselves in the same bits of matter.

The Greeks could never abide the idea of a cosmic Nothing, so they tended to atomize it. Both Plato's conception of the Forms and the Pythagorean notion of numbers as the numinous sources of all physical things are variants of the idea, as Schopenhauer recognized. And in their materialist personification of "atoms and the Void," the emphasis of the gestalt in the ontologies of Democritus and Lucretius is most emphatically on the atoms and not the Void.

The antiquity of the idea, furthermore, is attested by the presence of those painted animal archetypes haunting the Paleolithic caves of Lascaux and Les Trois Freres, for *these* are the true ancestors of Plato's Forms. In this case, the allegory of Plato's cave is reversed, for the world of darkness below is the protogenetic womb containing the numinous sources of the animals, while the sunny world of the plains up above is that of the transitory herds which come and go, into the Dark and out of it again as they are slain by the hunters.

The great German anthropologist Leo Frobenius, in his still untranslated book *Unknown Africa*, gave an account of a hunting ritual he witnessed one morning amongst the pygmies. Three men and one woman went out to a clearing before dawn and drew an image of an antelope on the ground. When the first rays of the sun struck the drawing, one of the men stepped forward with his bow and shot an arrow into the neck of the antelope as the woman shouted something in her native tongue. Then the men went off to hunt and came back later in the day with an antelope which they had shot through the neck in exactly the same spot as in the diagram. They returned to the image and poured some of the animal's blood on it, then erased it, lest its unpropitiated ghost take vengeance on them and cause a hunting accident.[5]

This image of the momentary concrescence of the Antelope archetype, rising, as it were, out of the ground like those ghostly letters materializing on the child's belly in *The Exorcist*, demonstrates how primordial man envisioned the animal archetypes as embedded within the womb of Mother Earth. There is undoubtedly a continuity of thought between the hunting ritual of these pygmies and the womb-like atmosphere of the Paleolithic caves, in which the animal Forms rest like embryos within the Mother.

Plato's vision of the timeless Forms upon which the shadow copies of the world are imperfectly modeled represents the continuation of this ancient notion into the structure of high civilization. The Neo-Platonic philosopher Plotinus, in the third century C.E., placed the Forms within the Mind of the world, from out of which the *anima mundi* emanated and in turn projected the physical plane of corporeality. This conception of the *anima mundi* then became the ontological basis for the sacred disciplines of alchemy, astrology and hermetic magic throughout the medieval and early renaissance periods, where it was carried on into the scientific revolution as far as Giordano Bruno, before disappearing in the seventeenth century and going underground into the esoteric brotherhoods of the Freemasons and the Rosicrucians.

But like a crystal which is now translucent, now opaque, the idea was reincarnated in the scientific minds of the Baroque as the materialist substratum of the world, to which the skeleton key lay in mathematics, at least since the time of Galileo. For it was the precision and clarity of mathematics which inspired Descartes, Newton and Leibniz to revisualize the invisible world as a kind of latticework composed of densely layered equations like radiant arabesques. The priesthood of the modern world was now composed of scientists, whose faith in the pious formulae embodying the secret forces of the cosmos was evidence that it was the language of mathematics, not Latin, that was the true idiom for capturing the numinous dimension. For the initiate into this priesthood, the equations of physics were numeric hieroglyphs of the sacred forces of the universe, and he alone possessed the capability for invoking the realm of the universal constants. The magical belief that the powers of the world can be summoned to do your bidding is as old as shamanism, for whether it takes on the form of the hunting rituals of the pygmy, the mass of the Catholic priest, or the experiments of the physicist, it is all the same as far as the archetypal structure of the human imagination goes.

The idea of the invisible dimension would seem to constitute the nucleus of the human mind, for its presence in the thought of Paleolithic man as well as in the contemporary scientist would not seem to be susceptible of any other explanation.

The presence of the idea as a kind of metaphysical canvas upon which the thinkers of this book paint their visions should not, therefore, come as a surprise. But what is different about their inflection of the idea in comparison with the scientific conception of a materialist substratum — be it Newtonian atoms, mass-energy, or unified field — is the fact that they have drawn inspiration from traditional thought systems that most contemporary scientists would regard as outdated. For these people as scientists to welcome the imagery of the mythic imagination absolutely sets them apart from mechanists like Stephen Hawking or Marvin Minsky or Daniel Dennett, none of whom would sit comfortably with the thought of any contamination of their "universal constants" and "forces of nature" with "religious" ideas.

Whether we are discussing Rupert Sheldrake's scientific translation of the Neoplatonic Mind of the world; Ralph Abraham's vibration theory; Deepak Chopra's revival of *Ayurvedic* medicine, complete with its conception of *Brahman* as the noumenal ground of our being which, when touched by human consciousness through meditation, can allow a reprogramming of the body to expel illness; Stanislav Grof's encounters in holotropic therapy with the realm of Bardo; Brian Swimme's Spinozistic conception of the mind of God; Terence McKenna's contact with the Gaian Overmind; or William Irwin Thompson's vision of the resurgence of the astral plane in electronic technology, we are inhabiting the same field of ideas, wherein the materialist conception of the invisible world has undergone transubstantiation into a more etheric conception of the nature of ultimate reality.

Carl Sagan, Murray Gellmann and Richard Dawkins belong in the same noosphere; Brian Swimme, Deepak Chopra and Stanislav Grof in another altogether. It is not even a question of "atheism" versus "theism" here, for many of the scientists which I have listed in the introduction of this book also share this phase space and are comfortable, to varying degrees, with admitting that they have drawn inspiration from the world of myth. Lynn Margulis, for example, is an avowed atheist, but she certainly welcomes the cultural amplifications of William Irwin Thompson, who holds up the X-ray lens of mythology to illuminate the presence of the mythic skeleton in her work in microbiology. Thompson's perception, for example, of the structural resonance shared by Margulis's historical descriptions of how anaerobic bacteria were thrust down into the depths of the ocean by fierce, oxygen-powered aerobes, with the myth of Michael slaying the dragon and casting him into the abyss, is a connection which she certainly enjoys.[6]

And so there is a resonance between not only the thinkers profiled in this book, but those that I have listed in the introduction, as well, since they all share a portion of the noosphere in which myth and science comfortably overlap, whereas the mainstream does not. The thinkers of this book, furthermore, have in common a similar etherialization of the materialist substratum in their revisioning of the cosmos, and so I see the shift from mechanistic science to their work as directly analogous to the transubstantiation of the wine and the bread of the mass as the priest calls forth the divine Logos to pour down through the world ceiling and take up its residence there.

IV. Toward a Mythic Science

What I mean by the transubstantiation of science is not a fusion of science and religion. I have stressed throughout the book that the two spheres have entirely separate functions. Rather, since science is becoming concerned with holistic images of the cosmos which are *inclusive* of human beings, then the general climate of ideas will be more sympathetic to the mythological imagination, rather than hostile. It is only *mechanistic* science that is incompatible with spirituality. Since that is changing, perhaps the two spheres can engage in a more fruitful exchange of ideas.

There is an image from a paper by Ralph Abraham which I would like to sketch as the concluding vision of this book, for it is a perfect example of this kind of cross-fertilization of science and religion. In Abraham's description, a two-acre Bioshelter would be created within the attic of the Cathedral of Saint John the Divine in New York City. The architect

Santiago Calatrava dreamed up a kind of Gothic architecture which actually includes columns blending with real trees from the amazon rain forests, while a self-enclosed water system would recycle sewage from the toilettes through the use of John Todd's living machines. William Irwin Thompson, in a talk given at the cathedral, articulated a vision for the creation of an electronic rose window as a giant, liquid crystal display upon which would be projected visions of Lynn Margulis's film footage of cyanobacteria and spirochetes. More conventional monitors would "make the invisible parameters of Gaian physiology visible" by displaying read-outs of temperature, humidity, oxygen, carbon dioxide levels, and so forth.[7] Dean James Morton was in charge of the cathedral during the period in the early nineties when this was envisioned. Though he has since left the cathedral to establish Interfaith, he is a paragon of the kind of priestly philanthropist that the church requires if it is to survive into the twenty-first century as anything more than a holdout for fundamentalist revivals.[8]

What science can borrow from religiosity are mythic *images* that will help to create more intuitive rather than abstract cosmologies that will serve to link us to the universe rather than divorce us from it. The visionary imagination is a conduit of energies pouring forth from the *anima mundi* itself. The Gaia hypothesis is an example of this, because science has borrowed an intuitive image from Greek mythology to express with ideographic brevity what would otherwise be stated as "a cybernetic system with homeostatic tendencies as detected by chemical anomalies in the earth's atmosphere."

The transformation of scientific theories into mythic analogs will create a more affective language for science, and the imagination, consequently, will be more receptive to theories which are presented to it as images. The native tongue of the intellect is abstract language, but the rest of the mind thrives on images, for that is how it communicates to us at night through dreams. The language of science, then, should be enriched by this exchange.

What religion can borrow from science, on the other hand, is new *knowledge* about the universe that it, in turn, can transform through the mythic imagination. This is what Chardin attempted to accomplish in his life's work, and the Church could not accept his fusion of science and Catholicism, so his work was published posthumously. The future of the

Church seems less viable if it cannot adapt to our present images of the cosmos. After all, the myths of Christianity which were brought into being in the first couple of centuries C.E. were based upon the scientific knowledge of that era. The world was a three-tiered hierarchy of heaven, earth and hell, with angels above and demons below, and the planets were spun about the earth as God sat on his throne in the Empyrean and watched his machine run. The history of the cosmos was unfolded in a three-act play, consisting of genesis, crucifixion and apocalypse, and each of these events was unique and never to be repeated. *That* was the science of the first century C.E.

So now it would seem that religion must catch up with science, for science is already returning to its ground of origins in myth. What brood of children their marriage will produce to populate the earth remains the mystery and the promise of the twenty-first century.

ACKNOWLEDGMENTS

In an age in which the cinema and rock and roll are the preeminent art forms, almost every undertaking is a collective endeavor to which no one individual can assume full credit, and the case is no less so with the present book. As the opening epigraph indicates, I owe the primary vision of the book to the final chapter of Oswald Spengler's *Decline of the West,* Volume One, on "Faustian and Apollonian Nature Knowledge," which demonstrates that there is no such thing as "nature" per se, only varying descriptions of it as perceived through that epistemological lens which we call "myth," and by which we normally mean to depreciate the cosmologies of other cultures. It was Spengler's genius to perceive that what we call "science" is actually an extremely recondite and highly textured variation of "mythology."

And to Joseph Campbell perhaps more than anyone I owe a great debt for the inspiration of his "Copernican" vision of mythology, in which the Biblical cosmos is seen as merely one planet amongst many whirling around the great mystery which we think of as "God." I also owe thanks to The Joseph Campbell Foundation for their financial support.

To Arthur Young, I owe the structure of the book's evolution-involution arc, and to William Irwin Thompson I owe an even greater debt for introducing me to the post-Campbell world of contemporary science and culture.

To F. David Peat I owe a somewhat astonished thanks for writing the foreword to a book whose author might just as well have been Adam.

And for looking over the manuscript and making various comments and suggestions I owe many thanks to the following: John Lobell, Stephen Larsen, Ray Grasse and Ralph White.

And for their generosity in granting me the time to interview, I thank my co-authors: Brian Swimme, Rupert Sheldrake, Ralph Abraham, Lynn Margulis, Terence McKenna, Stanislav Grof, Deepak Chopra and once again, Bill Thompson.

And then there's that friend out in Minnesota, Robert Warner, whose enthusiasm and kind encouragement made my days go easier; the incipient fiction writer Kheir Fakhreldin, whose book *Elvis Redivivus: A Myth* is destined to make him famous; my mother, for the immense sacrifices which she made in raising my brother Tom and me; and Melynda Christoff, since I probably would not have written this book without her persistent encouragement and the many discussions we had concerning it. Her innate charm, warmth and sensitivity provided me with the fuel to undertake the project to begin with, and then her careful and thoughtful criticisms of each of these chapters helped to keep me on the rails throughout.

INTRODUCTION

[1] See Jung (1976) pp.67-68. For more of Jung's comments on his meeting, see *Selected Letters of C.G. Jung, 1909-1961*, edited by Gerhard Adler, (1984), p.116; and *C.G. Jung Speaking: Interviews and Encounters*, edited by William McGuire and R.F.C. Hull (1977), p.326.

[2] *Wandlungen und Symbole der Libido*, later translated as *Symbols of Transformation*.

[3] See Serres (1982), pp.125-26.

[4] This video series is available from Mystic Fire.

[5] See Gimpel (1976), pp.149-153.

[6] See Peterson (1993), Ch.2, esp. pp.23-30.

[7] Gimpel, ibid. p.153.

[8] See Spengler (1929), vol II., p.502.

[9] Spengler (1932), pp.84-85.

[10] Neumann (1974), pp.94-95.

[11] Campbell (1988a), p.8.

[12] Rifkin (1981), p.33.

[13] The four parts of Wagner's opera *The Ring* were completed in phases between 1869 and 1876. Hebbel's dramatic trilogy *Die Nibelungen* dates from about 1862. But Wagner had been working on earlier drafts of his *Ring* cycle as far back as 1848. Ibsen's early plays, likewise, of the period about 1855-67 drew from Norse myths and Viking legends. Rudolf Clausius, meanwhile, in 1850, was the first to formulate the entropy principle after Carnot's work and the following year, Kelvin formulated it independently, although both men had read Carnot. The word "entropy" was coined by Clausius in 1865.

[14] Adams (1961), pp.380-81.

[15] Lessing (1974), pp.287-88.

[16] See the essay by Heinrich Zimmer, "On the Significance of the Indian Tantric Yoga" in Campbell, ed. (1960), p.39.

[17] Neumann (1974), p. 110.

[18] In fact, I have structured this book according to the process theory outlined by Young in *The Reflexive Universe*. I have divided it into two sections, "The Descent to Earth" and "The Return to the Source" in deliberate evocation of the V-shaped seven-stage outline which Young discusses in his book. In that model, the creation of the universe at the top of the left side of the V, the realm of pure matter governed by mechanistic laws at the nadir, and an increasing sense of freedom which consciousness develops for itself as it evolves upwards from the mineral world into that of plants, then animals, and with human beings, recapturing the potential to achieve the same kind of unlimited freedom demonstrated by particles of light at the Big Bang; all of this is paralleled in my book with Brian Swimme's discussion of the Big Bang at the start, Lynn Margulis's elucidation of the origins of Gaia at the nadir, and the wide-ranging intellectual freedom of Thompson at the opposite end. The myth as Young outlines it is that of fall, capture and liberation, exactly as envisioned by the various Gnostic and mystery cults of the Hellenistic era, as well as in the Hermetic and Neo-Platonic traditions that grew out of them. This book is meant to echo that myth in its essential structure. I have also drawn inspiration on this point from William Irwin Thompson's discussion of the myth in his book *The Time Falling Bodies Take to Light*.

[19] Arthur Zajonc is the author of *Catching the Light: the Entwined History of Light and Mind*. He has recently published a work on the science of Goethe, and has taken over as President of the Lindisfarne Association.

[20] I actually interviewed Richard Tarnas, the author of *The Passion of the Western Mind*, for this book, but because the core of the interview concerned the subject matter of a book he has been working on for many years — *Cosmos and Psyche: Intimations of a New World View* — he withdrew from the present collection, feeling that many of his statements concerning astrology might be unsupported lacking the context of his book.

[21] Nancy Todd's phrase.

COSMOLOGY

[1] "[Think of] Descartes withdrawing from the world, calling all into doubt, having the initiatic vision of the mathematics behind appearances, and then going forth again to study the world with the new method of science. Notice, however, just how mythic is the structure of Descartes' *Discourse on Method*; it has what Joseph Campbell would call the 'monomythic pattern' of separation, initiation, and return." See William Irwin Thompson (1991a), pp.20-21.

[2] For an introduction to Thomas Berry, see the article "Thomas Berry and a New Creation Story" by Marjorie Hope and James Young (1989), pp. 750-753.

[3] For an explanation of this see *The Sixth Extinction, Patterns of Life and the Future of Humankind*, by Richard Leakey and Roger Lewin, (1995).

[4] For example, the monism of the 17th century philosopher Benedict Spinoza (1632-1677), who attempted to overcome the Cartesian dualism of matter and mind by postulating that both were simply two different modalities of the one universal Substance of Nature which, in fact, was God himself. His most famous work is the posthumously published *Ethics Demonstrated According to the Geometrical Order* (1677). Plotinus, Giordano Bruno, Friedrich Schelling, Arthur Schopenhauer and the Romantics in general shared this essentially Neo-Platonist view of the *anima mundi* or world soul, which happens also to be the common ontological foundation of the paradigm shared by the various thinkers profiled in this book.

[5] For example, the steady state theory proposed by Hermann Bondi, Thomas Gold and Fred Hoyle, in which matter is continually created and therefore drives the expansion of the universe.

[6] These tiny asymmetries at the birth of the universe which give rise at the macro-scale to the formation of galaxies and stars brings cosmology remarkably in line with chaos theory, one of the fundamental insights of which is that there is an exquisite sensitivity to initial conditions in the life cycles of unfolding systems. This is known as non-linearity, in which small causes explode into huge effects which are out of all proportion to their causes. Popularizations of chaos theory like the one produced by NOVA for PBS convey this idea with the old cliche of the straw that broke the camel's back. It is better known, perhaps, as the Butterfly Effect — the central cliche of chaos theory — in which a butterfly that flaps its wings on one side of the world can send out ripples that explode into storms on the other side. See the Ralph Abraham interview below for a discussion of chaos theory.

BIOLOGY

[1] For an illustration of morphic resonance see Sheldrake (1995a), p.97 and p.103.

[2] See, for example, Jung (1969a), p.181: ". . . a predominantly scientific and technological education . . . can also bring about a spiritual regression and a considerable increase of psychic dissociation. . . . Loss of roots and lack of tradition neuroticize the masses and prepare them for collective hysteria. . . ."

[3] Sheldrake (1974).

[4] Campbell (1988), p. 102.

[5] As Ralph Abraham writes, ". . . while staying at the ashram of Neem Karoli Baba at Kainichi, in the Himalayan foothills of North India, I abstracted . . . a mathematical model for morphogenesis. . . . During this same period of time, Rupert Sheldrake was writing his first book on morphogenesis in the ashram of Dom Bede Griffiths, in Tamil Nadu, South India. Both of us were undoubt-

edly influenced by the Hindu theories of the *akasha*, that is, an infinite, vibrational field of intelligence." See Abraham (1996).

[6] Brown and McClenn (1993), p. 9.

[7] Sheldrake (1988), pp. 220-222.

[8] Stevenson (1974).

[9] See the section "Psychic Protoplasm" in Arthur Young's *The Reflexive Universe* (1976), pp.136-146, and esp. p.145 for an example of the phenomenon Sheldrake is referring to.

[10] Sheldrake (1997).

[11] Jahn and Dunne (1987).

MATHEMATICS

[1] For Newton and William Whiston see Abraham (1994), pp. 180-86.

[2] Compare with the Kant-Laplace theory of the origin of the solar system, in which it was stated that the sun and planets had evolved from the condensation of a vast nebular cloud of dust and gas, the increasing rate of rotation of which eventually spun the planets into being.

[3] The Western recovery of the Hermetic Tradition occured in two phases. The second, to which Abraham is referring, transpired in 1453 when Constantinople fell to the Turks, spilling forth Greek-speaking Byzantine scholars and monks, some of whom were received by the Medici family in Florence. These scholars brought with them many esoteric writings from the Greco-Roman Hellenistic world which had been lost to the West after the fall of Rome in the fifth century and the closing of Plato's Academy under the Byzantine Emperor Justinian in the sixth.

Subsequently, the learning of the Greek language was lost to the West with the sole exception of the monasteries of the Irish Celtic monks who mastered the language and synthesized their own version of Neoplatonism and Christianity, culminating in the masterwork of the Irish philosopher John Scotus Erigena, entitled *De divisione naturae* (c.865-870 a.d.). The Irish Celtic Christian world was ended by centuries of Viking invasions, beginning with the sacking of the Lindisfarne monastery in the eighth century and continuing to the tenth. The recovery of such texts as *The Corpus Hermeticum* and the dialogues of Plato during the fifteenth century inspired Cosimo de Medici to open an Academy of learning based on Plato's, and thus began the restoration of the learning of Greek by such scholars as Marsilio Ficino and Pico della Mirandola.

The first phase of this recovery, however, had already taken place in the twelfth century during the Crusades when Spanish scholars had recovered from the Arabs the entire corpus of Aristotle along with the literature of alchemy, which constitutes one thread of the Hermetic Tradition. The subsequent impact of alchemy on the West was considerable: its first students were men such as Albertus Magnus, Roger Bacon and Thomas Aquinas. The extent of its reach continued down through Newton, Goethe and Carl Jung.

[4] See Dobbs (1975).

[5] For illustrations of Paleolithic goddess figurines in association with snakes and vortices, see illustrations 127 and 128 on p.72 of Joseph Campbell (1988a).

[6] For an exposition of these ideas see the paper "Chaos in Myth and Science," by Ralph Abraham (1988) pp.193-210.

[7] For a popular presentation of catastrophe theory that includes a synopsis of Thom's views, see Woodcock and Davis (1978).

[8] In this essay, "The Four Cultural Ecologies of the West," Thompson articulates his theory of Western civilization as a sequence of four distinct phases, each with its own kind of mathematics, technology and world view. These are, respectively, the Riverrine (or Mesopotamian), Meditteranean (Greco-Roman), Atlantic (Northern European) and Pacific (or global civilization). The corresponding forms of mathematic are: arithmetic, Euclidean geometry, calculus, and dynamical systems theory. See Thompson's book *Pacific Shift* (1985) pp. 65-151.

Abraham and Thompson are collaborating on a book together. Abraham describes it as follows: "It deals with interactions between mathematics and art history. The first chapter would be a reprint of his chapter on the four cultural ecologies in *Pacific Shift*. And then there would be four other chapters, one for each shift. For the first one, about the Paleolithic, we've analyzed this prehistoric sculpture, the *Venus of Lespugues*, for its dimensions and found the Greek Doric scale represented there almost entire. And now we have a similar analysis of a Fra Angelico painting done in 1434 [*Cortona Annunciation*] which prefigures the discoveries of modern mathematics."

[9] Thompson and Abraham are employed by The Ross School, founded by Courtney Ross, heiress of Time-Warner. See Shnayerson (1996), p.190 and esp. pp. 194 and 234 for Abraham and Thompson.

[10] For example, see the paper by Abraham, "Vibrations: Communication Through a Morphic Field." (1996).

[11] William Irwin Thompson, on the other hand, has a decidedly different view of the value of Sheldrake's contributions: ". . . all the scientists that I do know and respect, because of the level of their achievements in science, have considered Sheldrake's work, and they tell me it is not good science. . . . I notice that the people who are the most enthusiastic followers of Sheldrake are generally people who are not practicing in science but are devotees of the New Age or therapists of some sort." See pp.98-100 of his *Reimagination of the World* (1991c).

[12] Abraham (1995).

GEOSCIENCES

[1] See *The Universe Story* pp.85-95.

[2] Among the marginalia which Margulis scrawled while correcting the early draft of this chapter, she wrote: "I want no part of Swimme's 'Theogony.'"

[3] This fusion occurs under anoxic conditions, according to Margulis.

[4] For William Irwin Thompson's mythical amplifications of this material, see his book *Imaginary Landscape: Making Worlds of Myth and Science*, pp. 55-62. ". . . for the excretions of the photosynthesizing bacteria accumulated as a poison to the anaerobes and they had to retreat from those who fed on light and oxygen to sink down into the darkness of the slime at the bottom of lakes . . . here was the war of Michael the Archangel fighting against Satan and driving him down to chain him to the underworld." (ibid. p.59).

[5] The above quotes and much of the following material is based on Chapter Two of Margulis's *Symbiotic Planet*. See pp.17-19 for quotes.

[6] Lovelock, J.E., and L. Margulis. "Atmospheric Homeostasis by and for the Biosphere: The Gaia Hypothesis." *Tellus* 26:2-10.

[7] The period of the trilobites is that of the Cambrian, currently dated to about 540 million years ago.

[8] The three most important astronomical factors are, according to Ralph Abraham, the stretch, tilt and wobble of the earth's orbit around the sun: every 100,000 years the earth's orbit stretches from a more nearly circular to a more nearly elliptical one; the wobble of the earth as it spins about its axis is known as the precession of the equinoxes and the duration of one complete wobble is 25,920 years; and every 41,000 years, the earth's axial tilt shifts from approximately 22 to 24 degrees. See Abraham (1994), pp.204-205.

[9] Margulis's footnote: "Indeed, Paul Hoffman at the Harvard University Department of Geosciences presents massive and compelling information to support his hypothesis of the iceball earth. During the Vendian (Neoproterozoic eon, the latest pre-Cambrian) glaciers formed at sea level in the tropics and the entire surface of the earth froze. Removal of atmospheric CO_2 and other biologically modulated greenhouse gases were in part responsible."

Immanuel Velikovsky — who was one of Carl Sagan's favorite pinatas — was already as far back as 1955, discussing the evidence for the presence of glaciers in the tropics. See his *Earth in Upheaval*, 1973 edition, pp.47-48, "Ice Age in the Tropics." Velikovsky is still too often dismissed as a crackpot, whereas, in reality, he was a kind of prophet of the current catastrophist vogue that is sweeping through the astronomical and geological sciences. His work is filled with fresh and original ideas, many of which are presently turning up as "new" theories or hypotheses, such as the role of comets in geological history. Scientists are lothe to credit him in any way, for the aura of "heretic" still glows around his name, despite the present vindication of much of his work. See Ralph Abraham interview above.

[10] See Margulis's comments in John Brockman's *The Third Culture* p.140 (Simon and Schuster, 1995); see also Jan Sapp, *Evolution by Association*, pp. 196-97 (Oxford University Press: 1994).

PART TWO   THE RETURN TO THE SOURCE
ETHNOBOTANY

[1] Gibson and Sterling (1992), p. 117.

[2] See, for example, *The Mayan Factor* by Jose Arguelles (1987), p. 86.

[3] According to McKenna's software, *Timewave Zero*, history is composed of a series of Novelty waves, in which new inventions spring up at the end of a cycle. Since the *I Ching* is composed of 64 hexagrams, dates in history can be divided by that number to yield Novelty points. For example, 1.3 billion years ago marks the invention of sexual reproduction by eukaryotic organisms. Divide that number by 64 to yield a cycle beginning 18 million years ago within the Miocene epoch at the height of the age of the mammals (and perhaps not coincidently, 15 million years ago, a great catastrophe was initiated by the impact of some planetoid). Divide that by 64 to yield a figure around 200,000, a date associated with the advent of the Neanderthal populations. Divided by 64 again yields a figure around 4,300, which is the beginning of the Kurgan invasions of the goddess civilizations of Old Europe, the prologue to the rise of high civilization a thousand or so years later. The last of these Novelty cycles begins on August 5, 1945 — a day before the Hiroshima bombing — and ends on December 21, 2012 C.E. See the paper, "Temporal Resonance" in McKenna (1991), pp.104-113. See also Arguelles, ibid., although McKenna claims that *he* introduced the 2012 idea to Arguelles.

[4] For an illustration of this intercalation process, see fig. 9, p.76 in McKenna, Terence and McKenna, Dennis (1993).

[5] Jaynes (1976).

[6] For illustrations of these hallucinogenic figures see McKenna (1992), pp.72-73. Also, see the illustration in Campbell (1988a), p.83, fig.146. Regarding the significance of the art of the Tassili plateau, Campbell quotes from the work of scholar Henri Lhote: "'It seems,' states Lhote in discussion of these finds, 'as though we are confronted with the earliest works of negro art — indeed, one is tempted to say, with its origin.'"

[7] For example, William Irwin Thompson writes: "Unfortunately, the California-hippie way . . . is to become the typical American consumer and think that the way to enlightenment is through consuming mushrooms and enjoying illumination without all the hard work of yogic *sadhana*." See Thompson (1996), p.189. See also Endnote 6, of the Grof interview below for Ken Wilber's comment.

[8] Contrast with Thompson: "I think the main problem with virtual reality is that it's a toxic technology, a rape of your frontal lobes. I think it's going to give people health effects like early Alzheimer's. When I was a kid, I used to go into shoe stores and stick my toes in X-ray machines. What seemed to be progress and groovy was actually giving people cancer." See Brown and McClen (1995), p.297.

PSYCHOLOGY

[1] See "Freud and the Future" in *Essays* by Thomas Mann (1957).

[2] Richard Tarnas's phrase.

[3] Hofmann (1981).

[4] Although this oversimplifies Grof's views, some acquaintance with these matrices is necessary here for understanding certain questions which follow. The reader is advised to consult Grof's books before making a judgement based only on my synopsis.

[5] For example, in a workshop which I attended with Grof, he recounted an episode of animal identi-fication during ingestion of LSD, in which he experienced himself as an herbivorous dinosaur which was attacked by a carnivorous one, and felt himself dying in the mud as he was torn apart and eaten. He also recounted an episode of identification with a Venus fly trap, and vividly recalls his mingled revulsion and satisfaction at the memory of digesting a fly.

[6] "'It's a fundamental error to assume that moving into the higher stages of spiritual development is easy — something you can do in a weekend workshop or by reading a book or by taking LSD. Only through long-term disciplines can you make these experiences stable, permanent structures of con-sciousness.'" Thus Ken Wilber in Tony Schwartz (1995), p. 364.

[7] A Japanese film made in 1976 by Nagisa Oshima. It was rated X for its depiction of explicit sexual obsession.

[8] See the film *Mishima: A Life in Four Chapters*, directed by Paul Schrader (1985).

[9] For Ken Wilber's criticisms of Grof, see *The Eye of Spirit: An Integral Vision for a World Gone Slightly Mad* (1997) Chapter 7: "Born Again: Stan Grof and the Holotropic Mind," pp. 165-85. See also Wilber's *Sex, Ecology, Spirituality: The Spirit of Evolution* (1995) pp. 741-51. For Grof on Wilber, see Grof's *Beyond the Brain: Birth, Death and Transcendence in Psychotherapy.* (1985) pp.131-37. See also, *Ken Wilber in Dialogue* (1998).

[10] See my interview with Terence McKenna above.

[11] Grof himself was put under hypnosis and actually recalled his past life as a Russian monk. For his account of these experiences see *The Holotropic Mind* (1992), pp. 128-131.

[12] Stevenson (1987).

[13] "And thus every new Culture is awakened in and with a new view of the world, that is, a sudden glimpse of death as the secret of the perceivable world. It was when the idea of the impending end of the world spread over Western Europe (about the year 1000) that the Faustian soul of this reli-gion was born." See Spengler (1926), p. 167.

MEDICINE

[1] Wagner had at one time thought of composing an opera about the life of the Buddha, while Nietzsche's first book *The Birth of Tragedy* , owes a great debt to his predecessors Wagner and Schopenhauer, particularly insofar as they were both inspired by Hinduism and Buddhism. Nietzsche, of course, later reversed his attitude toward the East altogether, making the very same mistake both his mentors had in oversimplifying its doctrines to a purely world renunciatory ethic. But unlike them, Nietzsche dismissed it as of no value for those who wish to embrace life. It must be said that unlike certain journalists today these great philosophers of the West may be excused for their oversimplifications because not much was known about the complexities of Hindu and Buddhist thought in the 19th century. However, the mistakes made by the editors of *What is Enlightenment?* magazine in their interviews and scattered comments on Deepak Chopra cannot be excused on the grounds of Western cultural ignorance. The errors here are due to individual igno-rance and misplaced trust in facile, media-microwaved packaging of Chopra. See Hal Blacker (1997) p.39 and Susan Bridle (1997), pp. 46-52.

[2] Leland and Power (1997), pp. 53-58.

[3] Bridle (1997), ibid.; Leland and Power (1997), ibid.

[4] ". . . the main problem is, what is *moksa?* Is it release from the world? or is it release from ignorance? If it is the latter and if *atman* is *in* the world, release from the world is superfluous and may even represent a wrong notion about the nature of *moksa.* . . . If one knows of the immanence of *atman-Brahman* in all things, then what if one responds to desire? I should gladly go crazy with desire, knowing of its divinity. . . ." See Joseph Campbell (1995), pp. 171-72.

[5] See Campbell (1962) p. 351.

[6] *Brahman* is the Hindu conception of Absolute Reality, the ontological ground of being of which all forms in the world are a manifestation. *Brahman*, however, is inscrutable, unknowable and ulti-mately a mystery to the intellect, though it is to be experienced in the yogic trance state of *samad-*

hi, wherein the mind is catapulted beyond all names, forms, visions and pairs-of-opposites to an experience of this ultimate One that is the ground of all being in space and time. *Atman,* which is often mistranslated as "soul," is the personal ground of mystery embodied by the individual. *Brahman-atman* thus form a pair of concepts — the mystery as macrocosm underlying the universe and as microcosm underlying the human soul — that is to be transcended by the non-dual experience of *samadhi,* whereby the two become one, *brahmatman.* It is not quite true to say, however, that no predicates can be attached to *Brahman,* since its etymological root is the prefix *brh-* which means "energy." Some schools, therefore, attach three predicates to *Brahman,* known as *sat, cit, ananda. Sat* is "being," *cit* is "consciousness" and *ananda* is "rapture."

[7] The longest-lived case on record in the West is that of Thomas Parr, who was born in 1483 and died in 1635 at the age of 152! At the age of 130, he was said to have threshed corn.

HISTORY

[1] For Goethe's brief paper see Campbell (1968), pp. 378-79.

[2] Sri Aurobindo's major work *Life Divine* was published in the same year, as was, incredibly, Erich Neumann's *Origins and History of Consciousness* and Joseph Campbell's classic *The Hero with a Thousand Faces.* Carl Jung, upon reading these latter two spin-offs of his work, was then moved to revise his 1912 book *Psychology of the Unconscious,* which he then published in 1952 as *Symbols of Transformation.* Teilhard de Chardin's *The Phenomenon of Man* appeared posthumously in 1955, though most of the manuscript had been completed by 1938. Gebser's work explicates only those levels of consciousness pertaining to Chardin's "noosphere" and so Chardin's book, which covers the unfolding of the cosmos, is more comprehensive, if less detailed. Owen Barfield is little read these days, but his work belongs in the same category and forms the link back to Rudolf Steiner, who influenced him enormously. Barfield's first two books, *History in English Words* (1926) and *Poetic Diction* (1927) came out of the British milieu of Eliot, Tolkien and C.S. Lewis, who were friends of his, but Barfield's work was radically different from theirs in seeing language as an archaeological record of the evolution of consciousness. His next important work was *Saving the Appearances* (1957). Bergson's *Creative Evolution* (1907) should not be forgotten here, either, since it was one of the first sketches of the different organs of perception consciousness grows for itself as it evolves through nature.

[3] See Thompson (1989), p.134.

[4] See "The Quest for the Holy Grail," in Thompson (1997) p.103.

For Thompson's elaboration of this see his and David Spangler's *Reimagination of the World: A Critique of the New Age, Science and Popular Culture.* (1991) pp. 3-9.

[5] For Thompson's adventures at Esalen, see the chapter "Going Beyond it at Big Sur," in *At the Edge of History.* (1971) pp. 27-66.

[6] For a series of talks representative of Lindisfarne's first phase, see Thompson (1977). For a series representative of the second phase, see Thompson (1987) and (1991).

[7] For a further amplification of this theme, see the essay "The Return of the Middle Ages" by Umberto Eco in his *Travels in Hyperreality,* NY: Harcourt Brace, 1986.

[8] For Thompson on non-fiction as an art form, see his "Foreword" to his novel *Islands Out of Time: A Memoir of the Last Days of Atlantis.* (1990) pp. vii-xii.

[9] See Thompson (1993).

[10] The Ross School, founded by Courtney Ross, heiress of Time-Warner. See Shnayerson (1996), p. 190, esp. pp. 194 and 234 for Thompson and Abraham.

[11] "If we are to blame 'Sesame Street' for anything, it is for the pretense that it is an ally of the classroom. . . . As a television show, and a good one, 'Sesame Street' does not encourage children to love school or anything about school. It encourages them to love television." See Postman (1985), p.144.

[12] For more on Cronenberg, see Thompson (1989), pp.166-67. For Cronenberg and Pynchon, see the essay "Visions of a Biomechanical Apocalypse," by John David Ebert (1997), pp. 67-71.

[13] Doris Lessing is one of the truly great writers of the 20th century. She has composed a string of mas-

terpieces, the most famous of which are *The Golden Notebook* (1962) and her *Children of Violence* novels (1950-1969), and for the latter, the overarching paradigm is exactly that of this book, namely, the shift from our 19th century legacy of materialist philosophies such as communism and industrialism, to the more spiritually inclined capacities and paranormal potentials of the human being. But it is her great magnum opus *Canopus in Argos* (1979-1983) that in my opinion is her finest achievement. In this series of five novels she resurrects Gnostic mythology in the form of a kind of science fiction space opera that consists of a darkly apocalyptic vision of the state of contemporary man. The first volume of her autobiography was published in 1994, entitled, *Under My Skin: Volume One of My Autobiography to 1949*. The second volume, chronicling her life up to the writing of *The Golden Notebook* was published in 1997. For Thompson's reflections on Lessing's work, see the following: *Passages About Earth* (1974), pp. 132-139 and *Pacific Shift* (1985), pp.11-12.

[14] *Solaris* (1972) is a film directed by the great Russian filmmaker Andrei Tarkovsky, who also directed the famous *Andrei Rublev*. The story concerns a Russian space station that is orbiting a planet covered entirely by water. When a psychologist is sent to try and salvage whatever information remains in the minds of its dying cosmonauts, only two of whom are still living, the psychologist soon discovers that a ghost is haunting the abandoned space station, a ghost which turns out to be that of his dead wife. We discover that the ghost is in fact the Gaian Overmind of the planet which is trying to communicate with the astronauts by assuming the human form of their most intimate love relationships.

It is interesting how scientific theories often cast their shadows backward in time, appearing first in the imagination of poets and artists. *Solaris* the novel was published in 1961 and provides certain important details that are left out of the film. We are told, for instance, that the planet is orbiting between two suns and that the gravitational pressures exerted upon it should not only preclude the formation of life but should, over time, send the planet's orbit into chaos and cause it to crash into one of the suns. The scientists conclude, however, that the evolution of the planet's sentient ocean has enabled it to defy these predictions, since it has apparently learned how to make corrections in its own orbit in order to avoid crashing into one of the suns. Lem's vision would seem thus to represent the earliest clear formulation of the Gaia hypothesis in the Western imagination. Even the phrase he uses to describe his creation, "homeostatic ocean" is amazingly close to the language scientists use to describe Gaia.

[15] See pp. 12-13 in Thompson (1996).

[16] At the time Thompson was teaching at California Institute of Integral Studies Brian Swimme, Stanislav Grof and Richard Tarnas were colleagues.

[17] For the story of Treya's cancer and her relationship with Ken Wilber, see Wilber's *Grace and Grit: Spirituality and Healing in the Life and Death of Treya Killam Wilber* (1991).

[18] *Sex, Ecology, Spirituality: The Spirit of Evolution*. (1995).

[19] It occurs to me that Ken Wilber and William Irwin Thompson are modern incarnations of an archetypal dichotomy of intellectual temperament. Aristotle and Plato are perhaps the earliest manifestation in Western culture, but it has continued right down the line in such pairs as Newton and Leibniz, Kant and Goethe, Hegel and Schopenhauer. The Wilber type is the Systematist for whom the world is capable of reduction to a single clear architecture. There is *one* set of truths, eternal and unchanging, which the Systematist, whether he is Kant or Hegel, Newton or Aristotle, believes he has been uniquely privileged to discover. Everything is assigned to its niche, like the saints and apostles in a Gothic cathedral, and one system contains all the necessary answers for any question that should arise.

For Wilber, consequently, there is only one theory that is articulated over and over again in each of his books, all of which repeat the same schemas and diagrams endlessly. His work can be neatly divided in two halves, for *Sex, Ecology, Spirituality* marks the birth of his new Final Theory, in the light of which his earlier works are to be taken as precursors. Everything since that book contains a carbon copy of the same four-fold diagram of quadrants, as though consciousness can be mapped as neatly as the trajectory of a parabola on a Cartesian grid.

For the Thompson-Schopenhauer-Goethe-Leibniz-Plato type, the world is in flux and its truths are changing along with it. The ideas of these thinkers are never finished, always subject to revision, and constantly undergoing transformation as new truths are tested, or new theories acquired. The world is a state of perpetual Becoming and no system or body of knowledge can ever hope to be complete, capturing all that there is to know at last. No scholar has ever succeeded, for example, in capturing the fine nuances of Plato's ideas as they evolve through the course of his dialogues. Nothing but actually reading them through chronologically can replicate the experience of watching his thought ripen to full maturity. Plato, like Nietzsche, was not afraid of contradicting himself, for the two were alike in their manner of constantly trying out new ideas on themselves to see what the resulting points of view would look like.

Something of this dichotomy is embodied, also, by Michelangelo and Leonardo da Vinci. For the former, working in the medium of stone meant the production of complete masterpieces. Michelangelo almost always finished what he started — until his later years, that is — and consequently we possess only a handful of unfinished works. The Sistine Chapel constitutes a veritable System of the Christian cosmos, complete in every respect from Genesis to Apocalypse. For Leonardo, on the other hand, the world was ever changing and so were his views. Rarely did he finish what he began. Each painting is a sort of test of an entirely provisional theory. His notebooks are unsystematic and no one has ever really managed to capture their full complexity in a synopsis.

Thompson, likewise, must be read in his entirety, every book, in order to grasp the substance of his vision, which is always changing. He is unsystematic, but always innovative, incorporating fresh insights with each new volume. Every book is a unique experience. For him, consequently, Wilber personifies that which Thompson most dreads: the Final Theory Engraved in Stone.

CONCLUSION

[1] See Campbell (1988b), fig. 1 on pp.40-41 for illustration. I should point out here that not all scholars of Indian history and culture agree on the antiquity of the Jains. In fact, the majority have assumed that the Jains originated in the fifth century B.C.E., about contemporary with the Buddha. Heinrich Zimmer and Joseph Campbell, however, believe them to date clear back to the Dravidian civilization. See the chapter on Jainism in Heinrich Zimmer's *Philosophies of India.*, edited by Joseph Campbell. Bollingen Series XXVI, Princeton: Princeton University Press. See also Campbell (1962), p. 219.

[2] Chopra (1989), pp.225-26 for kitten experiments.

[3] See Bergson (1944), pp.102-04.

[4] See Campbell (1988a), p.13 for original Hindu verison.

[5] Campbell quotes Frobenius's account in *Primitive Mythology* (1959), pp.296-97. Jean Gebser paraphrases the same account as a paradigmatic example of the Magical structure of consciousness in his masterwork *The Ever-Present Origin* (1985), p.47.

[6] See Thompson (1989), pp. 59-62.

[7] See Abraham (1992).

[8] For an illustration of this vision, see Nancy and John Todd's *Bioshelters, Ocean Arks, City Farming: Ecology as the Basis of Design* (1984) pp. 88-89.

The following list does not pretend to be complete, for no such list ever can be, despite the posturing of "authorities" who compose them. I have inevitably neglected someone, due to my personal tastes, prejudices or other such species of ignorance. But the major landmarks as I am aware of them are these:

1894..Rudolf Steiner, *The Philosophy of Freedom.* The first of Steiner's four "foundational" books is rooted in the stream of German Romantic philosophy and its distinction between thinking and intuition. Steiner is generally regarded as the first prophet of the New Age, since his work forms a bridge between such academic figures as Kant, Goethe, Schopenhauer and Nietzsche, and certain motifs normally associated with New Age thinking, such as clairvoyance, karma, Hinduism, the astral plane and astrology.

1896..Henri Bergson, *Matter and Memory.* First non-material theory of memory. Important figure for Rupert Sheldrake.

1900..Sigmund Freud, *Interpretation of Dreams.* Birth of the psychoanalytic movement. Freud's work represents one of the final statements of 19th century materialism.

1904..Steiner, *Theosophy* and *How to Know Higher Worlds.* The second and third of Steiner's "foundational" books. The former attempts to liberate the concept of "theosophy" from identification with Madame Blavatsky's movement. (Steiner broke from the theosophists when they announced Jiddu Krishnamurti as the reincarnation of Christ.) The second book describes the possibilities of attaining clairvoyant powers.

1907..Henri Bergson, *Creative Evolution.* One of the first books to begin separating the machine metaphor from that of the organic. Bergson was a key figure for both Oswald Spengler and Carl Jung.

1909..Steiner, *Outline of Occult Science.* Synopsis of the main points of Anthroposophy, Steiner's blend of Goethian science and mysticism. The reach of Steiner's influence is felt well into the New Age movement of the 60s and 70s, as he becomes an important figure for counter cultural philosophers like William Irwin Thompson and such scientists as Hans Jenny and Arthur Zajonc.

1911-12..Carl Jung, *The Psychology of the Unconscious.* Decisively marks the break from Freud with Jung's revisioning of the "libido" concept as psychic, rather than exclusively sexual, energy. Jung's discussion of the hero myth contains the seed from out of which Joseph Campbell's *Hero With a Thousand Faces* grew.

1912..P.D. Ouspensky, *Tertium Organum.* A Russian mathematician whose acquaintance with the mystic G.I. Gurdjieff transformed his world view.

1914..Ouspensky's *A New Model of the Universe.*

1918..Freud, *Totem and Taboo.* Freud's response to Jung's work on the libido was to invent his own myth for explaining the origins of myth. Somewhere in the dawn of pre-history, the original sin upon which all of myth and ritual is based occurred when the leader of a clan was slain by his sons, who then ingested his power through their ritual cannibalism of him.

Oswald Spengler, *The Decline of the West, Volume One: Form and Actuality.* Spengler rejects the "Ptolemaic" schema of history as a sequence of Ancient-Medieval-Modern in favor of his "Copernican" model: each civilization is a self-contained superorganism with its own predetermined life cycle. The West at present is about where the Classical world of the Greeks was, just prior to the collapse of the Roman Republic and the advent of the Caesars. The "Second Religiousness" was imminent. Spengler's influence on Joseph Campbell, particularly on *The Masks of God* is enormous, and too often overlooked in favor of Campbell's "Jungianism."

1921..Jung's *Psychological Types* articulates the theory of the extroverted and introverted personalities.

1925..Alfred North Whitehead, *Science and the Modern World.* One of the first works by a scientist to perceive that something was missing from science, namely, the animistic world view described by the Romantic poets Keats, Shelley, Worsdworth, et. al. William Irwin Thompson claims that reading this book as a teenager convalescing from cancer was his call to adventure.

1929..Whitehead's forbiddingly difficult *Process and Reality* was influential on Thompson, Ken Wilber, Sheldrake and others.

1934-37..Arnold Toynbee, *A Study of History.* Spengler's British counterpart develops his empiricist theory of the rise and breakdown of civilizations.

1935..Ludwik Fleck, *The Genesis and Development of a Scientific Fact.* This book would probably have sunk into oblivion if Thomas Kuhn had not mentioned it in the prologue to *The Structure of Scientific Revolutions.* Kuhn's book is largely based on this little work written by an obscure Jewish doctor who survived the concentration camps. Fleck's book, which is more profound than Kuhn's, demonstrates that there is no such thing as a scientific "fact" but that each "fact" depends for its existence on a theory, just as a flame requires an atmosphere in which to burn. Fleck is an important figure for Lynn Margulis and William Irwin Thompson.

1936..A.O. Lovejoy, *The Great Chain of Being.* Helped Ken Wilber develop his hierarchical model.

1938..Freud's *Moses and Monotheism* puts forth a radical, and enormously influential theory of Moses as an Egyptian priest in the service of the pharaoh Akhenaton. The origins of monotheism stem from Akhenaton's substitution of the worship of the sun in place of the gods themselves. When Akhenaton's priesthood collapses, Moses flees with this cult into the deserts of Sinai, taking "monotheism" with him. He is there murdered by the Hebrews and devoured in communion meal.

1948..Heinrich Zimmer, *The King and the Corpse: Tales of the Soul's Conquest of Evil.* Zimmer was an important Indologist and friend of both Carl Jung and Joseph Campbell. At his death in 1943, his German posthuma were bequeathed to Jung, while his unfinished American writings were handed over to Campbell. This particular publication edited by Joseph Campbell is one of his most important, though little read, works. Zimmer's theory that the images of myth and fairy tale should not be approached with any preconceived formulae of interpretation, and that the stories should be allowed to speak for themselves and to surprise the reader with unexpected revelations, foreshadows James Hillman's approach to the images of the psyche. For Campbell, this is also an important prologue to his *Hero With a Thousand Faces*, published the following year, although with an entirely different (i.e., "Jungian" / formulaic) approach.

1949..The year of symbolic "coincidences":

Jean Gebser, *The Ever-Present Origin, Volume One: Foundations of the Aperspectival World.* Articulates the theory of the evolution of human cultural consciousness as a sequence of stages from the Archaic, to the Magical, Mythical, Rational and Aperspectival, the latter having originated in the nineteenth century cubism of Cezanne and the rise of relativity in Einstein's physics. Gebser's influence on William Irwin Thompson and Ken Wilber is prodigious.

Joseph Campbell, *The Hero With a Thousand Faces.* One of the last developments of what Gebser would term the "Perspectival" structure of consciousness, Campbell constructs the "monomyth" out of insights gleaned from *Finnegan's Wake*, *The Psychology of the Unconscious*, the work of Leo Frobenius, Arnold van Gennep and others. One of the most influential books of the century.

Erich Neumann, *The Origins and History of Consciousness.* Neumann maps the stages of the Cosmogonic cycle over the ontogentic development of the individual psyche. Figures in the writings of Ken Wilber.

Sri Aurobindo, *The Life Divine.* Philosophy of the evolution of consciousness from the Hindu point of view. Another important figure for Wilber.

1950..Immanuel Velikovsky, *Worlds in Collision.* Banned by the astronomical community even before it was published, Velikovsky's work has turned out to be prophetic. Velikovsky foresaw our current apocalyptic obsessions with comets and bolides crashing into the earth. Taking his departure from Freud's *Moses and Monotheism*, he is somewhat of a literalist and those who take him that way — the planet Venus having begun as a comet in 1500 B.C.E. that nearly destroyed the earth — miss out on the importance of his catastrophist visions. Influence on Ralph Abraham.

1951..Marshall McLuhan, *The Mechanical Bride.* The first truly Aperspectival work of scholarship. McLuhan points out that its chapters can be read in any order, for it develops a non-sequential argument designed to illustrate the end of the Perspectival world view of linear, left-brain reasoning cultivated through the study of books written in the abstract alphabetic languages of the West. McLuhan is an important figure in the thinking of William Irwin Thompson and Terence McKenna.

1952..Carl Jung, after having read the two spin-offs of his work by Neumann and Campbell, is inspired to rework his earlier *Psychology of the Unconscious* as *Symbols of Transformation.*

Synchronicity: An Acausal Connecting Principle. For all its brevity, this is one of the most powerful and influential works on the twentieth century imagination, period. It has spawned theories for the explanation of astrology, works on the decline of causality in science, and countless inferior imitations. Perhaps the most important bridge to transcending the subjective-objective gap bequeathed by the Cartesian world view. The simultaneous manifestation of an archetype in the mind and in the outer world suggests a new theory that the archetypes transcend even the collective unconscious and reside somewhere "beyond" time and space.

1955..Teilhard de Chardin, *The Phenomenon of Man.* Published posthumously, this book is a Catholic priest's vision of the evolution of the universe from Creation to Omega Point. By contrast with Gebser, Neumann and Aurobindo, the book is surprisingly dull. Important, however, for its influence on Brian Swimme, Thomas Berry, Matthew Fox and others.

1957..Joseph Campbell, "The Symbol Without Meaning." Probably Campbell's most important essay, this was based on a talk delivered at the Eranos conferences in Ascona, Switzerland, and is often overlooked when Campbell's detractors dismiss him as "Jungian," since in this essay he deconstructs the mandala archetype, insisting that there is little evidence of its appearance in Paleolithic art, and therefore it cannot be an innate structure of the psyche but one that arose out of historical contingency when civilization began to develop around 4000 B.C.E. and the human individual became an organelle in the overall architecture of civilization. The mandala first begins to appear in the art of this time, Campbell insists, as a means of integrating the individual within a larger cultural membrane. This is the prologue to his next great endeavor *The Masks of God.*

Owen Barfield, *Saving the Appearances.* Barfield carries the Steinerian tradition on into the more turgid field of British academic literature. Barfield was a personal friend of both C.S. Lewis and J.R.R. Tolkien and is presently in his nineties.

1959-68..The first volume of Joseph Campbell's magnum opus, *The Masks of God* appeared in 1959 under the title, *Primitive Mythology.* Subsequent volumes appeared in 1962 (*Oriental Mythology*), 1964 (*Occidental Mythology*), and in 1968 (*Creative Mythology*). In this much neglected series, Campbell switches mentors from Jung to Spengler as he sets out to examine the differences between mythologies, rather than their similarities, for Spengler had emphasized the various uniquenesses embodied by each society, and the essential gulfs of misunderstanding between them. *The Masks of God,* after *The Hero With a Thousand Faces,* is the second of Campbell's "foundational" works.

1960..Immanuel Velikovsky, *Oedipus and Akhenaton: Myth and History.* The second volume of Velikovsky's Ages in Chaos series, this is actually an early work that Freud's *Moses and Monotheism* had inspired him to write but which had been preempted by his fascination with catastrophes. The thesis is that the pharaoh Akhenaton and the mythic Oedipus were actually the same figure, the latter being a Greek mythologization of the former's bloody deed of murdering his father and sleeping with his mother. Fascinating development of Freud's mythologies of history.

1961..Jung's autobiography *Memories, Dreams, Reflections* describes his strange and intense experiences with the supernatural realm throughout his life. Jung's confessions of living in a world filled with ghosts, synchronicities, clairvoyance, astral travel and the like essentially foretells what our "picture" of the world will look like as the mechanical metaphors collapse.

1962..McLuhan's *The Gutenberg Galaxy* describes the meltdown of the age of the book beneath the onslaught of electronic technologies.

Thomas Kuhn, *The Structure of Scientific Revolutions.* One of the most influential books of the century, Kuhn articulates his theory of paradigm shifts.

1964..McLuhan's *Understanding Media* announces that "the medium is the message," not the content of the medium. McLuhan also describes his theories of media hot and cool.

James Hillman, *Suicide and the Soul.* With this book, we cross over the threshold to the realm of the protagonists studied in the present work. This is the book that launched the "soul" movement currently in vogue.

1967..Lynn Margulis, "The Origin of Mitosing Cells." The publication of this paper marked the crystallization of Margulis's theory of cellular symbiosis.

Arthur Koestler, *The Ghost in the Machine.* As the title indicates, the ghosts are on their way, and machines will never look the same again. As the mechanical metaphor is absorbed by the animistic one (thus essentially reversing the position of the nineteenth century) our machines will become more and more personified as living sentient beings, as they are in James Cameron's "Terminator" films or in George Lucas's *The Phantom Menace.*

1968..Ludwig von Bertalanffy, *General Systems Theory.* Important for Fritjof Capra, Joanna Macy and others.

1969..James Lovelock first proposes, but does not name, the Gaia hypothesis.

The French philosopher Michel Serres publishes the first of his Hermes volumes. Serres's investigations of the interrelationships between myth, information theory, thermodynamics, and literature marks him as one of the first to begin to contemplate the deep structures shared by myth and science.

Hertha von Dechend and Giorgio de Santillana, *Hamlet's Mill: An Essay Investigating the Origins of Human Knowledge and Its Transmission Through Myth.* Von Dechend develops an intriguing thesis that ancient myth is a way of encoding astronomical knowledge. Von Dechend was teaching at MIT while William Irwin Thompson was teaching English there, and her thesis helped him to develop one level of his multi-layered reading of the Rapunzel story in *Imaginary Landscape.*

1970..Lynn Margulis expands her short paper on symbiosis to book length as *The Origins of the Eukaryotic Cell.*

John Anthony West, *The Case for Astrology.* One of the best and most well-reasoned arguments in defense of what was thought to be an outmoded paradigm. This book may mark the turning point for the re-inclusion of astrology within our scientific world picture.

1971..Karl Pribram, *Languages of the Brain.* The neurosurgeon who developed the holographic theory of memory.

William Irwin Thompson, *At the Edge of History.* Thompson chronicles the beginnings of his restless search for a new planetary mythology that will transcend the narrow confines of materialism and industrialism. He leaves MIT at this time.

Joseph Chilton Pearce, *The Crack in the Cosmic Egg.*

1972..James Lovelock names his hypothesis in the paper, "Gaia as Seen Through the Atmosphere."

James Hillman, *The Myth of Analysis.* Hillman begins his deconstruction of Jungian psychology. Also, during 1972, Hillman delivers the Terry Lectures at Yale, which would become the basis for his *Revisioning Psychology.*

Gregory Bateson, *Steps to An Ecology of Mind.* Bateson was a figure who spent his final years at Esalen, and his synthesis of anthropology, biology and cybernetics was influential upon William Irwin Thompson, Stanislav Grof, Francisco Varela, Fritjof Capra and many others.

Mary Catherine Bateson, *Our Own Metaphor: A Personal Account of a Conference on Conscious Purpose and Human Adaptation.* Bateson's daughter publishes her first general non-fiction book.

Rene Thom, *Structural Stability and Morphogenesis.* The birth of catastrophe theory; this book introduces "processual" mathematics. Important figure for Ralph Abraham.

1973..Ivan Illich, *Tools for Conviviality.* A former Catholic priest outlines a critique of technology and the institutions that dominate contemporary life.

1974..Joseph Campbell, *The Mythic Image.* Campbell begins to wind down his career with the third of his "foundational" books, demonstrating his thesis that myths are essentially based upon images, rather than linguistics.

Ralph Abraham, "Vibrations and the Realization of Form." Abraham returns from India with a synthesis of his studies in mathematics and Hindu philosophy.

Ian Stevenson, *Twenty Cases Suggestive of Reincarnation*. Stevenson is a mainstream psychiatrist who has devoted his life's work to researching the phenomenon of reincarnation.

Donnella Meadows, *The Limits to Growth*.

Ivan Illich, *Energy and Equity*. The dehumanizing effects of technology.

1975..Stanislav Grof, *Realms of the Human Unconscious*. Grof's first book presents his model of the perinatal matrices sandwiched in between the Freudian personal unconscious and the Jungian collective.

Terence and Dennis McKenna, *The Invisible Landscape*. McKenna's first book synthesizes shamanism, the *I Ching* and chemistry to produce the Time Wave model.

James Hillman, *Revisioning Psychology*. Hillman deconstructs the hero myth and ego psychology.

Fritjof Capra, *The Tao of Physics*. One of the first syntheses of Western science and Eastern wisdom.

Paul Feyerabend, *Against Method*. Introduces irrationalism and anarchism into science.

J.T. Fraser, *Of Time, Passion, and Knowledge*. An almost unknown masterpiece of academic philosophy, particularly important for its contributions to the study of the evolution of consciousness. Fraser revives the Great Chain of Being — in the manner of Ken Wilber, Arthur Young and Stanislav Grof — for a hierarchical theory of the genesis and evolution of time.

1976..Arthur Young, *The Reflexive Universe*. Young began as an engineer who developed the famous bubble-top Bell helicopter, but he was already becoming dissatisfied with the mechanist vision of the world and so began to experiment with yoga, Jungian psychology and other disciplines. *The Reflexive Universe* is a much neglected masterpiece of the evolution of consciousness in the tradition of Gebser, Neumann and Chardin, but in many respects it is even better than those. His process has influenced the structure of this book.

Zacharia Sitchin, *The 12th Planet*. Sitchin is, like Velikovsky, a literalist who develops his own mythology and then mistakes it for reality. His theory that earth was invaded by extraterrestrials in search of gold for their dying planet, and that these beings are what the Bible refers to as the "Nephilim," sounds fantastic, and it is, yet Sitchin unintentionally reveals "aliens" for what they are: what former cultures have called "the gods" have returned from the depths of our imagination as "extraterrestrials" because that is the only way materialistic science will allow "the gods" back into its picture of the universe.

1977..Ken Wilber, *The Spectrum of Consciousness*. In his first book, Wilber attempts to reconcile the various systems of Eastern philosophy with Western psychology by subsuming them all into one band of consciousness. Different therapies are aimed at individuals whose consciousness exists within a certain "bandwidth" of the spectrum.

1978..Ralph Abraham, *The Foundations of Mechanics*. Abraham's first book is a mathematical excursion on the stability of the solar system.

Arthur Koestler, *Janus: A Summing Up*. Koestler's articulation of the theory of "holons" becomes influential for scientists like Fritjof Capra, Rupert Sheldrake and others.

1979..Gregory Bateson's last book *Mind and Nature* was written while he was a scholar-in-residence at William Irwin Thompson's Lindisfarne.

James Hillman, *The Dream and the Underworld*. Hillman attempts to retranslate the concepts of psychology back into their mythic prototypes. The ego and the id become the "hero" and the "underworld."

James Lovelock's *Gaia: A New Look at Life on Earth* popularizes his ideas.

Francisco Varela, *Principles of Biological Autonomy*.

1980..Varela and Humberto Maturana, *Autopoiesis and Cognition*. These Chilean neurobiologists develop their theory that organisms are self-making and do not "adapt" to their environments but create them.

Ilya Prigogine, *From Being to Becoming*. The Belgian physicist develops his theory of "dissipative structures" by applying thermodynamics to biology. The theory of self-organizing structures that emerges begins to dissolve the mechanistic view of nature as dead matter that is pushed and pulled by external forces from the environment.

Erich Jantsch, *The Self-Organizing Universe*. This book is dedicated to Prigogine, and attempts to synopsize an overall view of the universe within which the various theories and ideas of Prigogine, Lovelock, Margulis, Varela and Maturana are given their place. Jantsch was a friend of Ralph Abraham.

Ken Wilber's *The Atman Project*.

David Bohm, *Wholeness and the Implicate Order*. Bohm develops his holographic theory of the universe as an attempt to resolve the epistemological problems of quantum mechanics with the postulation of an ontological ground of being which he terms "the implicate order."

1981..William Irwin Thompson, *The Time Falling Bodies Take to Light*. Thompson's first masterpiece walks the reader through the main phases of human culture history, from the Paleolithic to ancient Egypt, giving a fresh, multi-layered approach to the interpretation of mythic symbols, images and narratives.

Lynn Margulis, *Symbiosis in Cell Evolution*. The synopsis of her life's work.

Rupert Sheldrake, *A New Science of Life*.

Morris Berman, *The Reenchantment of the World*.

1982..James Hillman, "Anima Mundi: the Return of Soul to the World." One of Hillman's finest writings. A reimagination of the world as though it were live.

Ken Wilber, *Up From Eden*. Covers exactly the same terrain as Thompson's *Falling Bodies* or Campbell's *Masks of God*, but with a more conceptually-overburdened approach.

Fritjof Capra, *The Turning Point*. The clockwork paradigm comes to an end in favor of General Systems Theory.

1983..Joseph Campbell, *The Historical Atlas of World Mythology, Volume One: The Way of the Animal Powers*. Campbell publishes the first volume of his fourth "foundational work," essentially a rewrite of *The Masks of God* with the visual accompaniments utilized in *The Mythic Image*. A truly magnificent work of scholarship, this magnum opus was doomed to incompletion at Campbell's death in 1987.

1984..Mary Catherine Bateson, *With A Daughter's Eye: A Memoir of Margaret Mead and Gregory Bateson*.

Brian Swimme, *The Universe is a Green Dragon*.

Ilya Prigogine and Isabelle Stengers, *Order Out of Chaos*. Prigogine's popularization of his theory of "dissipative structures."

Nancy Jack Todd and John Todd, *Bioshelters, Ocean Arks, City Farming: Ecology as the Basis of Design*.

1985..Stanislav Grof, *Beyond the Brain*. One of the great classics of post-Jungian psychoanalytic literature.

Neil Postman, *Amusing Ourselves to Death: Discourse in the Age of Show Business*. Postman is an important development of the McLuhanesque tradition of describing how technology and the media, used unconsciously, become deterministic influences upon our thinking and behavior.

William Irwin Thompson, *Pacific Shift*. Contains "The Four Cultural Ecologies of the West," one of Thompson's finest writings.

1987..Francisco Varela and Humberto Maturana, *The Tree of Knowledge: The Biological Roots of Human Understanding*. Popularization of *Autopoiesis and Cognition*. Excellent and readable introduction to the difficult ideas of these two Chilean neurobiologists.

Deepak Chopra, *Creating Health*. Chopra's first attempt at a synthesis of Ayurvedic medicine, Transcendental Meditation and healthy living.

Robert G. Jahn and Brenda J. Dunne, *Margins of Reality: the Role of Consciousness in the Physical World*. Important validation of E.S.P., remote viewing and psychokinesis from the Princeton

Engineering Anomalies Research Program.

1988..Rupert Sheldrake, *The Presence of the Past: Morphic Resonance and the Habits of Nature.*

Joseph Campbell, *Historical Atlas of World Mythology, Volume Two: The Way of the Seeded Earth.* Posthumous publication. The other two projected volumes were to have been titled *The Way of the Celestial Lights* and *The Way of Man.*

Thomas Berry, *The Dream of the Earth.*

Percy Seymour, *Astrology: the Evidence of Science.* Astrology begins to make its way into mainstream science as this respectable astronomer develops his thesis that astrology works through planetary electromagnetic fields and genetics.

1989..William Irwin Thompson, *Imaginary Landscape: Making Worlds of Myth and Science.* One of the most important books on this list for its influence on the present author. Thompson's discussion of the fairy tale of Rapunzel is a classic in its own right.

Deepak Chopra, *Quantum Healing.* Still his best book.

Marija Gimbutas, *The Language of the Goddess.*

1990..Camille Paglia, *Sexual Personae: Art and Decadence from Nefertiti to Emily Dickinson.* Paglia's celebration of decadent culture is a refreshing and important reversal in the trend in academic philosophy that began with Nietzsche, the first to identify the emergence of decadent culture forms.

1991..Rupert Sheldrake, *The Rebirth of Nature.* Revival of animism; belongs in the tradition of Hillman's essay "Anima Mundi."

Francisco Varela, Evan Thompson, and Eleanor Rosch, *The Embodied Mind.* Varela teams up with William Irwin Thompson's son for a fusion of Buddhism, Merleau-Ponty and research into cognitive science and the immune system.

Joanna Macy, *World As Lover, World As Self.* Fusion of General Systems Theory, Buddhism and Deep Ecology.

Michael Talbot, *The Holographic Universe.* A popularization of David Bohm's and Karl Pribram's holographic models of the mind and the universe.

Marija Gimbutas, *The Civilization of the Goddess.*

1992..Brian Swimme and Thomas Berry, *The Universe Story: From the Primordial Flaring Forth to the Ecozoic Era, A Celebration of the Unfolding of the Cosmos.* Important work in the area of the cross-fertilization of myth and science.

Terence McKenna, *Food of the Gods.*

Neil Postman, *Technopoly: The Surrender of Culture to Technology.*

Michael Murphy, *The Future of the Body: Explorations into the Further Evolution of Human Nature.* The co-founder of Esalen discusses evidence for the paranormal capacities of human beings.

Thomas Moore, *The Care of the Soul.* Spengler predicted that the Second Religiousness will have settled in permanently when the soul's health becomes more important to people than worldly concerns. The enormous popularity of Moore's book indicates that the threshold has been crossed. And that this is no mere fad was indicated when Gary Zukav's *The Seat of the Soul* was featured on the Oprah Winfrey Show in 1998, causing it to become a bestseller when it had already been in print for a decade or so.

1993..Arthur Zajonc, *Catching the Light: The Entwined History of Light and Mind.* The quantum physicist who is now president of the Lindisfarne Association set up by William Irwin Thompson examines the cultural and physical history of light. The influence of Rudolf Steiner is present here.

Deepak Chopra, *Ageless Body, Timeless Mind: The Quantum Alternative to Growing Old.* Biological aging, the result of cultural programming? Impossible!

1994..Ralph Abraham, *Chaos, Gaia, Eros: A Chaos Pioneer Uncovers the Three Great Streams of History.*

1995..Ken Wilber, *Sex, Ecology, Spirituality: The Spirit of Evolution*. Wilber returns from the Underworld with this 800-page synopsis of his life's work.

Nicholas Campion, *The Great Year: Astrology, Millenarianism and History in the Western Tradition*. Though Campion's attitude is annoying, this is a fascinating look backward at the culture history of astrology and historiography.

1996..F. David Peat, Infinite Potential: the *Life and Times of David Bohm.*

Fritjof Capra, *The Web of Life: A New Scientific Understanding of Living Systems*. Popularization of Erich Jantsch's Self-Organizing Universe.

William Irwin Thompson, *Coming Into Being: Artifacts and Texts in the Evolution of Consciousness*. Check out Thompson's comparisons of McLuhan and Gebser, and his contrast between the latter and Ken Wilber.

Abraham, Ralph. 1988. "Chaos in Myth and Science." In *Doing Science: The Reality Club* 2. ed. John Brockman. New York: Prentice Hall Press.

- - - . 1992. "Cathedral Dreams." *Annals of Earth*, Dec. 1992.

- - - . 1994. *Chaos, Gaia, Eros: A Chaos Pioneer Uncovers the Three Great Streams of History*. San Francisco: Harper Collins.

- - - . 1996. "Vibrations: Communication Through a Morphic Field." Preprint for *Synthesis of Science and Religion*. Calcutta, India: 1996.

Abraham, Ralph H. and Marsden, Jerrold E. 1978. *The Foundations of Mechanics*, 2d ed. Reading, MA: Addison-Wesley.

Abraham, Ralph., McKenna, Terence., and Sheldrake, Rupert. 1992. *Trialogues at the Edge of the West*. Santa Fe, NM: Bear & Co.

Abraham, Ralph H. and Shaw, Christopher D. 1992. *Dynamics, the Geometry of Behavior*, 2d ed. Reading, MA: Addison-Wesley.

Adams, Henry. 1961. *The Education of Henry Adams*. Boston, Mass: Houghton Mifflin.

Arguelles, Jose. 1987. *The Mayan Factor*. Santa Fe, NM: Bear & Co.

Badiner, Alan Hunt. "Chaos and Karma." *Yoga Journal*. March-April.

Bergson, Henri. 1944. *Creative Evolution*. Arthur Mitchell trans. Modern Library Series. New York: Random House.

Blacker, Hal. "An Interview with George Feuerstein." *What is Enlightenment?* (fall / winter), pp. 35-43, 1997.

Bridle, Susan. "Deepak Chopra: the Man With the Golden Tongue." *What is Enlightenment?* (fall / winter), pp. 45-52, 1997.

Brown, David J. and McClen, Rebecca. "What the Universe Remembers: An Interview with Rupert Sheldrake." *The Sun*. 211:6, 1993.

- - - . 1995. *Voices From the Edge*. Freedom, CA: The Crossing Press.

Campbell, Joseph. "Review of *Der Weg zum Selbst*." *Review of Religion*, 11, no. 3, 1947.

- - - . 1949. *The Hero With a Thousand Faces*. Princeton: Princeton University Press.

- - - . 1959. *Primitive Mythology*. New York: Viking-Penguin.

- - - . 1960. (ed.) *Spiritual Disciplines. Papers from the Eranos Notebooks*. Bollingen Series XXX, vol. 4. Princeton: Princeton University Press.

- - - . 1962. *Oriental Mythology*. New York: Viking-Penguin.

- - - . 1964. *Occidental Mythology*. New York: Viking-Penguin.

- - - . 1968. *Creative Mythology*. New York: Viking-Penguin.

- - - . 1988a. *The Historical Atlas of World Mythology, Vol. I: The Way of the Animal Powers, Part 1: Mythologies of the Primitive Hunters and Gatherers*. NY: Harper Collins.

- - - . 1988b. *The Inner Reaches of Outer Space*. New York: Harper & Row.

- - - . 1995. *Baksheesh and Brahman: Indian Journal 1954-55*. ed. Robin & Stephen Larsen & Antony Van Couvering. New York: Harper Collins.

Chardin, Teilhard de. 1959. *The Phenomenon of Man*. New York: Harper & Row.

Chopra, Deepak. 1987. *Creating Health: Beyond Prevention, Toward Perfection*. New York: Houghton Mifflin.

- - - . 1988. *Return of the Rishi: A Doctor's Search for the Ultimate Healer*. New York: Houghton Mifflin.

- - - . 1989. *Quantum Healing: Exploring the Frontiers of Mind/Body Medicine*. New York: Bantam.

- - - . 1993. *Ageless Body, Timeless Mind: the Quantum Alternative to Growing Old.* New York: Harmony.

Dobbs, Betty Jo Teeter. 1975. *The Foundations of Newton's Alchemy.* Cambridge: Cambridge University Press.

Ebert, John David. "Visions of a Biomechanical Apocalypse." *Lapis* 5:67, 1997.

Fox, Matthew, and Sheldrake, Rupert. 1996a. *Natural Grace: Dialogues on Creation, Darkness and the Soul in Spirituality and Science.* NY: Doubleday.

- - - . 1996b. *The Physics of Angels.* SF: Harper San Francisco.

Gebser, Jean. 1985. *The Ever-Present Origin.* Noel Barstad and Algis Mickunas trans. Athens: Ohio University Press.

Gibson, William and Sterling, Bruce. 1992. *The Difference Engine.* New York: Bantam.

Gimpel, Jean. 1976. *The Medieval Machine: the Industrial Revolution of the Middle Ages.* New York: Viking Penguin Books.

Grof, S. 1975. *Realms of the Human Unconscious: Observations from LSD Research.* New York: Viking Press.

- - - . 1980. *LSD Pyschotherapy.* Pomona, Cal.: Hunter House.

- - - . 1985. *Beyond the Brain: Birth, Death and Transcendence in Psychotherapy.* Albany, New York: State University of New York Press.

- - - . 1988. *The Adventure of Self Discovery: Dimensions of Consciousness and New Perspectives in Psychotherapy and Inner Exploration.* Albany, NY: State University of New York Press.

Grof, S. and Bennett, Hal Zina. 1992. *The Holotropic Mind: the Three Levels of Human Consciousness and How They Shape Our Lives.* NY: Harper Collins.

Hofmann, Albert. "Interview: Albert Hofmann." *Omni*, 1981.

Hope, Marjorie and Young, James. "Thomas Berry and a New Creation Story." *The Christian Century.* August 16-23, 1989.

Huxley, Aldous. 1954. *The Doors of Perception.* NY: Harper.

Jahn, Robert G. and Dunne, Brenda J. 1987. *Margins of Reality: the Role of Consciousness in the Physical World.* New York: Harcourt, Brace, Jovanovich.

Jaynes, Julian. 1976. *The Origins of Consciousness in the Breakdown of the Bicameral Mind.* Boston: Houghton Mifflin.

Jeffers, Robinson. 1991. *The Collected Poetry of Robinson Jeffers*, vol. 3, ed. Tim Hunt. Stanford, CA: Stanford University Press.

Jung, C.G. 1953. "On the Psychology of the Unconscious." In: *Two Essays on Analytical Psychology.* Collected Works, vol. 7, Bollingen Series XX, Princeton: Princeton University Press.

- - - . 1956. *Symbols of Transformation.* Collected Works, vol. 5, Bollingen Series XX, Princeton: Princeton University Press.

- - - . 1969a. *Aion: Researches Into the Phenomenology of the Self.* Collected Works, vol. 9, Bollingen Series XX, Princeton: Princeton University Press.

- - - . 1969b. *Psychology and Religion: West and East.* Collected Works, vol. 11, Bollingen Series XX, Princeton: Princeton University Press.

- - - . 1971a. *The Portable Jung.* ed. Joseph Campbell. NY: Viking Penguin.

- - - . 1971b. *Psychological Types.* Collected Works, vol. 6, Bollingen Series XX, Princeton: Princeton University Press.

- - - . 1976. *The Symbolic Life: Miscellaneous Writings.* Collected Works, vol. 18, Bollingen Series XX, Princeton: Princeton University Press.

- - - . 1978. "Commentary to 'The Secret of the Golden Flower." In *Psychology and the East.* From Collected Works, vols. 10, 11, 13 and 18, Bollingen Series XX, Princeton: Princeton University Press.

Leland, John and Power, Carla. "Deepak's Instant Karma." *Newsweek*, Oct. 20, 1997. pp. 53-58.

Lessing, Doris. 1974. *The Temptation of Jack Orkney and Other Stories*. NY: Bantam.

Mann, Thomas. 1957. *Essays*. New York: Vintage.

McKenna, Terence. 1991. *The Archaic Revival*. NY: Harper Collins.

- - - . 1992. *Food of the Gods: The Search for the Original Tree of Knowledge; a Radical History of Plants, Drugs and Human Evolution*. NY: Bantam New Age.

- - - . 1993. *True Hallucinations: Being an Account of the Author's Extraordinary Adventures in the Devil's Paradise*. SF: Harper San Francisco.

McKenna, Terence and McKenna, Dennis. 1993. *The Invisible Landscape: Mind, Hallucinogens and the I Ching*. San Francisco: Harper San Francisco.

Neumann, Erich. 1954. *The Origins and History of Consciousness*. Bollingen Series XLII, Princeton: Princeton University Press.

- - - . 1974. *Art and the Creative Unconscious*. Bollingen Series LXI, Princeton: Princeton University Press.

Peterson, Ivars. 1993. *Newton's Clock: Chaos in the Solar System*. NY: W.H. Freeman and Company.

Postman, Neil. 1985. *Amusing Ourselves to Death: Public Discourse in the Age of Show Business*. New York: Viking, 1985.

Rifkin, Jeremy. 1981. *Entropy: A New World View*. NY: Bantam.

Schwartz, Tony. 1995. *What Really Matters: Searching for Wisdom in America*. New York: Bantam.

Serres, Michel. 1982. *Hermes: Literature, Science, Philosophy*. Baltimore, MD: The Johns Hopkins University Press.

Sheldrake, Rupert. "The Ageing, Growth and Death of Cells," *Nature* 250: 381, 1974.

- - - . 1988. *The Presence of the Past: Morphic Resonance and the Habits of Nature*. Rochester: Park Street Press.

- - - . 1994. *The Rebirth of Nature: the Greening of Science and God*. Rochester, VT: Park Street Press.

- - - . 1995a. *A New Science of Life: The Hypothesis of Morphic Resonance*. Rochester, VT: Park Street Press.

- - - . 1995b. *Seven Experiments that Could Change the World: A Do-It Yourself Guide to Revolutionary Science*. NY: Riverhead Books.

- - - . "Experimenter Effects in Scientific Research: How Widely Are They Neglected?" *Journal of Scientific Exploration* 11, 1997.

Shnayerson, Michael. "Life After Steve," *Vanity Fair* Nov. 1996.

Spengler, Oswald. 1929. *The Decline of the West*, vol. I., Charles Francis Atkinson trans., NY: Alfred A. Knopf.

- - - . 1932. *Man and Technics*. Charles Francis Atkinson trans., NY: Alfred A. Knopf.

Stevenson, Ian. 1974. *Twenty Cases Suggestive of Reincarnation*. Charlottesville: University of Virginia Press.

- - - . 1987. *Children Who Remember Previous Lives*. Charlottesville, VA: University Press of Virginia.

Strozier, Charles. 1994. *Apocalypse: On the Psychology of Fundamentalism in America*. Boston, Mass: Beacon Press.

Swimme, Brian. 1984. *The Universe is a Green Dragon: A Cosmic Creation Story*. Santa Fe, NM: Bear & Co.

- - - . 1996. *The Hidden Heart of the Cosmos: Humanity and the New Story*. Maryknoll, NY: Orbis Books.

Swimme, Brian and Berry, Thomas. 1992. *The Universe Story: From the Primordial Flaring Forth to the Ecozoic Era, A Celebration of the Unfolding of the Cosmos*. NY: Harper Collins.

Thompson, William Irwin. 1971. *At the Edge of History*. New York: Harper & Row.

- - - . 1977a. (ed.) *Earth's Answer: Explorations of Planetary Culture at the Lindisfarne Conferences*. New

York: Harper & Row / Lindisfarne.

- - - . 1977b. *Evil and World Order*. NY: Harper & Row.

- - - . 1981. *The Time Falling Bodies Take to Light*. NY: St. Martin's Press.

- - - . 1985. *Pacific Shift*. San Francisco: Sierra Club Books.

- - - . 1987. (ed.) *Gaia: A Way of Knowing, Political Implications of the New Biology*. New York: Lindisfarne Books.

- - - . 1989. *Imaginary Landscape: Making Worlds of Myth and Science*. New York: St. Martin's Press.

- - - . 1990. *Islands Out of Time: A Memoir of the Last Days of Atlantis*. Santa Fe, NM: Bear & Co.

- - - . 1991a. *The American Replacement of Nature: The Everyday Acts and Outrageous Evolution of Economic Life*. NY: Doubleday Currency.

- - - . 1991b. (ed.) *Gaia 2: Emergence, The New Science of Becoming*. New York: Lindisfarne Books.

- - - . 1991c. *Reimagination of the World: A Critique of the New Age, Science and Popular Culture*. Santa Fe: Bear & Co.

- - - . 1993. "Of Angels, Extraterrestrials, Lost Continents, and other Strange Attractors: A Conversation with Ralph Abraham and William Irwin Thompson," *Annals of Earth*. Vol. XI, No. 2.

- - - . 1996. *Coming Into Being: Artifacts and Texts in the Evolution of Consciousness*. New York: St. Martin's Press.

- - - . 1997. *Worlds Interpenetrating and Apart: Collected Poems 1959-1996*. Hudson, New York: Lindisfarne Books.

Velikovsky, Immanuel. 1950. *Worlds in Collision*. NY: Doubleday.

Wilber, Ken. 1995. *Sex, Ecology, Spirituality: The Spirit of Evolution*. Boston, Mass.: Shambhala.

- - - . 1997. *The Eye of Spirit: An Integral Vision for a World Gone Slightly Mad*. Boston, Mass.: Shambhala.

- - - . 1998. *Ken Wilber in Dialogue*. D. Rothberg and S. Kelly, eds. Wheaton, IL: Theosophical Publishing House.

Woodcock, Alexander and Davis Monte. 1978. *Catastrophe Theory*. New York: Avon Books.

Young, Arthur. 1976. *The Reflexive Universe*. San Francisco: Robert Briggs Associates.

INDEX

Brahman, 90, 131, 134-135, 168, 171, 174
brain, chemistry, 132; physiology, 132
Brand, Stewart, 79
breathwork. *See* Holotropic Breathwork
Brihadharanyaka Upanishad, 22, 127
Bruno, Giordano, 55, 57, 64, 173
Buddha, Gautama, 136
Buddhism, 21-22; Mahayana, 132-132;
    Tibetan, 92, 132
Buddhist philosophy, 14, 140

C

Calatrava, Santiago, 176
Caldean Oracles, The, 57
calendar, astronomical, 6; Mayan, 95
California Institute of Integral Studies, 19, 21
California, University of, at Santa Cruz, 54
Campbell, Joseph, 21, 24, 43, 93, 149-150
Canaan, 64
cannons, invention of, 7
Canopus in Argus series, 18
Canticle to the Cosmos, 29, 34
capitalism, 16, 152-153
Capra, Fritjof, 5, 20, 23, 48, 124
Carnot, Sadi, 10-12
Carson, Rachel, 21
Cartesian, 169-170
"Cartesian-Newtonian materialistic world view,"
    124, 143
Casting Nets Into the Sea of Mind, 94, 104
catastrophe theory, 53, 61-62
cells, bacterial, 68; eukaryotic, 68; nucleated, 68
cellular symbiosis, 41
Center for Eastern Wisdom and Western
    Science, 152
Center for Intercultural Documentation, 150
centrioles, 71
Cezanne, Paul, 13, 161
Chandler, Raymond, 159
Chaos, Gaia, Eros, 54-55, 60, 62
Chaos in Discrete Dynamical Systems, 67
Chaos theory, 4, 26, 51-55, 59-61, 65-67, 73,
    104, 134
Chardin. *See* Teilhard de Chardin, Pierre
Chinese inventors, 6
chloroplasts, 70-71, 79
Chomsky, Noam, 148, 153
Chopra, Deepak, 5, 19, 89, 127-141, 165, 174
Christ, 65, 141; birth of, 66; body of, 166;
    temptation of, 7; vision of, 12
Christian, art, 8; cosmos, 169; Middle Ages, 16
Christianity, 3, 27, 42, 58, 177
Civilization and its Discontents, 99

Clarke, Arthur C., 170
Clausius, Rudolf, 11
COBE satellite, 32-32
Coevolution Quarterly, 79
coffee as drug replacement, 93
cognitive, commitment, premature, 166;
    science, 22
Columbus, Christopher, 8, 92
compass, the, 7
comet theory, 55
Coming Into Being, 146, 161
communication, 104-105
communism, 16
Composing a Life, 21
consciousness, 46, 49, 93-94, 98, 100, 106,
    132-133, 143, 174; cosmic, 109; evolution,
    125, 145, 161; transformation of, 28
consumerism, 35
Contact, 86
continental drift theory, 56
Copernicus, Nicolaus, 15
Cornell University, 147
Corpus Hermeticum, The, 57, 58
cosmic, allurement, 36; architect, 52; egg, 27
Cosmic Game, The, 125
Cosmic Memory, 26
cosmology, 27-38, 169; cyclic, 33; Western, 52
Couette-Taylor. *See* experiment
Crash, 117
Creating Health, 130
creation, epic, Babylonian, 9; of the universe,
    26
Creative Evolution, 167
creativity, goddess of, 60
Crete, Minoan, 53, 101, 164
Crick, Francis, 83
Critchlow, Keith, 144, 158-159
Critique of Pure Reason, The, 39
Cronenberg, David, 13, 160
Crying of Lot 49, The, 160
Cubism, 99
cults, beer, 102
cultural programming, 99
culture, 103, 124, 142, 144, 157; history, 20,
    60, 62, 64, 147, 161; new planetary, 151,
    158; Western, 169
cyanobacteria, 76, 79, 84, 176
cytoplasm, 71

D

da Gama, Vasco, 8
da Vinci, Leonardo, 8, 26, 92
Dalai Lama, the, 3, 5

Dali, Salvador, 108
Dante, 5
Darkness and Scattered Light, 145, 153
Darling, David, 23
Darwin, Charles, 15, 40, 44, 74, 106, 135
Dass, Ram, 54
datura, 92
Davies, Paul, 5, 23
Dawkins, Richard, 174
Dawn of the Dead, 169
Decline of the West, 4, 16, 142
Deism, 30, 49
de Kooning, Willem, 14
de Lubicz, Schwaller, 158
de Medici, Cosimo, 58
Demiurge, Plato's, 9, 51, 89
Democritus, 52, 165, 172
Dennett, Daniel, 157, 174
depression, 116
De Rerum Natura, 8
Descartes, Rene, 8, 55, 169, 173
detachment, 136
De Vosjoli, Phillipe, 94, 104
Diaz, 8
Dick, Philip K., 160
diet, affecting mutation, 100
Difference Engine, The, 91
dimethyltryptamine, 92, 97
dinosaurs, 44, 56
diploid, 77
Dirichlet, 59
disease, origin of, 138
DMT. *See* dimethyltryptamine
DNA, 70, 83, 94-96; cultural, 93
Doors of Perception, The, 91
doshas, three, 130
Dossey, Larry, 4, 23
dreams, 107
drug, abuse, 35-36; addiction, 138
Dunne, Brenda, 4, 23
Durckheim, Karlfried Graf, 24
dvija, 121
dynamatrons, 54
dynamical, historiography, 62-63; literacy, 62; sciences, 152; systems theory, 54, 61, 65, 145
Dynamics, 54

E

Early Life, 71
Earth, Mother, 173
Earth's Imagination, The, 29
Earth Systems Science, 80

Easter Rebellion, the, 147
Eckhart, Meister, 32
Ecology, Deep, 21
ecosystem, 75, 81
Ecozoic Era, 37-38
Edge of History, At the, 144, 148-149
Egypt, 27, 64; Middle Kingdom, 53
Einstein, Albert, 2-3, 13, 50, 53, 60, 107, 168
Eldredge, Niles, 30
"Electrodynamics of Moving Bodies, On the," 2
electromagnetic fields, 41, 135
electron capture detector, 21
electronic latifundia, 154
Eliade, Mircea, 102, 127
Eliot, T.S., 40, 127
emanation, theories, 58, 60
energies, emotional, 28, 121
engine, Carnot's, 12; Platonic heat, 10; steam, 7, 9-10, 12, 27, 165
Enlightenment, 59, 102
entropy, 3, 11
Enuma Elish, 9, 51
epistemology, 22
"Epochs of the Spirit," 142
ergot, 101
Eranos, conferences, 128
Esalen, 144, 150
ESP, 46
ESS. *See* Earth Systems Science
ethnobotany, 91-105
Euclid, 55
Euclid Project, The, 55, 67
Euclid's Voyage into Chaos, 67
Euglena, 70
Ever-Present Origin, 4, 143
Evil and World Order, 145, 153
evolution, 49; cosmic, 36; of Gaia, 68
Evolutionary Mind, The, 42, 54, 94
Exorcist, The, 173
expansion, of the galaxies, 34
experiment, blind, 48; Couette-Taylor stirring, 55
extinction, of the dinosaurs, 56; mass, 44; sixth great, 30
Eye of the Spirit, 119
eyeglasses, invention of, 7

F

Faraday, Michael, 42
Faust, 7, 11
feminism, 21
Ferguson, Kitty, 5
Fermat's Last Theorem, 59

fermenters, 69-70
Ficino, Marsilio, 57-58, 64
Findhorn, 151-152
Finkelstein, David, 151
Finnegan's Wake, 142
Fire in the Equations, The, 5
Fire in the Sky, A, 118
Fleck, Ludwik, 4
fluctuation, 32; macro, 31; quantum, 31
Food of the Gods, 99-101, 104
forces, 36
forests, 76
Foster, Jodie, 86
Foundations of Mechanics, The, 53, 55
Four Ages of Man, 142
"Four Cultural Ecologies of the West, The," 145, 159
four, basic transformations, 145; elements, theory of the, 8; fundamental interactions, 36; humors, 130; matrices. (*see* perinatal matrices)
fourth mentality, 145-146, 158
Fox, Matthew, 3, 28, 42, 48, 50
fractals, 52, 61
Frankenstein, 68
Frazer, James, 3, 4, 102
Freemasons, 173
Freud, Sigmund, 2, 40, 92, 97, 99, 106-108, 110, 156
Friedrich, Caspar David, 15
Frobenius, Leo, 172
Fuller, Buckminster, 149-150
fungi, 70, 81

G

Gabriel, the angel, 8, 66
Gaia anthologies, 5
Gaia, 26, 54, 75-77, 79-81, 98, 164; the goddess, 52; hypothesis, 4, 21, 33, 41, 71-73, 176
Gaian, "fevers," 76; intelligence, 98; Overmind, 89, 98, 174; physiology, 176
Galen, 92
Galileo, 9, 92, 158, 169, 173
galvanoscope, 121
Gamow, George, 31
Garden of Microbial Delights, The, 71
Gassendi, 8
Gauquelin, Michel, 23
Gebser, Jean, 4, 24, 143, 161
Gehrig, Lou, 170
General Systems Theory, 21
genes, cytoplasmic, 70

Genesis, 51, 55, 168, 170
Genesis and Development of a Scientific Fact, 4
genetic, engineering, 41
genetics, science of, 70
Gentle Bridges, 5
geological, uniformitarianism, 15
geometry, sacred, 158
geosciences, 68-87
Gerber, Richard, 4, 23
Ghost in the Machine, The, 18
ghosts, 18, 26, 42, 44-45; mathematical 133
Gibson, William, 4, 91, 159
Gimbutas, Marija, 23
Gimpel, Jean, 6
Glass, Philip, 160
Glenn, John, 139
global, civilization, 30
God, 37, 39, 169, 171, 177; mind of, 174
God and the New Physics, 5
Goddess, 58; culture, 101, 164-165; tradition, 60
Godhead, 32
Goethe, Johann Wolfgang, 128, 142
Golden Age, 41, 95
Golden Bough, The, 3, 102
Golding, William, 72
gravitational, attraction, 36-37; field, 58, 60
gravitation, force of, 106, 135; theory of universal, 59
Greece, 27, 95, 101
Greek, mythology, 176; philosophy, 172; statuary, 143
greenhouse, effect, 152; gas, 76
Grof, Stanislav, 19-20, 22, 89, 97, 106-126, 165, 174
Grof, Christina, 109, 113
Grossetteste, Robert, 5
Guenon, Rene, 158
gunas, three, 130
guns, invention of, 7
Gutenberg, Johann, 143, 153

H

Hagen, Steve, 23
hallucinogens, 89, 92, 97, 99-102
Harman, Willis, 23
Harner, Michael, 23
hashish, 92
Hawking, Stephen, 31, 174
Healing Gaia, 76
health, experience of, 137; origins of, 138
Heaven's Gate, 124
Hebbel, 12

hebephrenia, 113
Heidegger, Martin, 14
Heisenberg, Werner, 155
Hellenistic epoch, 6
hemp, 102
Henry the Navigator, Prince, 8
Hermes, 58
Hermetic, corpus, 58; philosophers, 59, 64; tradition, 57, 59-60
heroin, 93
Hesiod, 52, 152
Hidden Heart of the Cosmos, The, 29, 35
Hillman, James, 18, 22-23
Hindu, creation myth, 168; mathematician, 6; philosophy, 3, 14, 43, 54, 128, 134, 140, 171; spirituality, 131
Hiroshima, the bombing of, 16
history, 142-162, 177
Hitchcock, Alfred, 139
Hitler, Adolf, 16
Hobbes, 8
Hofmann, Albert, 107-108, 111
holism, 49
Hollow Man, The, 40
holograms, 45
holographic, cosmos, 4
Holographic Universe, 5
Holotropic Breathwork, 109-110, 113, 115, 120, 122, 174
Holotropic Mind, The, 110
Homeorhetic Mechanism of Planetary Dynamics, The, 72
Homer, 128
homunculus, Leibnezian, 11
Horney, Karen, 122
Hubbard, L. Ron, 121
Hutton, 15
Huxley, Aldous, 91-93, 126
Huxley, T.H., 91

I

Ice Age, 69, 76
I Ching, 94-95
Illich, Ivan, 150
Imaginary Landscape, 18, 84, 146, 159
imagination, 142, 145, 170, 176
Imagination of an Insurrection, The, 143, 147
immortality, 140
immunology, 22
India, 17, 43; Dravidian, 53; philosophy of, 67
Industrial nation state, 152
inertia, 106
Institute of World Order, 151

Integral, stage, 4
intention, 135
intentional, community, 151
intercalation, 96
Internet, the, 66, 153
Introductory Letters in Psychoanalysis, 110
Invisible Landscape, The, 93-94, 96
Ireland, 147
IS Journal, 159
Islands Out of Time, 145, 159

J

Jahn, Robert, 23, 48
Jains, the, 164-165
Jantsch, Eric, 22-23
Jas, Frank, 55
Jaynes, Julian, 98
Joachim of Floris, 142
John, Robert, 4
Journal of the American Medical Association, 130, 138
Journal of Theoretical Biology, The, 71
Joyce, James, 91, 128, 142, 147
Jung, Carl, 2-3, 8, 18, 22, 24, 65, 94, 96, 107-109, 119, 121, 127-128
Jupiter, 53
Jurasic Park, 44

K

Kalanos, 127
Kalidasa, 128
Kampf, Louis, 148
Kant, Immanuel, 15, 39-40, 106-107, 128, 155, 172
kapha. (*see doshas*)
karma, 127
karmic, realm, 120
"Karyotypic Fissioning and Lemur Evolution," 79
Kauffman, Stuart, , 23
Keller, Evelyn Fox, 85
Kelvin, William Thomson, 11
Kepler, Johannes, 9, 169
kinetochores, 79
Klee, Paul, 13
Knights Templar, 154
Koestler, Arthur, 18, 128
Koran, the, 141
Krippner, Stanley, 23
Krishna, Lord, 135
Krishnamurti, Jiddu, 3
Kuhn, Thomas, 63
Kundalini, yoga, 5

L

Lacan, 157
Lamarck, 135
Langer, Ellen, 139
language, 104, 176
Laocöon, sculptures of, 8
Laplace, Pierre Simon, 15, 56, 59
Larkin, Emmett, 148
Laszlo, Ervin, 23
Law of Falling Bodies, the, 9
Lawson, Alvin, 119
Lee, Alexander, 139
Leeuwenhoek, Anton van, 42
Leibniz, Gottfried, 4, 11, 13, 171, 173
Lem, Stanislaw, 160
Lemaître, Abbé Georges, 26, 27, 31, 168
LeShan, Lawrence, 23
Lessing, Doris, 14-15, 18, 142, 160, 166
Levi-Strauss, Claude, 157
light, speed, 2, 13
Lindisfarne, 144-146, 150-151, 153, 158
Lives of a Cell, 155
Living Being, Plato's, 9
Locke, John, 171
Lovelock, James, 18, 21, 23, 33, 71-72, 76, 79, 81, 146, 151, 158
LSD, 22, 54, 97, 107-114, 116, 120, 126
"LSD and the Cosmic Game," 126
LSD Psychotherapy, 110
Lucretius, 8, 172
lunar, rocks, 74

M

machine, 29, 168, 177; living, 176
macrocosm, 94-95
Macy, Joanna, 23
Madhyamika Sastra, 132
Madonna, 21
Magellan, Ferdinand, 8. 92
magic, 4
Magical stage, 4
magnetism, 7
Mahesh, Maharishi, 130
Manifesto for a Global Civilization, 28
Mann, Thomas, 106-107
Maplethorpe, 21
Marduk, the solar god, 51
Margulis, Lynn, 19-20, 26, 33, 68-87, 146, 151, 158, 165, 174-176
Markandeya, 90
Mars, 40, 53, 72, 80, 92
Marx, Karl, 16, 40, 99, 148

Maryland Psychiatric Research Center, 108
materialism, 18, 35, 132, 144, 149, 151, 174
mathematicians of solar dynamics, 57
mathematics, 51-67, 145, 158, 173
Mather, 32
matter, 32, 169; anti-, 32; in motion, 2; organic,74
Matter in Memory, 43
Maturana, Humberto, 22-23
Max Planck Institute, 155
Maxwell, James Clerk, 11-12
Mayan, architecture, 143; culture, 95
McKenna, Dennis, 92-94, 96
McKenna, Terence, 19-20, 41-42, 54, 89, 91-105, 120, 125, 127, 174
McLuhan, Marshall, 24, 54, 143, 149-150, 160
Mead, Margaret, 20
mechanical, clocks, 6, 9; universe, 5, 13, 17; world view, 23-24
mechanics, Newtonian, 10, 13, 169; quantum, 13, 15
Medieval pattern, 154-155
medical accidents, 138
medicine, 127-141. (*see also* Ayurveda)
meditation, 132, 174
Memories, Dreams, Reflections, 18
memory, 45-46; collective, 46; past-life, 109; perinatal, 116-117; storage, 96
Mendel, Gregor Johann, 42
Meno, 89
mescalin, 91
Mesopotamia, 63
metabolism, 96; time seen as, 94
metanoiac, shift, 18
metaphysical dimension, 132
metaphysics, science of, 39
Michelangelo, 8
microcosm, 94-95
microcosmologies, ancient, 5
Milankovitch effect 77
Milky Way, The, 30, 32
Mind and Nature, 20
Minsky, Marvin, 174
Miro, Joan, 13
mirrors, invention of, 7
Mishima, Yukio, 118
MIT, 144, 148-150, 152
mitochondria, 70-71
Mohammed, 66, 141
Monera, 70
monks, Gothic, 5; Zen, 145
Moody, Raymond, 23